DATE DUE

GAYLORD			PRINTED IN U.S.A.

RUSSIA AND THE WEIMAR REPUBLIC

RUSSIA
AND THE
WEIMAR REPUBLIC

LIONEL KOCHAN

BOWES & BOWES

First published in 1954 by
BOWES AND BOWES PUBLISHERS LIMITED
CAMBRIDGE

To

WINKLE

In Recognition of Her Forbearance

327.430947
K81r

Feb. '64

46,402

PRINTED IN GREAT BRITAIN BY
WILLMER BROTHERS AND CO. LTD. BIRKENHEAD

CONTENTS

CONTENTS

INTRODUCTORY NOTE

In the main this book speaks for itself. It is an attempt to trace the varying relationship between Soviet Russia and the Germany of 1919-1934, that is, roughly the period of the Weimar Republic. The relationship itself was compounded of three elements—diplomatic, political (i.e. the connection between the Comintern and the German Communist Party), and military. There was some inter-action between all three, but not to such an extent that they cannot be separated for the purposes of study. All three were in existence during the fourteen or fifteen years covered by the book ; similarly all three ceased to pursue their joint existence after 1934.

Owing to the relative lack of attention given to the period, some of the detailed narrative will no doubt be unfamiliar to the reader. It seems, therefore, that the most apt form an introductory note may take is a short conspectus of the principal conclusions reached.

Briefly, then, the beginning of the period is characterised by the Russian belief in an imminent revolution in Germany, a country that Lenin in 1918 compared to a rotting tree. The Soviet leaders had little or no conception that in Germany, of all countries, they might be confronted with a capitalist and not a communist régime. This optimistic view predominated, although with declining vigour, until 1923, when the abortive German Revolution in November of that year finally ended the prospect of a communist Germany within any measurable or reasonable period of time.

Thenceforward, the emphasis changed in favour of normal diplomatic contact, with revolutionary hopes at a discount. The one side of the medal was represented by the doctrine of socialism in one country, first enunciated by Stalin in the autumn of 1924. The obverse was represented by the strengthening of the Russo-German Treaty of Rapallo which, although signed early in 1922, did not take on its full importance until two years later.

What was this importance ? It varied in each case. To Russia, Rapallo denoted primarily an assurance that the capitalist world was disunited. Germany was often referred to by Soviet spokesmen and publicists as a *point d'appui*, a foothold in the enemy's

camp. Come what may, Germany would always be the missing
link in any concerted action that might be attempted by the non-
communist powers. In other words, Germany was neutralised as
far as Russia was concerned. Beyond the Western borders of
the Soviet Union, there stretched a vast belt of neutralised
territory.

This was primarily a defensive aim. To Germany, on the other
hand, Rapallo's significance was primarily offensive. It was a
weapon in the struggle against Versailles. It was a threat to the
Western powers that, should alleviations of Versailles not be
granted, Germany would always be able to enter into closer
relations with Soviet Russia. This German policy of using the
East against the West (as also the West against the East) was
associated particularly with Stresemann. The support that the
Bolsheviks gave to the German national struggle against Versailles
was the price they had to pay for German neutrality.

The future development of Rapallo took place against the background of European diplomacy and the changing balance of
power. Indeed, events in Western Europe had possibly a greater
effect on that development than any intrinsic factor. If Rapallo is
looked at from this point of view, then the two outstanding events
were the Dawes Plan and Locarno in 1925, and the Young Plan
and the evacuation of the Rhineland in 1929-1930. The effect in
both cases was sensibly to lighten the burden of reparations and to
give Germany greater freedom of action. A further result was
to weaken Rapallo, for if this had its origin in opposition to
Versailles, then it could not but lose in value as the structure of
Versailles itself was weakened. On each occasion, accordingly,
there took place a certain swing away from Russia by Germany.
It was barely noticeable in 1925 but well to the fore in 1929-1930.
Of course the Russo-German Treaty of Berlin of 1926 and its
renewal in 1931 compensated for the temporary German
defection. They restored the balance.

Yet hardly was this last phase overcome than towards the
second half of 1931 Rapallo came gradually to be overshadowed
by the growth of Nazism and the emergence of a German right
wing under Brüning that had no use for the Russian connection.
Over a period of some two and a half years, the Soviets had to
reckon with the possible loss of their German *point d'appui*. But
not until 1934, when Hitler decisively rejected Russian overtures
for a continuation of the old relationship, did Stalin decide to

throw in his lot with the Western powers. Such was the end of Rapallo. It is at this parting of the ways that this book also ends.

Its significance does not only relate to the actual events that it narrates. A period can at the best of times be but a label that may obscure an underlying continuity. What is the continuity in this case ? It may be briefly outlined as follows: the same pattern that had determined Russo-German relations in 1925 and 1930 was repeated, albeit on a far larger scale, from 1931-1939. Hitler, as the anti-Bolshevik *par excellence*, was enabled to secure concessions from the West that Stresemann had only been able to envisage in his wildest dreams: the occupation of the Rhineland, the Anschluss with Austria, the annexation of Czechoslovakia. This was the culminating point of a development the latest phase of which begun in 1931. Then came the British guarantee to Poland in 1939. Hitler was temporarily baulked. Willy-nilly he had to do what Stresemann had done in similar circumstances— he had to turn to Russia, i.e. resurrect Rapallo. The situation that had arisen in 1925 over the Dawes Plan and Locarno, in 1930 over the Young Plan and the evacuation of the Rhineland, was repeated in 1939. On each occasion Germany, after obtaining certain concessions in the West swung away from Russia and then swung back again. In 1925-26 the swing was very slight; in 1929-1930 it was perceptibly greater; in 1931-1939 it was plain for all to see. Nevertheless, even though the last swing had brought Germany into an enormously stronger position than at any time previously, she was still unable to forgo the Russian connection.

Russian policy, like German, had also continued on its accustomed path. From 1931 onwards, Stalin had perceived the possibility of danger from a resurgent Germany which he and Litvinov had attempted to parry by lining up with the Western powers. But by 1939 not a single worthwhile success had been achieved. Almost every possibility of a reconciliation with the West was exhausted; there was no longer any point in barking up that particular tree. Stalin showed the same patience in dealing with the West in 1939 that he had shown in dealing with Germany in 1931-1934. Before changing sides, he waited until he could be reasonably sure that the Western door was barred. Only then were the Germans admitted by the Eastern door. Stalin had succeeded in getting his capitalist *point d'appui*.

It was of course no part of Stalin's design that he would thereby strengthen an aggressor; as little as it was Stresemann's design that his policy would turn into Hitler's, or Sir Austen Chamberlain's that the Locarno policy would turn into appeasement. But history does not deal with motives and intentions—only with results.

The task of writing this book has been immeasurably lightened by the resources placed at my disposal by Chatham House; and in particular by the skilled assistance of Mrs Degras in tracking down much Russian material. I owe a similar debt of gratitude to the Wiener Library, and especially to Mrs Löwenthal in respect of German material. Both the Foreign Office and Mr Isaac Deutscher very kindly placed at my disposal certain material not available elsewhere. Finally, and most important, I wish to express my appreciation to Professor Sir Charles Webster for the most generous help and encouragement he gave me in the task of writing the dissertation in which the present book had its origin.

LIONEL KOCHAN.

London,
January, 1953.

CHAPTER I

From Brest-Litovsk (March 1918) to the Russo-Polish War
(Summer 1920)

By the summer of 1918, the Germans had realised the dream of Mitteleuropa. They stood, for a few brief months, on the verge of success. The main instrument of their achievement was the Treaty of Brest-Litovsk, imposed on a defeated Russia in March 1918. The Treaty gave to Germany a position of domination in Lithuania, the Baltic, Poland and the Ukraine. It promised, too, the possibility of transferring troops from the Eastern front to the hard-pressed West. Later in the same year, the Peace of Bucharest reduced Rumania to a state of economic servitude; Bulgaria was a German ally so weak as to be easily dominated; and in July-August 1918 the Austro-Hungarian Empire was forced into accepting a customs and economic union with Germany.

The reverse side to this grandiose structure of domination was formed of Russian weakness, most obviously expressed in the Treaty of Brest-Litovsk. Moreover, even after its signature, the German advance into Russia was maintained. The little Soviet Republic, in existence a mere six months or so, was menaced abroad no less than at home. To an outside observer it would have seemed destined to disappear into obscurity as swiftly as it had emerged from obscurity.

Until August 1918 the main agent of this fate was taken, not unnaturally, to be Germany. It was from there that the greatest danger was expected.[1] But soon afterwards fear of Germany was eclipsed in importance by fear of the Entente. The sustaining power, necessary to the structure of German hegemony, declined at the same time that Allied intervention got under way. The threat from one quarter was slowly being replaced by that from another. In the Far East, American troops began to disembark in Siberia; Archangel in the North and Baku in the South were occupied by the British; and in the East the Czechoslovak Legion, formed of escaped Austro-Hungarian prisoners of war, began its advance on to the Volga.

[1] G. V. Chicherin: *Vneshnaya Politika Sovietskoi Rossii za dva goda (Two Years of Soviet Foreign Policy)*, Moscow, 1920, p. 7.

The reaction to these new Allied threats was of the same kind as had been the reaction to the German threats at Brest-Litovsk. Trotsky, as Commissar for Foreign Affairs, had then tried to secure arms and military instructors from Great Britain and the United States. His successor in office, George Chicherin, descendant of an aristocratic Russian family, polyglot and music-lover, now tried an exactly similar policy. He attempted to parry the threat from the Allied Powers by securing aid from Germany. To Helfferich, the German Ambassador at Moscow, he proposed that German troops cover St Petersburg while Russia withdrew her troops around Vologda in order to protect Moscow. Both in the North and in the South, Chicherin thought that an 'actual parallel-action' on this basis would be possible.[1]

Chicherin's effort *vis-à-vis* Germany was as fruitless as had been Trotsky's effort *vis-à-vis* the Allies. A few days later Helfferich returned to Berlin. He had only been in Moscow from July 28 to August 6.[2] As the war in the West ended, the Soviets were completely isolated, inside a territory that was little larger than the Grand Duchy of Muscovy in the fifteenth century.

Fear at this prospect was blended with the hope and expectation of world revolution. 'It seems to me', said Lenin in October 1918, 'that our present position, with all its contradictions, can be expressed thus: firstly, we were never so near to the international proletarian revolution as we are now; and secondly, we were never in a more dangerous position than we are now'.[3] Lenin, in fact, expected joint Entente-German action against the Bolsheviks[4] and when the Armistice was signed he told Chicherin in private: 'World Capital itself is now coming for us'.[5]

The answer to world capital was world revolution. This had been rather soft-pedalled during most of 1918, but as the threat from the Allies grew, so did the Russian appeals to the European masses. Attention was concentrated on Germany, no longer 'a mighty empire', said Lenin on October 22, but a 'rotting tree'.[6] In Berlin, Adolf Joffe, the Soviet Ambassador, had long been in touch with members of the German Left, aiding them in the

---

[1] Karl Helfferich: *Der Weltkrieg*, Vol. III, Berlin, 1919, pp. 466-7.

[2] Ibid., p. 487.

[3] Lenin: *Sochineniya*, Vol. 23, p. 288.

[4] Ibid., p. 268.

[5] Chicherin in *Izvestya*, November 7, 1923.

[6] Lenin: *Sochineniya*, Vol. 23, p. 238.

distribution of pamphlets and funds.[1] From Russia he now began to receive publicly expressed moral support, that verged at times on the mystical. On October 3 the Central Committee saw 'the German working-class irresistibly thrusting for power'.[2] Towards the end of the month greetings were sent to Liebknecht, the German Spartacist, on his release from prison;[3] and on November 1 *Pravda's* headlines read: 'The world revolution has begun. . . . Nothing can hold up the iron tread of revolution.' Radek rather incautiously committed himself to the prediction that by the Spring of 1919 all Europe would be Soviet.[4]

Under these circumstances Joffe's activities in Berlin became so important that even *after* the German request to the Allies for an Armistice, the cash indemnity due to Germany by the Treaty of Brest-Litovsk continued to be paid. It was hoped to deprive the German Government of any excuse for expelling the Soviet Ambassador.[5] At the same time grain was assembled for transport to a Germany suffering under the Allied Blockade.[6]

All this was in vain. On November 5 the German Government expelled the Russian Ambassador; and on November 19 it refused the Russian offer of grain, fearing in both cases to jeopardise its relations with the Entente. As one Russian writer put it: 'The fraternal hand extended by the Russian Government remained hanging in the air.'[7] At the time this might well have seemed to the Russians a damper on their hopes of a German revolution, of a proletarian Russia and a proletarian Germany marching arm in arm. But it was not so.

Nothing daunted, on December 5 Lenin hurriedly assembled a five-man delegation, consisting of the expelled Joffe together with Radek, Bukharin, Rakovsky and Ignatov, to participate in the Berlin Congress of Workers' and Soldiers' Councils, themselves formed on the Soviet model. This move was also forestalled by the German Government. On December 23 it refused to admit any representatives of the Bolsheviks, including those

---

[1] These activities had little influence on the course of events. Joffe said afterwards: '. . . we accomplished little . . . of permanent value. We were too weak to provoke a revolution' (Louis Fischer: *Men and Politics*, London, 1941, p. 31).

[2] *Pravda*, October 4, 1918.

[3] *Ibid.*, October 27, 1918.

[4] *Ibid.*, Dec. 5, 1918.

[5] Radek's article in *Krasnaya Nov*, No. 10, 1926, p. 140.

[6] Lenin: *Sochineniya*, Vol. 23, p. 216.

[7] M. Tanin: *10 let Vnyeshnei Politiki S.S.S.R. 1917-1927* (*Ten Years of the Foreign Policy of the U.S.S.R. 1917-1927*), Moscow, 1927, p. 40.

from the Red Cross.[1] Only by disguising himself as an Austrian prisoner-of-war was Radek able to get through the German lines and to set out for the chaos of post-Armistice Berlin.[2] There we leave comrade Radek for the moment—en route for Berlin.

If the Bolsheviks had designs on Germany, the same applied to the Allies. Point 12 of the Armistice agreement of November 11, 1918, stipulated that the German troops on the Eastern Front were to continue to hold their positions, which at this time straggled south-east from Narva on the Baltic to Rostov near the mouth of the River Don.[3] They were only to return 'to within the frontiers of Germany as soon as the Allies shall think the moment suitable, having regard to the internal situation of these territories'. Lenin's prophecy of joint Entente-German action against the Bolsheviks was fulfilled. This was the first time that the Germans became the defenders of Western Europe against the Bolsheviks.[4] The role has since become more familiar. But neither in 1919 nor in subsequent years were the Germans slow to take advantage of the position.

Their first opportunity to turn the Allied initiative to their own benefit came in the Baltic. Here, during 1919, an indescribable chaos prevailed. German troops, Allied Military Missions, Esthonian, Latvian and Lithuanian troops, Russian and native Bolsheviks, pro-German Russian Whites and pro-Entente Russian Whites all jostled each other in confusion. But one fact stands out —it was here that the Germans made their first attempt to come into contact with Russia.

The initial plan to this end was simplicity itself. It was merely to screen East Prussia by holding the line Libau-Kovno-Grodno.[5] This was a strictly defensive policy and would have entailed leaving the Baltic coast open to the Bolsheviks, advancing further to the North East. The intention of General von Seeckt, at this time chief of staff to Armee Oberkommando Nord—the organisation entrusted with the execution of the plan—was in fact to let the Russians back into the Baltic and not to participate in the

---

[1] G. V. Chicherin: *The Foreign Policy of Soviet Russia—Report of Narkomindel to the 7th All-Russian Congress of Soviets*, Eng. trans., London, 1920, p. 22.

[2] This journey is described in *Krasnaya Nov*, No. 10, 1926, pp. 143 ff.

[3] *Die Rückführung des Ostheeres*, Berlin, 1936, Map 1.

[4] cf. *The Times*, October 27, 1919: 'The Allies at the time of the Armistice endeavoured to make use of this Army of Occupation as a protection for Western Europe against the Bolsheviks and did not stipulate for an immediate evacuation, as there were no local forces considered capable of making head against Bolshevik aggression.'

[5] F. von Rabenau: *Seeckt-Aus Seinem Leben 1918-1936*, Leipzig, 1940, pp. 120-121.

Allied plan to erect a *cordon sanitaire* between Russia and Germany.[1]

The same General Seeckt was later to play a part of the greatest importance in the development of Germany's relations with Russia. But to what extent this was clear to him in early 1919 cannot be ascertained. In any event, there was at this time no widespread conception of any arrangement between a right-wing Germany and a left-wing Russia, such as Seeckt might possibly have had in mind. The ideological barrier in both countries had first to be surmounted.

In the development of the Baltic campaign as far as Germany was concerned this fact very soon became apparent. Seeckt's defensive policy was quickly abandoned for greater vigour. On February 1, 1919, General von der Goltz arrived in Libau to become commander of the 6th Reserve Corps. His orders from Armee Oberkommando Nord were to conduct a defensive battle.[2] Instead, he and his subordinates in the field went over to the offensive. Goltz hoped, he writes, 'after securing a base in Latvia-Lithuania, to crush Bolshevism in Russia with a large army, to install a "White" Government and to acquire in it a sure friend for Germany. . . . Together Russia and Germany . . . should then throw down a challenge to the Western powers and free us from Versailles.'[3] One of Goltz's subordinate commanders, Major Fletcher of the Baltische Landeswehr, was no less hopeful. An order to his troops of June 16, 1919, reads: 'From news just received from England it may be concluded with certainty that English aims are . . . to make impossible every endeavour of Germany becoming strong and to frustrate by all means the coming alliance of Germany with Russia.' England, he says, hopes 'to steal from Germany the opportunity of having before long a great and powerful ally—Russia'.[4] A third German commander, Major Bisschof of the so-called Iron Division, also looked forward to breaking the encirclement of Germany by collaborating with the Whites inside Russia.[5]

Seeckt opposed this plan from the start[6] and later in the year he went to East Prussia to try and cut off the flow of supplies across

---

[1] See 'Tschunke's Letter,' p. 60 below.
[2] R. von der Goltz: *Als Politischer General im Osten,* Leipzig, 1936, pp. 82-83.
[3] Ibid., p. 165.
[4] Robert Hale: *Report of the Mission to Finland, Esthonia, Latvia and Lithuania on the Situation in the Baltic Provinces, Washington,* 1919, pp. 23-24.
[5] Major J. Bisschof: *Die Letzte Front,* Berlin, 1935, pp. 52-53.
[6] F. von Rabenau: *Seeckt-Aus Seinem Leben 1918-1936,* Leipzig, 1940, p. 125.

the frontier.[1] These efforts were in vain. By Article 433 of the Versailles Treaty the Allies stipulated that the German troops in the Baltic were to continue to remain there, 'having regard to the internal situation of these territories'.[2] Not until the second half of 1919 was the German Baltic coast blockaded and pressure brought on the German Government to recall Goltz. He had never got further East than Riga. The first attempt of Germany to contact Russia ended in complete failure. But it had shown the way the wind was blowing.

When Radek reached Berlin his first action was to attend the foundation congress of the German Communist Party (the K.P.D.) on December 31, 1918. He was not altogether a welcome visitor. Factional differences dating from the pre-war period divided him from Rosa Luxemburg, one of the leaders of the new party. More important than this was Rosa Luxemburg's attitude to the Russian Revolution. In a brochure written whilst still in prison in 1918, she had indicted the Bolsheviks on several counts. Her principal charge against them was their suppression of democracy. 'Of course, every democratic institution has its limitations and weaknesses which it shares with all human institutions. But the cure that Lenin and Trotsky have found— the elimination of democracy altogether—is a worse evil than the one it is intended to avoid. . . . Freedom only for the supporters of the government, only for the members of a party, however numerous they are, is no freedom. Freedom is always the freedom of the person who thinks differently.'[3] Disillusioned by Social-Democracy's record during the war and by the Bolsheviks' behaviour in power, she sought a third way—a revolutionary mass-party that would achieve socialism through mass-strikes, avoiding the Red Terror.[4] The programme adopted by the young K.P.D. made no mention of the Bolsheviks and contained only the vaguest reference to international co-operation.[5] Again, Rosa Luxemburg instructed the German delegate to the foundation congress of the Third International in Moscow to vote against its formation.[6]

[1] *Documents on British Foreign Policy*, First Series, Vol. III, ed. Woodward & Butler, London, 1949, p. 207.
[2] *The Treaties of Peace*, pp. 255-256.
[3] R. Luxemburg: *Die Russische Revolution*, ed. Paul Levi, Berlin, 1922, pp. 108, 109.
[4] *Bericht uber den Gründungsparteitag der K.P.D.*, Berlin, n.d., pp. 33-34.
[5] Ibid., p. 55.
[6] See Zinoviev's remarks, *Protokolli VIII Syezda RKP (b)* (*Protocols of the 8th Congress of the Russian Communist Party (b)*), ed. Em. Yaroslavski, Moscow, 1933, pp. 137-138 and 144.

Radek's speech knew nothing of this—in full measure he brought with him the optimism of Moscow: 'We had to wait a whole year for the German Revolution. We armed, fought, defended ourselves and now we have lived to see the great day. . . . The day will come when the call with which I close will become reality, the day when world revolution will free the working-classes, when socialism will no longer be the aim of our fight but the object of our conscious work.'[1]

Shortly after this Radek was arrested and incarcerated in the Moabit prison in Berlin. In contrast with the treatment given to German communists—Liebknecht and Luxemburg were mur-dered in cold blood 'while attempting to escape'—the Russian Bolshevik was maintained in comparative comfort and became the object of some curiosity. While the embattled Reds were locked in desperate struggle with the Whites; while a state of quasi-civil war raged throughout Germany and street fighting flared up in Berlin; while ephemeral Soviet Governments came into power in Bavaria and Hungary; while the victors at Versailles deliberated over peace—Radek's prison-cell became an oasis of quiet in which the most far-reaching political ideas were discussed. Three years later they led to the Russo-German Treaty of Rapallo.

Radek's cell was a sort of 'political salon'.[2] Passes to visit him were obtained at the German Ministry of War.[3] Through this channel a series of distinguished visitors entered the salon. The first two, apparently, were Enver Pasha and Talaat Pasha. They were former leaders of the pro-German Young Turk Movement. After Turkey's defeat in the Great War they had fled to Berlin as political refugees. Radek had first met Talaat during the Brest-Litovsk negotiations where the latter had been a member of the Turkish delegation. Radek now advised Enver to go to Moscow[4]; and in October 1919 he set out on his journey. But the aeroplane had to make a forced landing in Lithuania and it was only with difficulty that Major Tschunke, an emissary of Seeckt in the Baltic, rescued Enver from an Entente prison.[5] The next visitor was

[1] K. Radek: *Die Russische und die deutsche Revolution und die Weltlage*, Berlin, 1919, p. 31.
[2] The expression is Radek's own, and is taken from his article in *Krasnaya Nov*.
[3] Ruth Fischer: *Stalin and German Communism*, Harvard, 1948, p. 206.
[4] *Krasnaya Nov*, No. 10, 1926, p. 164.
[5] F. von Rabenau: *Seeckt—Aus Seinem Leben 1918-1936*, Leipzig, 1940, p. 306. The date of Enver's departure is here given as April 1919, which seems impossible (see p. 20 below). In view of the fact that Enver was in touch with both Radek and Seeckt in 1919, it is likely that the latter two also met. On the other hand, their first *recorded* meeting did not take place till January 1922 (see p. 61 below). Seeckt and Enver had met when Seeckt was Chief of Staff to the Turkish Armies.

Walter Rathenau who later signed, though *à contre coeur*, the Rapallo Treaty. He expounded to Radek his theories of constructive socialism—a great advance on Marx, according to Rathenau—and predicted a time when the Bolsheviks in Moscow would have degenerated into wearing 'silken garments'. More to the point, Rathenau foresaw firstly, that the Soviets would win out against the interventionists, and, secondly, that no revolutionary developments would be possible in Germany for many years.[1]

After the industrialist came the soldier—Baron Reignitz, a former war-time colleague of Ludendorff's. He had broken with the latter and was, Radek writes, the first representative he met of the 'National-Bolsheviks'. By this Radek meant a bourgeois politician or soldier who was prepared to initiate a radical economic transformation of Germany as the price of an alliance with Soviet Russia against the Entente. At this time there was no prospect of any collaboration between a proletarian and a bourgeois state. Hence Reignitz propounded to Radek the concept of a union with Russia, based on a peaceful revolution in Germany, via the nationalisation of the means of production.[2]

At the end of 1919 Radek was released and went to stay in the Berlin apartment of Baron Reignitz. Here he was introduced to Colonel Max Bauer who had been propaganda chief at Ludendorff's Headquarters. Bauer too, was an adherent of Reignitz's ideas, for he looked forward to an arrangement between the officer-class, the communist party and the Soviet Union. The officers, he said, realise that Russia is unbeatable and is Germany's ally in the fight against the Entente and against Versailles.[3] Bauer, to put it mildly, was very impressed by Radek. 'He is a man', wrote the Colonel, 'who unites in himself really stupendous knowledge. Kant and Schopenhauer, Goethe and Shakespeare, Rousseau and Malthus, Napoleon and Frederick the Great are to him absolutely familiar figures. He particularly esteems Clausewitz in whom he sees his political mentor. . . .'[4] Admiral

[1] *Krasnaya Nov*, No. 10, 1926, p. 165.

[2] Ibid., p. 166.

[3] Ibid., pp. 169-170.

[4] Col. Max Bauer: *Das Land der roten Zaren*, Hamburg, 1925, p. 79. Others of Bauer's comments on Bolshevik leaders whom he met on a trip to Russia in the early twenties are not without interest: 'Trotsky is a born military organiser and leader. How he created a new army out of nothing, in the midst of heavy battles, and then organised and trained this army is absolutely Napoleonic . . . Dzerzhinski (the first chief of the Cheka) is perhaps just as powerful a nature and even more ruthless'. (Bauer, op. cit. pp. 80-82).

Hintze, the last German Foreign Minister before the request for an Armistice in November, 1918, was another of Radek's visitors who told him he saw the future in terms of a Russo-German *rapprochement*. Rathenau returned, this time in the company of Felix Deutsch, his fellow-director, on the board of the gigantic A.E.G. (Allgemeine Elektrizitätsgesellschaft).[1] It was at first intended that Radek should fly back to Moscow with Enver Pasha. But this plan was cancelled. He returned with Major Hey who later became counsellor of the German Embassy in Moscow.[2]

Amongst German left-wingers Radek was in touch with Ruth Fischer and Paul Levi, who led the K.P.D. after the murder of Luxemburg and Liebknecht.[3] Two Communist visitors from Hamburg-Lauffenberg and Wolfheim—were of particular significance. They put forward a version of 'National-Bolshevism' similar to that of Bauer and Reignitz. They proposed that the German communists should seize power and then, at the head of the German bourgeoisie and in alliance with Soviet Russia, repudiate Versailles.[4]

Towards the end of 1919 Radek wrote several articles that show the impact made on him by these varied encounters. Their general tenor was a pessimistic revaluation of the hopes of the German Revolution that he had seen at the beginning of the year. The first of these revaluations dates from October 1919. In a letter to the Congress of the K.P.D. that met that month at Heidelberg, he rejected the Lauffenberg-Wolfheim thesis of a revolutionary war against the West.[5] At the same time, while conceding that the world situation was as revolutionary as ever, he goes on: 'The world revolution is a very long process during which there will be more than one defeat. Yes, I do not doubt that in every country the proletariat will erect its dictatorship and will then see it collapse, before it is eventually victorious.'[6]

In a slightly later article Radek again rejected the National-

[1] *Krasnaya Nov*, No. 10, 1926, pp. 170-171.
[2] Ibid., p. 172.
[3] Ibid., pp. 167 ff.
[4] Ruth Fischer: *Stalin and German Communism*, Harvard, 1948, pp. 92-93. See also Lauffenberg and Wolfheim: *Revolutionärer Volkskrieg oder Konterrevolutionärer Bürgerkrieg*, Hamburg, 1920. Fischer also states (op. cit., p. 207) that Professor Otto Hoetzsch, German right-wing Russian expert was another of Radek's visitors.
[5] K. Radek: *Zur Taktik des Kommunismus*, Berlin, 1919, p. 11.
[6] Ibid., pp. 3-5. It is not impossible that Radek also had Soviet Russia in mind. October, when this was written, was the most critical month for the Bolsheviks with the Whites in the suburbs of Petrograd. Besides, earlier in 1919 the Soviet Republics of Bavaria and Hungary had lasted little more than a few weeks.

Bolshevism of Lauffenberg and Wolfheim. The German bourgeoisie, he wrote, would undoubtedly prefer a complete foreign occupation of Germany to a German Soviet Republic.[1] As for Russian foreign policy, the basic factor here was the delay in revolution in Western Europe and America. This altered the whole context in which that policy would have to operate. For the first time Radek envisaged the necessity of a *modus vivendi* with capitalism: 'The problem of the foreign policy of Soviet Russia . . . consists in attaining a *modus vivendi* with the capitalist states.'[2]

Elsewhere, reiterating his conviction that the world revolution will not be an 'explosion' but a 'disintegration' Radek again pleaded for a *modus vivendi* between capitalism and socialism.[3] The last step on this path was taken when he came out in favour of a restoration, as a temporary measure, of full diplomatic and commercial relations between Germany and Soviet Russia.[4] The wheel had turned full circle.

Some six years later Radek pointed to the wider significance of the situation prevailing at the end of 1919: the victory of the German bourgeoisie over the Communist threat—such as it was—coincided with the Bolshevik victory over the Whites.[5] In other words, the German bourgeoisie, having now nothing to fear from its own communists, could deal openly with the Bolsheviks, relieved of the horror that it might thereby become contaminated. And at the very same time, it became clear that it was the Bolsheviks with whom it would have to deal and not any kind of White régime; for at the end of 1919 Soviet power emerged consolidated from battle.

Two separate episodes in October 1919 show to what extent the German bourgeoisie was alive to the implications of the situation. The first of these episodes was the attempt of Enver Pasha to reach Moscow. In a brand new Junkers aeroplane he left Berlin on October 10. He was accompanied by another Turk and a Russo-Jewish interpreter. The pilot and mechanic of the aeroplane were both German. But they had to make a forced

---

[1] K. Radek: *Die Auswärtige Politik des deutschen Kommunismus und der Hamburger National—Bolschewismus*, (first published in *Die Internationale*, Heft 17-18, December 20, 1919), p. 16.
[2] Ibid., p. 9.
[3] K. Radek: *Die Auswärtige Politik Sowjet-Russlands*, Hamburg, 1921 (written December 1919), pp. 37-38.
[4] K. Radek: *Deutschland und Russland* (first published in *Die Zukunft*, No. 19, February 7, 1920).
[5] Radek in *Izvestya*, November 5, 1925.

landing and the crew and passengers were taken into custody by the British military authorities in Kovno, Lithuania. The principal document carried was a letter from Junkers enquiring about the legal position of their patent rights in Russia, the possibility of manufacturing Junkers aeroplanes on Russian territory, and the possibility of developing internal Russian air-lines. Another document was a map prepared by the Reichswehr and dated September 1, 1919. It informed the Bolsheviks of the number of troops that could be massed against them in all the countries hostile to them. In a very obscure reference Leonid Krassin, the Bolshevik Commissar of Foreign Trade is also mentioned.[1]

The other incident of October 1919 to illuminate the attitude of the German bourgeoisie *vis-à-vis* Russia was its reaction to the Allied invitation to Germany to enter the blockade of Russia. It was the nightmare of the peace-makers at Versailles that in one form or another Germany might link up with the Bolsheviks.[2] In consequence, the four Articles of the Versailles Treaty that refer to German-Russian relations—Articles 116, 117, 292 and 293—are all designed to prevent any such linking up. In the words of Dr Zitelmann, adviser on Russian political affairs to the Auswärtiges Amt: 'In their settlement of the Russian question all that has remained recognisable as the guiding thought of the Allied Powers is the effort to prevent, as much as possible, any *rapprochement* between Germany and Russia.'[3] In general terms, the four Articles in question oblige Germany both to accept the abrogation of Brest-Litovsk and to recognise in advance any treaties concluded between the Allied Powers with any present or future governments on Russian territory. In Article 116 the Allies even went so far as to reserve to Russia the right to claim

---

[1] All the foregoing is based on the despatch contained in *Documents on British Foreign Policy*, First Series, Vol. II, ed. Woodward & Butler, London, 1948, pp. 44 ff. In this despatch neither of the two 'Turkish gentlemen' apprehended is specifically identified as Enver. They both claimed to be members of the Turkish Red Cross in Russia. But since it is known that Enver was detained in Kovno on his way to Moscow (see Curt Okay: *Enver Pasha—der grosse Freund Deutschlands*, Leipzig, 1935, pp. 334-345, and Louis Fischer: *The Soviets in World Affairs*, London, 1930, pp. 384-385) and that the pilot of the aeroplane was carrying ' someone of great importance to the Bolshevik Government', there can be no doubt that Enver was one of the two 'gentlemen'.

[2] See, for example, Lloyd George's memorandum of March 25, 1919: 'The greatest danger that I can foresee in the present situation is that Germany may throw in her lot with Bolshevism, and place her power at the disposal of the revolutionary fanatics whose dream it is to conquer the world for Bolshevism by force of arms . . .' (Cmd. 1614, 1922, p. 4.)

[3] Dr F. C. Zitelmann: *Russland im Friedensvertrage von Versailles*, Berlin, 1920, p.3.

reparations from Germany[1]. The policy of erecting a *cordon sanitaire* of small states between Russia and Germany served the same purpose. The overall aim was to exclude Germany from exercising any influence in Eastern Europe.

Into the framework of this policy fits the Allied invitation to Germany to participate in the Russian blockade. A draft note on this subject was ready as early as August 21, 1919.[2] But it was not until September 29 that the Supreme Council in Paris decided to despatch the note to the neutral Powers.[3] Three weeks later, on October 20, Chicherin sent a bitter protest to Germany, warning her against the acceptance of the Allied invitation: ' . . . in the course of their hostile actions against the Russian masses the Entente Powers have also applied a system of the most barbaric blockade which aims at breaking the power of resistance of the Russian people by every kind of hardship to which even women and children are exposed. Should the German Government take an active part in this blockade, no matter in what manner, the Russian Soviet Government and the Russian masses will see in this a consciously hostile action on the part of the German Government. . . . The Soviet Government hopes that the German Government will reply to the profoundly unjust demand of the Entente powers with a decisive refusal.'[4]

In the event, the German Government was not so unwise as to reply with a 'decisive refusal'. But it refused all the same. The German note to the Allies explained that although Germany was prepared to take measures against the common danger from Bolshevism, she could only do so on the basis of an acknowledgment of reciprocal rights. 'It is difficult to admit that these conditions are realised so long as the Allied and Associated Governments consider it possible to proclaim blockade measure against the German coasts and German ships themselves at the very same time that they invite Germany to participate in the Russian blockade.'[5]

---

[1] *The Treaties of Peace*, pp. 83, 169.

[2] *Documents on British Foreign Policy*, First Series, Vol. I, ed. Woodward & Butler, London, 1947, pp. 501-502.

[3] Ibid., pp. 824-825 (For the actual text of the note see p. 830).

[4] *Mezhdunarodnaya Politika Novyeshevo Vremeni* (*Recent International Politics*), Part II, Klyuchnikov and Sabanin, Moscow, 1926, p. 398.

[5] Quoted from Dr Lucien Graux: *Histoire des Violations du Traité de Paix*, Vol. I, Paris, 1921, pp. 336-337. It has not been possible to trace the original of the German note. The Allied blockade of the German coasts mentioned is a reference to the measures taken by the Allies to enforce the return of the German troops still in the Baltic.

On October 23 and 24, the whole affair was ventilated in the Reichstag. The debate was a strange mixture of sob-stuff and Realpolitik, with the Social-Democrats specialising in the former and the right-wing deputies in the latter. The significant fact emerged that although not more than perhaps one right-wing deputy was prepared actually to recommend some sort of arrangement with a Bolshevik Russia, there were many others who were prepared to envisage this possibility and to take it into consideration.

The debate was opened by Hermann Müller, Social-Democratic Chancellor. Only a few days earlier he had warned the Reichstag against expecting any 'great economic advantages' from contact with Russia.[1] He now changed his tune: 'The strictest blockade is to be imposed on Soviet Russia, an economic boycott is to be applied. No one can say of us that we are friends of the Bolsheviks. In word and deed we have proved that we are determined to fight them. . . . In Bolshevik Russia and especially in Bolshevism as it has spread amongst us, we see great dangers for civilisation and economic welfare. On the other hand, also on the basis of our experience, we know that Bolshevism will only be encouraged if it is fought by the methods that the Allies now want to apply. On our own bodies we have learnt to know the starvation blockade. We have seen its cruel consequences in the sufferings of invalids, old people, mothers and children, and it is asking a lot of us to take part in this starvation blockade. For in this form of warfare it is not the political leaders who suffer first, but the masses . . . those people will suffer in Russia who are now being terrorised by the authorities and the Bolsheviks, and now they should be punished from abroad by imposing starvation and unemployment in Russia.'[2] Wels, another Social-Democrat, added that the world family of nations could only exist if its members did not intervene in each others' affairs.

It was now the turn of the right-wingers. Not one suggested that Germany join in the blockade. Dr Schultz of the German Nationalists said that Germany must be unprejudiced in her attitude to Russia. Dr Haussmann of the German Democratic Party—the party of which Rathenau was one of the founders—recommended a sympathetic but 'wait-and-see' policy towards Russia. The least enthusiastic about Russia was Dr Heinze of the

[1] Reichstag Debates, Vol. 330, p. 2958.
[2] This speech, like those that follow, is taken from Reichstag Debates, Vol. 330, pp. 3359 ff.

German People's Party; and the most enthusiastic Dr Pfeiffer of
the Catholic Centre: 'Our path lies Eastwards . . . the door to
the Western World is bolted against us. That seems to me to
impose on us the duty of knocking on the Eastern gate.'

At the time the German refusal to participate in the blockade
and the whole German attitude of neutrality during 1919 were
almost totally neglected by the Bolsheviks. Chicherin dismissed
it in a few words: 'It is also known that the German Government
has refused to join in the blockade of Soviet Russia. This refusal,
however, has no real value as Soviet Russia is no longer in
immediate contact with Germany.'[1]

Chicherin of course was right. In 1919 there was no contact
between Russia and Germany. German participation in the
blockade would have made no difference to Russia's position.
She was cut off from the world without that. The German stand
in the matter of the blockade, however, was significant for its
indication of the way a certain policy *vis-à-vis* Russia was evolving
out of the confused hostility that had marked the Baltic campaign
earlier in 1919. That the Russians did not see this was hardly
surprising, banking as they were (except Radek, of course) on an
imminent revolution in Germany. German neutrality in 1919
was one of those things the value of which is only appreciated when
it is on the point of being lost. What was completely passed over
at this time later became the cardinal principle of Russian
policy towards Germany. At almost all costs, the Russians
subsequently strove to keep Germany neutral, as a buffer between
themselves and the West.

When Radek returned to Moscow at the end of 1919, he was
replaced in Berlin by Vigdor Kopp. On February 20, 1920,
Kopp was recognised by the German Government as the official
Soviet plenipotentiary for prisoner-of-war matters.[2] In the spring
and early summer he signed three agreements on this subject.
His opposite number in Moscow was Hilger. Both were of uncertain diplomatic status, but later their position was defined more
closely. Kopp received authorisation from the Soviet Government
to initiate the exchange and transport of goods between Germany

---

[1] G. V. Chicherin: *Foreign Policy of Soviet Russia—Report of Narkomindel to 7th
All-Russian Congress of Soviets*, Engl. trans., London, 1920, p. 25.
[2] I. Maisky: *Vnyeshnaya Politika R.S.F.S.R. 1917-1922*, (*The Foreign Policy of the
R.S.F.S.R. 1917-1922*), Moscow, 1922, p. 106.

and Russia, and Hilger came to be regarded as a sort of temporary German Ambassador.[1]

When Hilger arrived in Moscow Chicherin told him, according to the German press, 'that Russia's attitude towards Germany would be dictated solely by the wish to establish closer economic political and cultural relations'.[2] This was a polite fiction. In 1919, as in the major part of 1920, world revolution was one of the main planks in the structure of Soviet Russia's foreign policy. The other main plank was peace, which culminated in the offer of terms amounting to complete capitulation. In a note of February 4, 1919, Chicherin offered to pay Russia's foreign debts, to lease concessions, to cover Russia's foreign obligations by the despatch of goods, and to make territorial concessions involving the occupation of areas forming part of the former Russian Empire by armies drawing their support from the Entente. If all this were agreed to, Russia pledged herself not to intervene in the internal affairs of the Powers.[3] But, of course, this was not agreed to. It had the disadvantage, from the Entente viewpoint, of involving the continued existence of Soviet Russia, on however limited a scale. Revolutionary propaganda continued unabated in an atmosphere of abundant optimism. Zinoviev, for example, the President of the Communist International, told the 8th Party Congress in March 1919 that in a Soviet Europe he was looking forward to transferring the seat of his organisation from Moscow to Paris.[4]

Chicherin's own contribution to this campaign was an open letter to the German workers, urging them to revolt: 'Time is pressing. The moment has come. There can be no more waiting.'[5] As Chicherin himself said: 'In that year (i.e. 1919) we sent fewer notes to Governments but more appeals to the working masses.'[6]

This atmosphere lasted well on into 1920. Radek on his return to Moscow from Berlin could have found no encouragement for

[1] On both points see Foreign Minister Simons's statement in the Reichstag, January 21, 1921 (Reichstag Debates, Vol. 346, pp. 1990-1992).
[2] Soviet Russia, August 14, 1920, p. 148. This was the official organ of the Soviet Government Bureau in New York.
[3] G. V. Chicherin: Foreign Policy of Soviet Russia—Report of Narkomindel to 7th All-Russian Congress of Soviets, pp. 5-6, Engl. trans., London, 1920, pp. 5-6.
[4] Protokolli VIII Syezda R.K.P. (b) (Proctocols of the 8th Congress of the Russian Communist Party (b)), ed. Em. Yaroslavski, Moscow, 1933, p. 139.
[5] G. V. Chicherin: An die deutschen Arbeiter, Moscow, 1919, p. 23.
[6] G. V. Chicherin: Vnyeshnaya Politika Sovetskoi Rossii za dva goda (Two Years of Soviet Foreign Policy), Moscow, 1920, p. 31.

his thesis of a *modus vivendi* between socialism and capitalism, between Russia and a bourgeois Germany or for any of the ideas discussed in the 'political salon'. All this went into cold storage till the end of the year. When it did re-emerge it was in a rather different form.

Nor was National-Bolshevism welcomed. Lenin called the theories of Lauffenberg and Wolfheim 'crying absurdities'. He explicitly warned the German communists against committing the tactical error of tying their hands in advance. On no account, said Lenin, should they undertake to repudiate the Versailles treaty as soon as they came to power.[1]

Lenin's belief in the Russian position was undiminished. The worst of the intervention was over. In January 1920 the Supreme Council lifted the blockade and in the next few months Russia concluded peace treaties with Esthonia, Latvia and Lithuania. On March 1, Lenin said: 'The international position of the Soviet Republic was never so favourable and victorious as it is now.'[2]

At the end of March, at the 9th Party Congress, Lenin was more precise in linking up the improvement in Russia's international position with the growth of revolution in Germany: ' . . . in the international sphere our position was never so advantageous as now, and what particularly fills us with joy and courage is the news that we receive every day from Germany, and which shows that with however great a strain and effort a socialist revolution is being born, proletarian soviet power in Germany is growing irresistibly. The German Kornilov-Affair has played the same role in Germany as in Russia. After the Kornilov-Affair began the swing-over to proletarian power not only amongst the masses of the town-workers but also amongst the agricultural proletariat of Germany, and this swing-over has a world-historical significance. It gives us not only again and again the absolute conviction of the correctness of our path; it gives us the certainty that the time is not far off when we shall march hand in hand with a German Soviet Government.'[3]

By the 'German Kornilov-Affair' Lenin meant the Kapp Putsch of March 1920. This comparison showed once again the

---

[1] Lenin: *Left Wing Communism—An Infantile Disorder*, Engl. trans., London, 1947, pp. 55-58.
[2] Lenin: *Sochineniya*, Vol. 25, p. 47.
[3] *Devyati Syezd R.K.P. (b) (9th Congress of the Russian Communist Party (b))*, ed. Meschtcheryakov, Moscow, 1934, p. 5; cf. also Bukharin's greetings to the German workers (ibid., pp. 10-11), and Lenin's later remarks (ibid., p. 23).

Bolsheviks' tendency to read the Western European situation in Russian terms. Whereas Kornilov's attempted Putsch in Russia in August 1917 was indeed the last come-back of the Russian right before the Revolution in October and did indeed rally the workers behind the Bolsheviks, the Kapp Putsch in Germany was a very different affair. It was the *first* come-back of the German right after their seeming defeat in November, 1918. It was accompanied for example by a campaign in the German nationalist press for Hindenburg as President.[1]

There was, nevertheless, a sense in which Lenin was right about Kapp—though he was hardly aware of this. The Putsch marked the last attempt, until 1933, by the anti-Russian German Right to seize power. It was a recapitulation of the split in their ranks that had first broken out in the Baltic the previous year and that had then been expressed in the differing attitudes of Seeckt and Goltz towards the campaign. Now matters came to a head.

As early as February 1919 Seeckt had warned Kapp, a high-ranking, super-patriotic Prussian civil servant, against any counter-revolutionary plans.[2] But the latter had persisted. When he eventually struck in March 1920 he was backed by a gang of generals and thugs who were not only anti-communist—Seeckt was that himself—but also anti-Russian. This Seeckt emphatically was not. On the contrary he had already written in January 1920: 'As I consider the future political and economic understanding with Great Russia the fixed aim of our policy, we must at least try not to antagonise Russia.'[3] The Kapp Generals on the other hand—primarily Ludendorff, Goltz and Lüttwitz—identified Russia with communism. Seeckt was 'the soul of the military opposition' with which they had to contend.[4]

Another motive for Seeckt's uncompromising opposition to the Kappists lay in the fact that they came to the brink of bringing the army into a head-on clash with the organised workers; for no sooner did Kapp proclaim himself Chancellor, than the trade unions declared a general strike. The possibility of an army trade union conflict was Seeckt's nightmare. Although the Reichwehr

---

[1] F. von Rabenau: *Seeckt—Aus Seinem Leben 1918-1936*, Leipzig, 1940, p. 128; F. Stampfer: *Die Vierzehn Jahre der ersten deutschen Republik*, Karlsbad, 1936, p. 153. Stampfer was the editor of *Vorwärts* (the Social-Democratic daily) a Reichstag deputy and a personal friend of Ebert.

[2] Ibid., p. 143, note 4.

[3] Ibid. p. 252.

[4] Gen. Lüttwitz: *Im Kampf gegen die November-Revolution*, Berlin, 1934, p. 122.

was used as an instrument of class war, it is also true that Seeckt, no less than Schleicher, his political adviser at this time, tried as far as possible to create an amicable relationship between the army and the people. The Kappists threatened to destroy this hope at the outset.

In the event, the conflict was avoided. After only a few days as Chancellor, Kapp collapsed in ignominy. No less ignominious was the defeat of Goltz and Ludendorff. This time they had stuck their necks out too far. Not until Hitler came to power did either play any significant part in German political life. Nor did either of them or any of their associates take any share in the creation of the new Reichswehr of 100,000 men.

This was Seeckt's work, initiated in June 1920 when he gathered into his own hands supreme military power as Chef der Heeresleitung. The new Commander-in-Chief of the Reichswehr was a Junker through and through. He had spent his youth in the aristocratic Alexander Regiment before being seconded to the General Staff. During the Great War he had initially been Chief of Staff to von Mackensen and was largely credited with the latter's break-through at Gorlice-Tarnowo in 1915. Later he became Chief of Staff to the Turkish Armies and was in Constantinople when the Turks collapsed. He left at once for Berlin and was on his way through the Ukraine when he heard of the Kaiser's abdication. This was the only occasion in decades to move Seeckt to tears. He lost all sense of time and place, so overwhelming was the loss.[1]

In appearance Seeckt resembled nothing more than one of George Grosz's brilliant caricatures in *Das Gesicht der Herrschenden Klassen*. But he was none the less clever for that. One example of his breadth of outlook may be cited: the introduction of what his biographer calls 'psycho-technical' tests for the selection of Reichswehr officers.[2] This is an interesting example of the invariable concomitant of scientific progress—the improvement in the technique of destruction. As Tolstoy once wrote: 'if the arrangement of society is bad (as ours is) and a small number of people have power over the majority and oppress it, every victory over Nature will inevitably serve only to increase that power and that oppression. This is what is actually happening.'

In foreign-political matters Seeckt, and with him the new

[1] F. von Rabenau: *Seeckt—Aus Seinem Leben 1918-1936*, Leipzig, 1940, p. 115.
[2] Ibid., pp. 490-491.

Reichswehr, were the foremost devotees of a *rapprochement* with Russia. His policy in the Baltic and his contact with Enver Pasha are two instances of this. In the letter of January 1920 already alluded to, he suggests that the collapse of Poland will be the seal of the desired *rapprochement*. 'I refuse to support Poland even in face of the danger that it is gobbled up. On the contrary, I am reckoning on that and if we cannot at the moment help Russia in the re-establishment of her former Imperial Frontiers, then we should certainly not hinder her in this.'[1]

These were prophetic words. Within six months the Russo-Polish war of the summer of 1920 put a Russo-German *rapprochement* fairly and squarely on the map. Pilsudski overplayed his hand very badly. In April 1920 he began to advance eastwards and on May 7 took Kiev in the Ukraine. Then the tide turned. In June the Poles were forced to evacuate Kiev. Soon afterwards the river Bug was reached, the rough ethnographical barrier between Russian Ukraine and Poland proper. In despair at the continued and wholly unexpected isolation of the Russian Revolution, Lenin now took the decision to carry the war into the Polish interior, hoping not only to stimulate revolution in Poland itself but, above all, in Germany.[2] A few weeks later the Red Army was sweeping back the retreating Poles. The Beresina was crossed, Vilno and Grodno fell. Local soviets emerged spontaneously all over Poland. Warsaw itself was threatened. The whole of the Western world seemed on the verge of succumbing to Bolshevism.

Zinoviev has left a graphic description of the atmosphere at the Second Congress of the Communist International meeting at this time in Moscow. 'In the hall of congress hung a large map on which every day the advance of our troops was pin-pointed. And every day the delegates stood with absorbed interest around this map. This was to a certain extent a symbol; the best representatives of the international proletariat followed with absorbed interest—one might also say with a clutch at their hearts—the advance of our armies. We all realised perfectly that if the war aims set before our armies were realised, this would signify an enormous acceleration of the international proletarian revolution. We all understood that on every step forward of our Red Army

---

[1] Ibid., p. 252.
[2] Lenin afterwards admitted that the advance on Warsaw was a mistake (see his remarks at the 10th Party Congress (*Desyati Syezd R.K.P. (b)—Stenographicheski otchet*, Moscow, 1921, p. 14).

there literally depended the fate of the international proletarian revolution.'[1]

But where stood Germany, the country most immediately affected? Once again, as in 1919, Germany was neutral, and once again German neutrality was consciously pro-Russian. On July 25 Dr Simons, the German Foreign Minister, actually forbade the transport across Germany of munitions from France to Poland.[2] Moreover, he and von Maltzan, the head of the Eastern Department in the Auswärtiges Amt, were also preparing to open diplomatic relations with Russia.[3] Posen, the pre-1918 Prussian part of Poland, was suspected of desiring to cut adrift from Warsaw.[4] Some people were watching the advance of the Soviet troops 'with feverish sympathy'.[5] Others even wanted Germany to attack Poland from the rear.[6] Seeckt himself went prudently on leave on August 1, confident that the Poles would succumb.[7] It was not only the German dockers in Danzig, who, by their refusal to trans-ship French munitions for Poland, were actively pro-Russian, but many of the right-wing as well. German neutrality was 'not without benevolence on the side of Lenin . . . ' wrote the Stinnes-owned *Kölnische Zeitung*.[8]

In the end, of course, Warsaw was saved. Pilsudski, a half-crazy military adventurer, became the saviour of the West. 'The ponderous balances have adjusted themselves to a new decision. Poland, like France, is not to perish, but to live. Europe, her liberties and her glories, are not to succumb to Kaiserism or to Communism.'[9] None the less, neither in Moscow nor in Berlin were the lessons of the Russo-Polish war forgotten. It was the decisive factor in clearing the ground for Rapallo.

[1] Ibid., p. 271.

[2] Ian F. D. Morrow: *The Peace Settlement in the German-Polish Borderlands*, London, 1936, p. 71. Lord d'Abernon, a member of the Allied Mission in Warsaw, remarked that the German ban made 'the question of how to get munitions through to Poland from the West one of immense difficulty.' (Lord d'Abernon: *The 18th Decisive Battle of the World*, London, 1931, p. 48.)

[3] Radek in *Pravda*, October 15, 1921.

[4] Lord d'Abernon, op. cit., p. 65.

[5] Chancellor Fehrenbach, Reichstag Debates, Vol. 345, pp. 786-787.

[6] E.g. the nationalist Count Ernst Reventlow, ibid., Vol. 381, p. 697.

[7] F. von Rabenau: *Seeckt—Aus Seinem Leben 1918-1936*, Leipzig, 1940, p. 253.

[8] Quoted in A. Erusalimski : *Germaniya, Antanta i S.S.S.R. (Germany, the Entente and the U.S.S.R.)*, Moscow, 1927, p. 83. 'The reactionary Germans', wrote Churchill, 'would of course be delighted to see the downfall of Poland at the hands of the Bolsheviks for they fully understand that a strong Poland standing between Germany and Russia is the one thing that will baulk their plans for (an imperialist) reconstruction and revenge' (*The World Crisis—the Aftermath*, London, 1929, p. 265).

[9] Churchill, op. cit., p. 270.

CHAPTER II

The Formation of Soviet Foreign Policy and its Relation to the Communist International

It is only from the end of the Russo-Polish War, say from the late summer of 1920, that a Russian foreign policy in the usual sense of the term can be said to have existed. Previously, at a time when world revolution was taken to be an imminent possibility, there existed no clear-cut necessity for any foreign policy. A Foreign Minister in the person of George Chicherin did indeed exist. But how little store he set by purely diplomatic activity was evidenced by his willingness to turn from diplomatic negotiation to revolutionary encouragement. His function being considered purely stop-gap, he could hardly be distinguished from Zinoviev, the President of the Communist International. The distinction was at best on paper.

However, a time was to come when the distinction would become very sharp, in the sense that circumstances would impose the necessity of choosing either foreign policy or revolution. In the last resort the two were incompatible. The seeds of the transformation whereby the People's Commissariat for Foreign Affairs —usually referred to by its Russian initials as Narkomindel— gradually took precedence over the claims of the Comintern were sown towards the end of 1920.

Where did Narkomindel's policy originate? There can be no doubt that the seat of its power lay in the Politburo of the Central Committee of the Russian Communist Party. At the 9th Party Congress in 1920 Lenin stated categorically that in the interval since the previous congress 'the Politburo decided all questions of international and internal policy'.[1] Two years later he spoke of this situation as 'an amalgamation' of a party institution (the Politburo) with a soviet institution (Narkomindel). This, he went on, 'was brought about at the very beginning. Have we not in the Politburo discussed from the party point of view many questions, both major and minor, concerning the "moves" we should make in reply to the "moves" of foreign powers in order to

[1] Lenin: *Sochineniya*, Vol. 25, p. 95.

forestall their, let us say, cunning, if we are not to use a less respectable term?' Lenin ended with the hope that what had become 'customary' in one sphere would soon apply to the 'machinery of state as a whole'.[1]

On the other hand, it was not necessarily the case that Narkomindel danced to Politburo's tune. According to an eye-witness of the latter's conduct of affairs in 1923-1924 the Politburo not only dealt first with the foreign-political items on its agenda but it also usually summoned to its deliberations Chicherin, the Minister of Foreign Affairs, and Litvinov, his chief deputy, possibly as much for the benefit of their advice as for the purpose of issuing instructions.[2] The same witness has left vivid pen-portraits of the Minister and his deputy. 'Chicherin came with a fat brief-case full of documents. He was always extraordinarily polite and behaved as shyly as a schoolboy. He had a thin voice, spoke rather quickly and slightly rolled his r's. His look was a little frightened; he was somewhat afraid of the members of the Politburo. . . . He was a very modest and pliable Minister.'

Litvinov, on the other hand, behaved himself very unpleasantly. 'With his hands in his trouser-pockets, untidy clothes and with an eternally dissatisfied expression. . . . He abruptly interrupts his interlocutor in order to speak himself.'[3]

The Politburo also exercised a great deal of influence on the policy of the Communist International. This came about through an historical evolution. In 1919, Zinoviev had considered the Comintern to be so little a Russian institution that he had envisaged the transfer of its headquarters to Paris.[4] In later years however it came increasingly to be dominated by Moscow. It was Rosa Luxemburg's foresight into this situation that caused her to instruct the K.P.D. delegate to the foundation congress of the Comintern to vote against its formation. At this period Lenin disagreed with her and characterised all accusations of undue Russian influence in the Comintern as 'eyewash'. 'As a matter of fact', he went on, 'the Executive Committee of the Communist

---

[1] Lenin: *Sochineniya*, Vol. 27, p. 413.
[2] Boris Bajanov: *Stalin—der rote Diktator*, Berlin, 1931, p. 110. Bajanov was at this time Stalin's secretary in the Politburo. Neither Chicherin nor Litvinov were ever members of the Politburo.
[3] Ibid. pp. 110-111.
[4] See above p. 25.

International consists of twenty members of whom only five are members of the Russian Communist Party'.[1]

Nevertheless, though this numerical proportion remained fairly constant, the weight of those five members became increasingly important. In a speech towards the end of his active career, Lenin came to realise this and to warn against it. At the end of 1922 he spoke to the Fourth Congress of the Comintern about a resolution that had been adopted the previous year on the organisational structure of the various national Communist parties. He complained to the Congress that everything in the resolution had been 'taken from Russian conditions'. It was 'too Russian', for which reason a foreigner would be 'unable to understand it. . . . We have not learnt to present our Russian experience to foreigners. All that has been said in the resolution has remained a dead letter.'[2]

Needless to say, the historical tendency, once under way, proved impossible to reverse. It was, in fact, intensified when a programme for the 'Bolshevisation' of the Communist parties was adopted in 1924. At approximately the same time, the relative degree of independence which the Comintern had enjoyed in policy matters began to decline. In 1923, in Germany, it had already been used to some extent as an instrument of Soviet foreign policy.[3] Later this position became more and more pronounced so that the Comintern came to reflect more and more the changes in Russian foreign policy rather than to base its activities on an independent analysis of the situation. To take one example only, the great change of 1928 can be traced over a period of a year from its first heralding in the columns of *Izvestya* to its appearance a year later in the Comintern.[4]

On what principle did the members of the Politburo base their activities? On precisely the same principle as did those who may be generally, albeit somewhat loosely, referred to as the Whites. On one occasion indeed Lenin himself pointed out this identity. His vade-mecum of communist political tactics—Left Wing Communism—An Infantile Disorder'—is dedicated: To the Right Honourable Mr Lloyd George as a token of my

[1] Lenin: *Sochineniya*, Vol. 25, p. 381.
[2] Ibid., Vol. 27, p. 354.
[3] For this point see below Chapter V.
[4] See below p. 138.

gratitude for his speech on March 18, 1920, which was almost Marxist and, in any case, exceedingly useful for Communists and Bolsheviks throughout the World.'[1]

[1] The speech of Lloyd George referred to was made to a gathering of Liberal M.Ps. in Westminster Hall. It formed part of Lloyd George's campaign to keep his coalition government together by appealing for the support of all groups of Liberals. The speech is reported in *The Times*, March 19, 1920.)

CHAPTER III

The Path to Rapallo (1920-1922)

NEITHER in Germany nor in Russia were the lessons of the Polish War lost. A common interest in the suppression of Poland had linked Russia and Germany throughout most of the nineteenth century. A similar common interest, though on a very different basis, was to bring them together again in the twentieth century. To Germany, largely at whose expense Poland had been created by the Versailles Treaty, the War was the most powerful argument possible in favour of a *rapprochement* with Russia; for had Poland fallen, the Treaty of Versailles would have fallen with her.[1] In a most graphic and convincing manner the Russo-Polish War brought a sudden spotlight to bear on all the possibilities latent in co-operation with the Bolsheviks.

The Bolsheviks were not of course interested in overthrowing the Versailles Treaty for the sake of restoring Imperial Germany. On the other hand, the War had for them a no less important application than it had for the Germans. It meant that they remained just as isolated in 1920 as in 1918. After almost two years of revolutionary agitation, of appeals to the masses of the world, culminating in the desperate attempt to carry revolution to the West at the bayonet point, no lasting Soviet success had been attained. Soviet isolation was as great as ever.

The consequence of this was to bring at once into the immediate foreground the problem of safeguarding the existence of the one Communist state in a capitalist world. It was a question that, in view of the expectation of a world revolution, had so far not been considered on any large scale. Only Radek in Berlin had so far considered the matter at all. Now Lenin too came to grips with it. For the ideological approach of world revolution he largely substituted the non-ideological approach of foreign policy.

There were, besides the experience of the Polish failure, solid reasons for this change of attitude. The most solid was of course

[1] cf. Churchill: 'Poland was the linch-pin of the Treaty of Versailles.' (*The World Crisis—the Aftermath*, London, 1929, p. 262); cf. also Lenin: 'If Poland had become Soviet . . . the Versailles peace would have been crushed and the whole international system forced by the victors on Germany would have collapsed' (*Sochineniya*, Vol. 25, p. 402).

36 RUSSIA AND THE WEIMAR REPUBLIC

the continued existence of capitalism. It had withstood, in the main, the most ferocious assaults of the Bolsheviks. But it had also been compelled to relax its hostility towards them. For one thing, the blockade had been lifted early in 1920 and Russia was at peace with all her Western border states. More important, active trade negotiations were in progress with Britain and Germany; and inside Russia, in the Autumn of 1920, Baron Wrangel, the last of the White generals, was driven from his stronghold in the Crimea. Very, very slowly Russia was coming to peace with the rest of the world. Lenin, for example, took the Polish war to be the last attack on Soviet Russia.[1]

A little later he considered the implications of this: 'We have shown ourselves to be in such a position that, without having obtained an international victory—the only stable one for us—we have won for ourselves the conditions in which we may exist side by side with capitalist states who are now forced to enter into trading relations with us. In the process of this struggle we have won for ourselves the right to an independent existence.

'Thus looking at our position as a whole, we see that we have won enormous successes, that we have not only a breathing space but something much more serious . . . we have a new phase when our basic international existence has been fought for and attained within the network of capitalist states . . . now we must already talk not only of a breathing-space but of a serious chance for reconstruction over a longer period of time.'[2]

This was the first occasion since the establishment of the Soviet Republic that Lenin permitted himself to talk in such terms. He had never before envisaged anything other than a 'breathing-space' as a prelude to war, or war itself, between the two systems of property. Now, some three years after the Revolution, he saw at last the prospect of peace between them. A real turning-point had arrived. It affected of course all Russia's relations with the outside world. But to Germany it had a special application.

Enver Pasha had been in Moscow in 1920 during the Russo-Polish War; and on August 26 of that year he wrote (in un-grammatical German) a letter to Seeckt. He spoke of having just seen 'Trotsky's really important aide' which is perhaps a reference to Sklyansky, Deputy Commissar for War. He continues: 'There is a party here which has real power, and Trotsky also belongs to

[1] Lenin: *Sochineniya,* Vol. 25, p. 401.
[2] Ibid., pp. 485-486.

this party, which is for an agreement with Germany. This party
would be ready to recognise the old German frontier of 1914.
And they see only one way out of the present world chaos—that is
co-operation with Germany and Turkey. In order to strengthen
the position of this party and to win the whole Soviet Government
for the cause, would it not be possible to give unofficial help, and
if possible sell arms? . . . I think it important that you should
come to an understanding with their representatives in order that
Germany's position also should be clear and certain. To help the
Russians one can, in the Corridor or in some suitable place, bring
into being a volunteer army or an insurrectionary movement. . . . '[1]

That Lenin's mind was moving in the same direction is evident
from various speeches delivered in the autumn and winter of 1920.

On three occasions in four months Lenin spoke of the
phenomenon of a pro-Bolshevik right-wing in Germany during
the Polish war. It must clearly have made a deep impression on
him. On September 22, he told a party conference: 'As our
troops approached Warsaw all Germany began to ferment. There
was reproduced there the picture which could be observed in
Russia in 1905, when the Black Hundreds aroused and called to
political activity extensive layers of the most reactionary peasantry,
who today march against the Bolsheviks but who tomorrow will
demand all the land from the land-owners. And in Germany we
saw a similar unnatural bloc of Black Hundreds and Bolsheviks.
There appeared a strange type of reactionary-revolutionary. . . . '[2]
On October 15, 1920 Lenin returned to the same theme. At the
time of the Russian advance on Warsaw, he said, 'everyone in
Germany, even the blackest reactionaries and monarchists said
that the Bolsheviks would save us, when they saw that the Versailles peace is splitting at all its seams, that it is the Red Army
which has declared war on all capitalists'.[3]

But it was in a speech in December 1920 that Lenin dealt in
full with the implications of the German phenomenon. At the
same time he gave an exposé of the decree on concessions of the
previous month. This was purely legal in form, laying down the

[1] Quoted in F. von Rabenau: *Seeckt—Aus Seinem Leben 1918-1936*, Leipzig, 1940,
p. 307.
[2] Lenin: *Sochineniya*, Vol. 25, p. 378. The 'Black Hundreds' in Russia were counter-
revolutionary gangs organised by the Tsar to break up workers' demonstrations and
to instigate anti-Jewish pogroms.
[3] Lenin, op. cit., p. 418.

conditions under which foreign investors would be entitled to lease concessions on Russian territory. Lenin now showed that it was also highly important from the angle of foreign policy. It was even more important from the angle of policy towards Germany. The speech is lengthy and extensive extracts require to be quoted.

Lenin began by repeating his conviction—one which he shared with all the Soviet leaders—that the Soviets owed their survival to the divisions prevailing amongst their enemies. The concessions to be offered under the terms of the decree would have the effect of intensifying these divisions. Should war be renewed, those capitalists with concessions in Russia would tend to find themselves on the Soviet side.[1]

Now for Germany: 'this country, bound by the Versailles Treaty, finds itself in circumstances that make its existence impossible. And in such a position Germany is naturally pushed into alliance with Russia. When the Russian troops advanced on Warsaw, all Germany was in a ferment. The alliance with Russia of this country, which is stifled [but] which is in position to set in motion gigantic productive forces—all this had as consequence that a political mix-up was produced in Germany. The German reactionaries marched with the Spartacists in sympathy with the Russian bolsheviks and this is fully understandable for it emerges from economic causes. This forms the basis of our economic position and of all our foreign policy.

Our foreign policy while we are alone and while the capitalist world is strong consists, on the one hand, in our exploiting contradictions. (To conquer all the imperialist powers would of course be the most desirable thing but we will not be in a position to do that for a rather long time). Our existence depends on there existing a radical divergence amongst the imperialist powers on the one hand and, on the other, that the victory of the Entente and the Versailles peace have made it impossible for the overwhelming majority of the German nations to live. The Versailles peace has created a position such that Germany cannot dream of a breathing-space, cannot dream of not being plundered, of not being deprived of the means of life, of her population not being condemned to hunger and starvation. Germany cannot dream of this and naturally her only means of saving herself is by an alliance with Soviet Russia, whither they are directing their

[1] Lenin: *Sochineniya*, Vol. 26, pp. 7-9.

glances. They madly attack Soviet Russia, they hate the Bolsheviks, they shoot their communists like real genuine White
Guards. The German bourgeois government madly hates the
Bolsheviks but the interests of its international position impel it
towards peace with Soviet Russia against its own wish. This,
comrades, is the second pillar of our international and foreign
policy: to prove to those peoples, conscious of the bourgeois yoke,
that there is no salvation for them outside the Soviet Republic.
And in so far as the Soviet Republic for three years has withstood
the pressure of the imperialists, this speaks of the fact that there
is one country in the world—and only one country—that successfully rejects this yoke of imperialism. . . .

The existence of Germany is impossible by virtue of the conditions created for her by the Entente. The people are dying
there . . . such a position pushes Germany towards a *rapprochement* with Soviet Russia. I do not know the details of the treaty
between Germany and the Entente. In any case it is well known
that in this treaty direct trading relations between Germany and
Soviet Russia are forbidden. The conditions of their existence
force the people of Germany as a whole, not excluding the German
reactionaries and capitalists, to seek relations with Soviet Russia.
Thus it is clear that we must put forward concessions, as an
economic method, even independently of how far we will succeed
in realising our plan. . . . We must pursue this policy because by
it we hamper a crusade of the imperialist countries against us. . . .

Our policy groups round the Soviet Republic capitalist countries
which imperialism is stifling. That is why this offer of concessions
has not only a capitalist significance, that is why this hand is
extended not only to the German capitalists—"Send us hundreds
of tractors and take 300 per cent rouble profits if you want them"
—but this hand is also extended to oppressed peoples and the
alliance of the oppressed masses, which is one of the factors of the
growing proletarian revolution.'[1]

In this way, the necessity of a *modus vivendi* with Germany, as
foreseen by Radek in 1919, re-emerged. But although it was on
the basis of a common Russo-German opposition to Versailles,
it differed from the earlier formulation in providing for revolution
in Germany. Lenin was trying to dance at two weddings at the

[1] Lenin: *Sochineniya*, Vol. 26, pp. 14-16. As a matter of fact, although the
Versailles Treaty between Germany and the Entente was aimed at keeping Russia
and Germany apart (see above p. 21) it did not explicitly forbid trading relations
between them.

same time. He was trying to effect a *rapprochement* with the German bourgeoisie at the same time as he was trying to win the support of the German workers. By opposing the Versailles 'Yoke of Imperialism' the Soviets would gain the sympathy of these suffering under this yoke; and by holding out favourable trading prospects to the German bourgeoisie he would give them a vested interest in the continued existence of the Soviets. He would also intensify the conflict amongst the capitalist powers.

Lenin, whose works include a brochure on Clausewitz, was fully aware that war and peace are relative terms. There exists no absolute distinction between them. There was therefore no reason why the same policy should not serve in both. That which had saved the Soviets in 1919—the lack of co-ordinated action amongst their enemies—would equally well save them in peace. As he once put it: 'while we remain economically and militarily weaker than the capitalist world we must stick to this rule: we must learn to exploit the contradictions and oppositions amongst the imperialists'.[1]

On the other hand, it was not possible for long both to exploit the contradiction between Germany and the West and to maintain the revolutionary overtones to the support of Germany. Lenin's aim of exposing the imperialist nature of Versailles to the German masses was not compatible with simultaneously backing the national struggle of the German bourgeoisie against the Treaty. This distinction speedily disappeared. Before long the Soviets found themselves supporting Germany without distinguishing between Germans. Only three years later, in 1923, Radek was even trying to bring the murderers of Liebknecht and Luxemburg into a Russo-German front.[2]

Theoretically, there was no reason why the Russians could not have worked with France or England in the same way as they were now preparing to work with Germany. But in point of fact only Germany was willing 'to knock on the Eastern gate' as Dr Pfeiffer had put it. Again a debate in the Reichstag was symptomatic. In January, 1921, Dr Simons, the German Foreign Minister, showed that he was as uninhibited in desiring to work with the Soviets as they were with him: 'Communism as such is no reason why a German republican and bourgeois Government should not trade with the Soviet Government.'[3]

[1] Lenin: *Sochineniya*, Vol. 25, p. 498.
[2] See below p. 77.
[3] Reichstag Debates, Vol. 346, p. 1994.

But Germany still had to tread very warily. There was as yet no independent German foreign policy. Entente pressure was still a factor to be reckoned with. New political forces were incubating, however, and these could not but be hostile to the Entente and Versailles Powers, hitherto predominant in Europe.

In February 1921 Kopp, who had apparently been in Germany uninterruptedly since his arrival in January 1920, returned to Moscow. To *Izvestya*, he gave the good news that 'in the near future the organisation of a (Russo-German) mutual trade representation will be established'.[1]

In March the 10th Party Congress re-affirmed the policy of commercial *rapprochement* with capitalism.[2] Lenin acknowledged that 'in comparison with last year the international revolution has taken a big step forward. . . . But if we were to deduce from this that within a short interval help will come to us from there [*i.e.* Western Europe] in the form of a stable proletarian revolution, then we would simply be mad and I am sure there are no such people in this hall. . . . And therefore we must learn so to co-ordinate our activity with the class-relationships inside our country and other countries that we may maintain over a lengthy period the dictatorship of the proletariat and, although gradually, heal the wounds and crises that have befallen us. This is the only correct and sober way to pose the question.'[3]

What now broke the ice in the relations between Russia and capitalism was the Anglo-Russian Trade Treaty of March 1921. It 'served as a door opening on the arena of world politics', writes one authoritative Russian source.[4] Two months later Germany also signed a Trade Treaty with Russia. Its main feature was an undertaking by Germany to recognise solely the Soviet Government as the Government of Russia and to refuse to maintain relations with any emigré claimants to authority. (At this time Berlin was swarming with Whites). The Treaty was greeted in Moscow as 'a new diplomatic success'.[5] Germany might have said the same; for the treaty was ostentatiously signed on May 6,

[1] *Izvestya*, February 1, 1921.
[2] *Desyati Syezd R.K.P. (b)—Stenographicheskii otchet (Tenth Congress of the Russian Communist Party (b)—Stenographic report)*, Moscow, 1921, p. 328.
[3] Ibid. pp. 17-18.
[4] I. Maisky: *Vneshnyaya Politika R.S.F.S.R. 1917-1922 (Foreign Policy of the R.S.F.S.R. 1917-1922)*, Moscow, 1922, p. 103.
[5] Steklov in *Izvestya*, May 10, 1921.

the day following the receipt of the London ultimatum on reparations. This obliged Germany to acknowledge her total reparation indebtedness of 132 billion gold marks and to accept the Allies' method of payment. In these circumstances the Russo-German Trade Treaty was a warning to the world that when hard-pressed in the West, Germany could always 'knock on the Eastern gate', or otherwise call in the new world to redress the balance of the old. This she now proceeded to do, with more and more success. During the rest of 1921 there took place a steady thickening of the Russo-German link. This was against a background of a steady, intermittent worsening in German-Allied relations that was to culminate in the occupation of the Ruhr in 1923.

At first this took a predominantly economic form. To the second half of 1921 belong the preliminary negotiations on several of the mixed companies and concessions that were later such a feature of Russo-German trade. The mixed companies were financed by capital from both countries. They included Derumetall, for the export of Russian scrap metal; Deruluft, for the organisation of air transport between the two countries; and Derutra, to handle all Russian transport in the Baltic. Of the concessions two of the most important were a Krupps agricultural concession in the area of the Manych River, a tributary of the Don; and a joint export-import company, whose German head was Louis Wolff, the Cologne industrialist. The two German directors of Derutra were Dr Melchior, a Hamburg banker, and Hildermann, of the Hamburg-America line.[1] By May 31, 1923 German capital was leading with ten ratified concessions. There were six each with the United States and Great Britain; and four each with Norway and Sweden. Including sundry others the total was twenty-nine.[2] Leonid Krassin, Commissar for Foreign Trade, had formerly been the managing director of the Siemens-Schuckert branch in St Petersburg.[3] The contacts he had then developed with the German official and industrial world now stood the Bolsheviks in good stead, for Krassin played a leading part in all the concessions negotiations.

---

[1] For all above see Dr Fuckner: *Russlands Neue Wirtschafts-politik*, Berlin and Leipzig, 1922, pp. 25-26; *Aus der Volkswirtschaft der Ud.S.S.R.—Sonderausgabe zu den deutschen Herbstmessen*, Berlin, 1923, p. 99; A. Erusalimski: *Germaniya, Antanta i S.S.S.R.*, Moscow, 1928, p. 89.

[2] *Izvestya*, May 31, 1923.

[3] Lyubov Krassin: *Leonid Krassin*, London, 1929, p. 40.

At the diplomatic level a further exchange of representatives took place. On September 19, Professor Arthur Wiedenfeld, the head of the foreign trade department of the German Foreign Office, arrived in Moscow; and on October 25 Nikolai Krestinski, former Commissar for Finance, arrived in Berlin.[1] Krestinski had been in Germany off and on during 1921. He had been concerned in the negotiations preceding the trade treaty signed in May;[2] and in July he had the misfortune to be arrested by the German police while taking the cure at the Bavarian spa of Bad Kissingen.[3] However, none the worse for his experience, we may suppose, on November 15 he handed over his credentials as Russian plenipotentiary representative to Reich Chancellor Wirth. His accompanying statement went considerably beyond the formula usual on such occasions: 'For the industrial reconstruction of Russia, torn by the imperialist and civil wars, as well as by intervention and blockade, a resumption and a many-sided widening of her relations with Germany are vitally necessary.

The post-war position of Germany also demands collaboration with Russia. These mutual interests found their first juridical expression in the treaty of May 6, 1921. In the name of the Soviet Government I express the hope that the mutual relations between Russia and Germany will not be limited by the framework of the treaty of May 6 but will lead to the closer collaboration of Russia and Germany, indispensable in the interests of the people of both countries.'

Wirth replied: 'For my part, I declare that I consider it my main task to strive for the consolidation of the relations of both peoples on the basis of their co-operation.'[4]

Two entirely separate and quite different events contributed powerfully to the fulfilment of Krestinski's hope. The first was the Russian famine of the second half of 1921. Nansen's appeals to the League of Nations received no official response, for the Western Powers hoped to exploit the situation to weaken the Bolsheviks—even at the cost of many lives. In his efforts to give relief Nansen was forced back on the generous though inadequate support of private individuals.[5] One delegate to the 9th Congress

[1] I. Maisky: *Vneshnaya Politika R.S.F.S.R. 1917-22*, Moscow, 1922, pp. 106-107.
[2] *Birmingham Post*, April 27, 1921.
[3] *Daily Telegraph*, July 12, 1921.
[4] *Izvestya*, November 27, 1921. Not until late in August 1922 did Krestinski present his credentials as Russian Ambassador to President Ebert, the head of the German state (*Russian Information and Review*, September 1, 1922, p. 554.)
[5] E. E. Reynolds: *Nansen*, Penguin ed., London 1949, pp. 225-231.

of Soviets in December 1921 bitterly referred to a speech made by
Colonel Wedgwood in the House of Commons, adding: 'if the
British Government had supplied only half the money it had
given to Kolchak and Denikin, there would not have been one
death from starvation in Russia. When it is necessary to attack
the Russian people they find uncountable milliards of roubles.
When it is necessary to help, they calculate with the greatest
cold-bloodedness, with really diabolical calmness.'[1]

Germany however, was the first country to offer help. Radek
contrasted the two attitudes in *Pravda*. After a bitter attack on
the indifference of the Western Powers he goes on: 'Can the
Allies not understand what sort of an impression this must make
on the masses of Russia at a time when the German Government
has been able to open credits to the German Red Cross and is
already loading a ship with medicines . . . ?'[2]

The other event to push Russia and Germany together and to
disillusion both with the West was the solution of the complicated
Upper Silesian question. This industrially valuable area was a
bone of contention between Germany and Poland. Eventually,
after a plebiscite under League auspices in March 1921, the area
was partitioned between the two countries. This took place in
October. Germany considered herself unfairly treated and Poland,
France's ally, to be unduly favoured. This brought about an
important change in personnel in the German Foreign Office.
The post of head of the Eastern Department was taken over by
von Maltzan, a foremost spokesman of the Eastern orientation,
and Behrendt, who favoured the White Russian cause, was
dismissed. After the Russian defeat in the Russo-Polish war,
when Maltzan had favoured opening diplomatic relations with
Russia, he had gone into temporary eclipse. After the Upper
Silesian award he now made a come-back.[3] The new head of the
Eastern Department was linked by marriage to an industrialist
family of Mannheim. Kuno Tiemann, who was at one time a
member of the Auswärtiges Amt, and later became a pacifist,

[1] *IX Vsyerossisski Syezd Sovetov* (9th All-Russian Congress of Soviets), Moscow,
1921, Pt. II, p. 15. The speech referred to is evidently that made by Col. Wedgwood
on November 8, 1921, part of which runs: 'we in this country are not entitled to allow
thirty-five million or even twenty million or ten million people to starve as long as
there is a penny in the pockets of the English people or a pound of food in the country.
Whether they are Russian or whether they are English makes no profound difference
to a Christian people . . .' (*House of Commons Debates*, 1921, Vol. 148, Col. 320).
[2] *Pravda*, August 17, 1921.
[3] Radek in *Pravda*, October 15 and November 11, 1921.

describes his former colleague as 'a superior mind, taciturn, sly, supple, immeasurably ambitious, yielding—even to the extreme— whenever and wherever he thinks this useful, but otherwise ruthless in the same degree'.[1] Lord D'Abernon called Maltzan 'perhaps the cleverest man who has worked in the Wilhelmstrasse since the war'.[2] Like Seeckt he was a Junker linked by marriage to industry and finance. (Seeckt's wife was the daughter of a Jewish banker.)

The World Economic Conference at Genoa now comes into perspective. Its pre-history is formed of two incompatible trends. The first was Chicherin's note of October 28th, 1921 to Great Britain, France, the United States, Japan and Italy suggesting a final settlement between them and the Soviets.[3] The second trend was the increasing need felt by the capitalist world to enter into commercial relations with Russia. This took the form of trying to organise a Consortium, a project discussed at Paris and London at the end of 1921. There were several varieties of Consortium in existence, but common to them all was the presupposition of co-ordinated capitalist action in the reconstruction of Russia. To this presupposition the Russians were unalterably opposed. They much preferred to deal with the capitalist states one by one. It took longer but was more advantageous in the long run since the balance of forces was more evenly distributed.[4] Chicherin was very quick in protesting against the idea of a Consortium. He said that although the Russians wanted to trade with the rest of the world, they rejected any co-operation with bourgeois states which 'took the form of economic domination over Russia'.[5]

None the less, at the January 1922 session of the Supreme Council at Cannes, Lloyd George artificially wove into one the Consortium Conception and the Russian desire to trade on a basis of equality with the capitalist world. Rathenau, one of the chief German delegates, though not at this time a member of the German government, expressed German willingness to adhere to the Consortium. Russia was not mentioned but Rathenau's speech was sufficiently explicit all the same: 'Germany is all the

[1] Die Weltbühne, Feb. 14, 1924, pp. 211-212.
[2] Lord d'Abernon: An Ambassador of Peace, Vol. II, London, 1929, p. 39.
[3] Mezhdunarodnaya Politika Noveshevo Vremeni (Recent International Politics), Vol. III, ed. Klyuchnikov and Sabanin, Moscow, 1928, pp. 140 ff.
[4] I. Maisky: Vneshnaya Politika R.S.F.S.R. 1917-1922, Moscow, 1922, p. 116.
[5] Izvestya, January 28, 1922.

more inclined to take part in reconstruction, as she is familiar with the technical and economic conditions and customs of the East. The path to be taken seems to me the right one. An international syndicate, above all, a private syndicate.'[1] In the end the Cannes Conference issued the invitations to Genoa, the most notable guests being Germany and Russia on a basis of complete equality with the other powers—and at the same time the Conference laid down six conditions for participation in Genoa.[2]

In 1914 Rathenau devoted his managerial talents to the mobilisation of raw materials for the war effort. He ended the war as a super-patriot, quarrelling with Ludendorff over the necessity of the German request for an armistice and calling for a *levée en masse* rather than submit to defeat.[3] When the fact of defeat was clear Rathenau had nothing more to live for. His refusal in 1922 to call in police protection, despite the many threatening letters he received, was a sort of suicide. It was an opportunity that the two well-briefed anti-semitic louts who murdered Rathenau found too good to miss.

In the post-war world Rathenau lost his bearings completely. He tossed uneasily between East and West. On January 1, 1919 he came out in favour of German-American friendship.[4] Later in the year he saw Radek in prison and discussed the prospects of German-Russian collaboration. This phase lasted until the beginning of 1920.[5] In 1921 Rathenau swung West again. In October of that year he concluded the famous agreement with Loucheur, the French Minister of Reconstruction, whereby German reparations would be made not in cash but in kind. Right at the end of 1921 he swung back East. In a conversation with Seeckt he said Germany must strengthen herself internally and then await the appropriate moment 'to strike'.[6] A few weeks later he appeared at Cannes to pledge German support for a Western European Consortium.

In the last resort Rathenau's industrial interests pulled him into the Western camp, the camp of the organisers of the

---

[1] W. Rathenau: *Gesammelte Reden*, Berlin, 1924, p. 373.

[2] These are given in Cmd. 1621, 1922.

[3] Ernst Troeltsch: *Spektator—Briefe*, Tübingen, 1924, p. 286; H. Kessler: *Walter Rathenau—His Life and Work*, Eng. trans., London, 1929, pp. 255-256.

[4] *Foreign Relations of the United States—Paris Peace Conference 1919*, Vol. II, Washington, 1942, p. 158.

[5] See two letters of January and March, 1920, quoted Kessler, op. cit. pp. 292-293.

[6] F. von Rabenau: *Seeckt—Aus Seinem Leben 1918-1936*, Leipzig, 1940, p. 310.

Consortium.[1] German light industry, whose spokesman Rathenau was, not only had affiliations with Western capital but also required imports of raw materials to satisfy its Western markets. German heavy industry, on the other hand, based on the coal and iron of the Ruhr, stood in no necessity of imported raw materials. Besides, its important markets lay in Central and Eastern Europe. It accordingly had no need for a Consortium and wanted to go ahead on its own. The *Deutsche Allgemeine Zeitung* for example, the organ of the Nationalist Party, wrote that as Russia was not interested in Versailles, Germany was 'under a moral obligation, and it is also in her political interests, to bring about a direct economic understanding with Russia before Genoa and to assist Russia in her reconstruction'.[2] Maltzan of the German Foreign Office put this view forward to Lord D'Abernon, the British Ambassador in Berlin, when he told him that trade with Russia should be organised on an individual basis by the great powers and not via an international syndicate.[3] Chancellor Wirth told the Reichstag the same thing in another way. He said Germany 'would have the greatest scruples against a policy that wished to consider and treat Russia as a colony'.[4]

In the same way as there was a conflicting approach between Germany and the West, there was no less a divergence between Britain and France. Hardly had the Cannes Conference laid the basis for Genoa than Briand, the French representative on the Supreme Council, was overthrown by Poincaré. The new French Premier was hostile in principle to Genoa. More than any other French politician, Poincaré supported the status quo as enshrined in the Treaty of Versailles. This was the law; any alteration could only be to France's disadvantage. A special meeting at Boulogne between Lloyd George and Poincaré was required before the latter was won over to support the Conference. Even then he only consented on condition that disarmament and reparations were excluded from the agenda.

Despite this fundamental divergence of view—for if reparations were excluded no serious discussion of economic topics was possible—a group of Allied experts met in London in March.

---

[1] The A.E.G. was the first German concern to receive a large U.S. loan after the war. It came from the New York bankers Kühn, Loeb to whom Felix Deutsch was linked by marriage.
[2] Quoted in *The Daily Telegraph*, February 21, 1922.
[3] Lord d'Abernon: *An Ambassador of Peace*, Vol. I, London, 1929, p. 238.
[4] Reichstag Debates, Vol. 352, p. 5562.

They prepared a memorandum giving the maximum of Allied demands on Russia if trade with that country was to be encouraged. Only one item had any practical importance—Point 6 of the memorandum mentioned, though only *en passant*, Article 116 of the Versailles Treaty.[1] This reserved to Russia the right to claim reparations from Germany. Later it was influential in hastening the conclusion of the Rapallo Treaty.

In Moscow meanwhile, a certain sobriety prevailed. The year 1921, the year that was to initiate a *rapprochement* with the capitalist world, had not brought much tangible result. A trade treaty with England, a trade treaty with Germany, and a few mixed companies and concessions—that was all. It was not very much. In an article in *Pravda* in December, Stalin, in one of his rare incursions into international affairs at this time, wrote that nothing more than an uneasy armistice prevailed between Russia and the capitalist world: 'we have entered a period of a sober calculation of forces, a period of molecular work for the preparation and accumulation of strength for future struggles'.[2] The prospect did not look very bright. It was the inevitable reaction to the collapse of the exuberant hopes of 1920. It was now clear that there was no short cut to socialism but that the road would be a long uphill grind.

Under the circumstances, a pro-German line—the only one that offered itself—was steered more than ever before. In handing over his credentials as plenipotentiary representative, Krestinsky had already come out in favour of a closer relationship between Germany and Russia. Two months later, in January and February 1922, a small Russian delegation consisting of Radek, Krassin and Rakovsky visited Berlin. They discussed Russian policy at Genoa and also threatened Germany with a Franco-Russian *rapprochement*, involving Russia's use of Article 116; *i.e.* Russia, in collaboration with France, might avail herself of the right to claim reparations from Germany.[3]

In Moscow the 11th Party Congress discussed Russian policy at Genoa. The important speech was made by Lenin. 'We go to Genoa', he said, 'not as Communists but as merchants. We must trade and they must trade. . . . We are going to Genoa

[1] Cmd. 1667, p. 7, 1922.
[2] Stalin: *Sochineniya*, Vol. 5, Moscow, 1947, pp. 117-118.
[3] Lord d'Abernon: *An Ambassador of Peace*, London, 1929, pp. 250-253 and 261. Radek's visit also had the purpose of negotiating a military agreement with Seeckt (see p. 61).

with a practical aim—to widen our trading relations. . . . '[1] The
practical keynote was stressed again by Chicherin in Riga. He
told an interviewer that Russian policy was 'economics and
production'.[2] Joffe, in another interview, pointed out the difference between the Russian attitude towards Brest-Litovsk
negotiations with the Germans in 1918 and their attitude towards
the forthcoming Genoa negotiations. From the latter they wanted
a genuine agreement to emerge; at Brest-Litovsk, on the other
hand, they had only been playing for time, pending the outbreak
of world Revolution.[3]

The question of signing a treaty with Germany was raised by
Litvinov with Lenin on the eve of the Russian delegation's
departure for Genoa. If the treaty was genuine, said Lenin,
'Litvinov had his blessing and should go ahead'.[4]

At much the same time as these words were spoken the project
of a separate Russo-German agreement was also being discussed
in the Reichstag. The two countries were coming ever closer
together. Lenin in Moscow was echoed by Stresemann in Berlin.
Stresemann, leader of the German People's Party and closely
connected with such a powerful representative of heavy industry
as Stinnes, specifically opposed German participation in any
international syndicate. The positive tone of his speech showed the
change in the atmosphere since the day when a German Foreign
Minister had cautiously told the Reichstag that 'Communism as
such is no reason why a Republican and bourgeois government
should not trade with the Soviet Government'.[5] Stresemann
warned the Germans against giving Russia 'the impression that
we look on her as a colony for international capital to exploit'.
Germany, he said, should not confront Russia 'as participant in
an international association economically hostile to her'.
Rathenau, now Foreign Minister, wavered characteristically in
his reply. Syndicates could be useful and Germany should not
cut herself off from them. 'On the other hand', he added, 'the
essential part of our reconstruction work will be for discussion
between us and Russia herself. Such discussions have taken place
and are again being held and I will further them by every means.'[6]

[1] Protokolli—odinatsati syezd R.K.P. (b) (Protocols of the 11th Congress of the Russian
Communist Party (b)), ed. N. N. Popov, Moscow, 1936, p. 12.
[2] Izvestya, April 1, 1922.
[3] Ibid., March 2, 1922.
[4] A. Upham Pope: Maxim Litvinov, New York, 1943, pp. 182-183.
[5] Reichstag Debates, Vol. 354, p. 6648.
[6] Ibid., pp. 6655-6656.

D

What specific discussions Rathenau was referring to are not known. What is certain, however, is that when the Russian delegation arrived in Berlin, en route for Genoa, they tried to come to a separate agreement with the Germans and so present the conference with a *fait accompli*.[1] To this Rathenau was the only obstacle, for despite what he had said to the Reichstag he clung to the hope of settling German-Russian relations within the framework of a Russo-European settlement. He also wanted to avoid affronting Britain.[2] All the same, the basis of what only a fortnight later was to become the Rapallo Treaty was drafted at these talks.[3] It was complete except for clauses 2 and 4 dealing respectively with socialised German property in Russia and most-favoured-nation treatment for Germany.[4] Despite the insistence of the Russians and of Maltzan, this was as far as Rathenau would go. 'Evidently', said Joffe afterwards to the Central Committee, 'the European atmosphere and, so to speak, the specific gravity of Russia had at that time still not sufficiently defined themselves for Germany to venture on such an important step'.[5]

Despite this refusal the Berlin talks strengthened considerably the Russian hand. The Soviets were going to Genoa with a Russo-German treaty in their pockets, known only to a very small circle and all but ready for signature. They were not going to face a united capitalist world. In Germany they had if not an ally, then the makings of a friend. It was a decisive improvement.

The Genoa World Economic Conference opened on April 10, 1922. Several hundred delegates were present from thirty-four nations. The gathering was reminiscent of Versailles. The difference lay in the presence of the 'two pariahs of Europe', as Lloyd George once called Germany and Russia, on a basis of equality with the other powers. This was the first such occasion since the war—indeed it was the Bolsheviks' first appearance at any international conference—and interest was correspondingly intense. The Russian delegation was a strong one—led by Chicherin, Commissar for Foreign Affairs, it included Litvinov, his

[1] Louis Fischer: *The Soviets in World Affairs*, London, 1930, p. 333.
[2] H. Kessler: *Walter Rathenau—His Life and Work*, Eng. trans., London, 1929, pp. 328-329.
[3] A. Joffe: *Ot Genui do Gaagi* (From Genoa to The Hague), Moscow and Petrograd, 1923, p. 16.
[4] Louis Fischer, op. cit., p. 332.
[5] Joffe, op. cit., p. 5.

deputy, Krassin, Commissar for Foreign Trade, Rakovsky, President of the Ukrainian Socialist Soviet Republic and Adolf Joffe, former Ambassador to Germany and now a high official in Narkomindel. The German delegation was led by the Reich Chancellor Josef Wirth and Rathenau, his Minister for Foreign Affairs. It also included Maltzan and General Hasse, the leading German negotiator on the military side.[1]

In his opening speech the cultured Chicherin showed the same ability to play the hypocrite as his bourgeois contemporaries. At the same time he made an artful bid for the sympathy of the German delegation. He emphasised the importance of disarmament as a means to peace and called for the outlawing of poisonous gases, aeroplanes, and means of attack against the civilian population.[2] These were the very instruments of war with which Russia was shortly to equip both the Reichwehr and herself.

Three days later, on April 13, Lloyd George played into Chicherin's hands, giving him an excellent opportunity to put increased pressure on the Germans. He invited the Russian delegation to his private residence, the Villa D'Albertis, for confidential talks.[3] Chicherin had little hope that these talks would result in any agreement. He used them rather as a means of bluffing the Germans with the prospect of a Russo-Allied settlement from which Germany would be excluded.[4]

In view of the importance of the Russian question, the Villa D'Albertis became the hub of the Conference whereas the Germans were isolated and remained on the periphery. In these circumstances they rapidly fell victim to the fear that Russia might be induced to make use of Article 116 and claim reparations from Germany. One of their delegates compares it to 'a sword of Damocles' hanging over Germany.[5] This fear was completely groundless. The talks at the Villa D'Albertis were entirely concerned with Russian pre-war debts, war debts, nationalised Allied property and possible credits for Russia.[6] The sole objective justification for the German fear was the mention of Article 116

---

[1] The last-named was taken along at Wirth's suggestion (F. von Rabenau: *Seeckt— Aus Seinem Leben 1918-1936*, Leipzig, 1940, p. 312 n.l).
[2] See the report of his speech in *Izvestya*, April 14, 1922.
[3] H. Kessler: *Walter Rathenau—His Life and Work*, Eng. trans., London, 1929, p. 332.
[4] Louis Fischer: *The Soviets in World Affairs*, London, 1930, p. 343.
[5] Carl Bergmann: *The History of Reparations*, Eng. trans., London, 1927, p. 126.
[6] A. Joffe: *Ot Genui do Gaagi,* Moscow and Petrograd, 1923, pp. 10-13.

in the memorandum prepared by the Allied experts in March.[1]

Nevertheless, inside the German delegation, Maltzan—who may or may not have been consciously deceiving Rathenau—was able to exploit the latter's fear that the Russians and Lloyd George were jointly planning an enormous addition to Germany's reparations burden.[2] This situation lasted for three days—April 13, 14 and 15. By then it had become clear to Chicherin that there was no more point in continuing to negotiate with the Allies. But he had to make sure that he closed with the Germans before they, in their turn, were invited to the Villa D'Albertis and Germany and Russia changed places.

It was late on the night of the 15th that the decision was taken. At 1.15 a.m. of the morning of the 16th Joffe telephoned the German delegation, inviting them to nearby Rapallo to complete the negotiations begun in Berlin.[3] Rathenau, the last obstacle to the proposed meeting, only gave way when he found himself isolated inside his delegation. He had never wanted a treaty with Russia at all.[4]

April 16, 1922 was Easter Sunday. Wirth, a Catholic of the Centre Party, went to Genoa Cathedral to attend High Mass.[5] Meanwhile the atheist Chicherin and the Jew Rathenau slipped quietly away to Rapallo where the Treaty was eventually signed. Lloyd George, by now aware of his mistake, tried to contact Rathenau by telephone.[6] It was too late—the bird had flown.

The terms of Rapallo were innocuous enough. By Articles I and II all mutual claims between the two countries were annulled i.e., Russia renounced her right to reparations from Germany under Article 116 and Germany renounced any claim to compensation for the property of German nationals nationalised by the Bolsheviks. By Article III full diplomatic and consular relations were re-established; Article IV introduced the principle of the most-favoured-nation clause into Russo-German commercial relations with the exception of the relations between Russia and territories formerly belonging to the Russian Empire, such as the

---

[1] See above p. 48.
[2] Louis Fischer: *The Soviets in World Affairs*, London, 1930, pp. 339-340.
[3] Louis Fischer, op. cit., p. 340.
[4] Krassin in *Izvestya*, June 27, 1922. Maltzan used to say that he 'raped' Rathenau at Rapallo (W. von Blücher: *Deutschlands Weg nach Rapallo*, Wiesbaden, 1951, p. 161, n.1).
[5] 'Augur': *Germany and Europe*, London, 1927, p. 75.
[6] Walter Rathenau: *Politische Briefe*, Dresden, 1929, p. 332.

Baltic States. Article V—the heart of the treaty—stipulated that 'the two Governments shall co-operate in a spirit of mutual goodwill in meeting the economic needs of both countries'.[1]

These terms were not technically a breach of the conditions to which Germany had pledged herself. But they were certainly contrary to their spirit. Lloyd George was furious, all the more so as only a few days before the opening of Genoa he had published a memorandum written to Clemenceau in 1919 in which he had warned the then French Premier that a harsh peace would drive Germany into Russia's arms.[2] In a stiff note to the German delegation he roundly accused them of a 'violation of the conditions to which Germany pledged herself in entering the Conference'.[3] In a speech to the House of Commons on his return from Genoa he called Rapallo 'a great error in judgement'. Later in the same speech he pointed out that it might ripen into 'a fierce friendship. . . . What does that mean? . . . Germany is disarmed and if necessary you could disarm her still more . . . you could render her perfectly impotent, but there is one thing you cannot do and that is to prevent the rearming of Russia if the nations are driven to despair. Germany cannot re-equip Russia economically. She has not the capital. It needs the West. That is not the case with armaments where you have every natural resource in one country and every technical skill in the other. It is necessary that we should look at all the possibilities of the situation.'[4]

The French were no less alarmed than the British and tried to secure the annulment of Rapallo. They referred it to the Reparations Commission on the grounds that Germany had violated Article 116, but received no response.[5]

The fact is that both the principal Versailles Powers saw their position threatened by the coming together of the outcasts. For this there was a large amount of justification. At Genoa Germany was punished by being excluded from any further discussion of the Russian question. But she became in reality the mediator between East and West.[6] This was a foretaste of the future.

By contrast with the very quick reaction of the Western

[1] L.N.T.S., Vol. 19, p. 248.
[2] Cmd. 1614, 1922, referred to above p. 21.
[3] Cmd. 1667, 1922, pp. 53-54.
[4] House of Commons Debates, Vol. 154, 1922, Cols. 1457-1458.
[5] A. Erusalimski: *Germaniya, Antanta i S.S.S.R.*, Moscow, 1928, p. 97.
[6] Walter Rathenau: *Politische Briefe*, Dresden, 1929, pp. 334-335.

Powers, the two Rapallo signatories themselves reacted very slowly and even contradictorily to their action. It is quite clear that neither the Russians nor the Germans were aware of the full implications of what they had done.

As far as the Russians were concerned there was an unmistakable divergence in the evaluation of Rapallo. Their interpretations fell under two main headings. There were, firstly, those who saw in the Treaty nothing more than the re-establishment of the most ordinary diplomatic relations between one country and another. Since the Soviet Republic, however regrettably, existed in isolation, it obviously required to have a certain minimum of relations with the outside world. Of this irreducible minimum Rapallo was the model. It was the ideal relationship between a Soviet and a bourgeois state.

As against this, other Soviet voices, while not denying their satisfaction at the nature of the relations established, spoke of Rapallo in quite different terms. They spoke of it in the usual terms of power-politics, drawing the conclusion that Russia had committed herself to the European balance of power.

Of the first interpretation Joffe, Kamenev and Trotsky were pre-eminently the spokesmen. In a lengthy report to the Central Committee, Joffe made not the slightest reference to the balance of power aspect of Rapallo. On the contrary, he saw its political significance in two main features. Firstly, it re-established normal diplomatic relations with a major European power. Secondly, Germany's renunciation of all her claims on Russia was 'the only possible solution' of the problem of Russian debts and in so doing, Germany had created 'a valuable precedent', breaking 'the united front of the world bourgeoisie in this basic, most important question'.[1] In view of Rapallo's later importance, entirely apart from the fact that it was backed by some of the most important elements in German society, Joffe's survey ended on a very surprising note: 'One could much rather . . . speak of the possible instability of the Rapallo Treaty which is more advantageous to Russia than to Germany. For that which is born of cowardice can equally well be destroyed by cowardice'.[2]

Under Joffe's guidance the Central Committee welcomed Rapallo in similar terms. Its resolution saw in the Treaty the only possible means of giving 'equality of rights of the two systems and

[1] A. Joffe: *Ot Genui do Gaagi*, Moscow and Petrograd, 1923, pp. 17, 31, 32.
[2] Ibid., p. 32.

agreement between them . . . until the whole world has advanced from private property . . . to a higher system of property'.[1]

Kamenev's interpretation also fell into this framework. He told *Pravda* that the Treaty was a 'model' agreement between Russia and any other state.[2]

Trotsky was the most vigorous in denying that the Treaty had anything to do with power-politics. The U.S. International News Service asked him this question: 'Is the Russo-German Treaty an alliance of Russia and Germany as a counterweight to the other groupings of the European Powers?' Trotsky replied: 'Germany is separated from the Soviet Republic by the same basic contradictions of property systems as the countries of the Entente. This means that the possibility of talking of the Rapallo Treaty as of some offensive-defensive alliance to counterbalance other states is excluded. It is a question of the re-establishment of the most elementary inter-state and economic relations. On the principles of the Rapallo Treaty, Soviet Russia is ready to sign today a treaty with any other country.'[3]

These people, Trotsky, Joffe, Kamenev, were the guardians of the ideological chastity of the Soviet Union. In other quarters the lady's virginity was considerably impugned. To Chicherin the Treaty marked 'the emergence of new international-political forces. The treaty of Rapallo marked the end of the first post-war period of the triumph of the victors.' Russia gained a *point d'appui*, a foothold in the capitalist world and Germany was enabled to safeguard her political independence despite Allied pressure. 'The real strength of Germany and of Soviet Russia could only increase from the conclusion of a treaty between them.'[4]

Curiously enough, it was Radek, in the later '20's a follower of Trotsky, who was Trotsky's counterpart in expounding most vigorously the balance of power aspect of Rapallo. He told the Fourth World Congress of the Communist International that 'the policy of throttling Germany implied as a matter of fact the destruction of Russia as a great power, for no matter how Russia is governed it is always her interest to see that Germany exists. A Russia which has been weakened to the utmost by the war could neither have continued as a great power nor acquired the economic and technical means for her industrial reconstruction

[1] *Izvestya*, May 18, 1922.
[2] *Pravda*, April 25, 1922.
[3] *Izvestya*, May 18, 1922
[4] Ibid. April 16, 1924.

unless she had in the existence of Germany a counter-balance against the supremacy of the Allies.'[1]

Between the two extreme views expressed by Trotsky and Radek wavered the unhappy Steklov, the editor of *Izvestya*. He clearly saw the dilemma with which Rapallo confronted the Soviet Union. One horn of the dilemma was represented by distaste for association with the German bourgeoisie. The other horn was the fact that if Russia did not associate with one of the bourgeois states she was isolated in a dangerous world. In his leader on April 21, 1922 he wrote that if Germany does not succumb to Allied pressure at Genoa, 'then the hegemony of militarist France forcibly imposed on Europe, will be broken'. He goes on: 'The German bourgeoisie is imperialist through and through . . . but in the first place, the position of Germany at the moment is such that in the near future she cannot dream of any aggressive plans. Secondly—and this is the most important thing—if she did cherish such plans then in this matter she could in no case count on support from Soviet Russia. . . . But it is quite another affair if it is a question of defence against Entente imperialism. If the latter refuses to enter into an agreement with Soviet Republic on terms acceptable to her . . . if, in this way, the question again arises before Soviet Russia of the defence of her right to existence, then of course, she will use all means and all forces for the maintenance of her political and economic independence.'[2] Two days later Steklov veered round to the other standpoint, and ceased to talk of Rapallo in the terms of power-politics or of what the Treaty meant to the Russian diplomatic position. Instead he used the same terms as Trotsky and Joffe. Russia, he wrote, was ready to sign treaties with countries based on different principles. 'But she can conclude these agreements only within the framework of her general policy of principle.' Such an agreement was exemplified in Rapallo.[3] After having thus identified the support given by Russia to 'the imperialist German bourgeoisie' in its struggle against 'militarist France' with Russia's 'policy of principle', Steklov swung back to his original interpretation. Three days later he again saw Rapallo as a blow at France's continental hegemony.[4]

---

[1] K. Radek: *The Winding-up of the Versailles Treaty—Report to the Fourth Congress of the Communist International*, Eng. trans., Hamburg, 1922, p. 16.
[2] *Izvestya*, April 21, 1922.
[3] Ibid., April 23, 1922.
[4] Ibid., April 26, 1922.

The Rapallo Treaty gave rise to some confusion in the German ranks no less than it had done in the Russian. The day following its publication the mood in the German Foreign Office was one of confusion and perplexity. One of the officials in the Russian department said: 'I wash my hands of the whole affair.' A visitor to Genoa found the German delegates 'slowly recovering from alarm at their boldness'.[1] Rathenau, in all probability, never made a complete recovery. His first question to General Hasse, after signing the Treaty, was: would Seeckt approve it?[1] Three weeks later Rathenau does not seem to have been over-enthusiatic about Rapallo. He wrote to a friend: 'I hope we will succeed in steering the Rapallo Treaty through all the rocks—I think it means something for our future.'[3]

Seeckt was no less surprised at Rapallo than everybody else. He was at Konstanz with his wife, celebrating his birthday, when Hasse brought the glad news. Curiously enough, Seeckt thought that the Russians had only signed with Germany because they were unable to reach agreement with the Western Powers.[4] But he was not the man to worry about *how* Rapallo had come about. The question was how to exploit the resulting situation. On this point he was in doubt. The Treaty must be played up for all it was worth. 'I do not see it [Rapallo] in its material content but in its moral effect. It is the first but very essential strengthening of German influence in the world. The reason is that more is suspected behind it than is actually justified. There are no politico-military agreements; but their possibility is believed in. . . . Is it in our interest to destroy this pale halo . . . ? It would be far better for unreasonable people to believe this. Our aim must certainly be to reach an agreement that will assure us aid. I will do everything to attain this; but until it is attained, appearances must help us. Our power is small. Our enemies' eyes must magnify it.'[5]

The German politicians were, on the whole, not so happy about Rapallo as the military men. Rathenau was not isolated in this. The reason was the fear of possible reprisals from the Western Powers, especially France. This applied in the case of Wirth, for example;[6] and in the Reichstag, introducing the Treaty in his

[1] H. von Dirksen: *Moskau—Tokio—London*, Stuttgart, 1949, p. 46.
[2] F. von Rabenau: *Seeckt—Aus Seinem Leben 1918-1936*, Leipzig, 1940, p. 312.
[3] Walter Rathenau: *Politische Briefe*, Dresden, 1929, pp. 336-337.
[4] F. von Rabenau: *Seeckt—Aus Seinem Leben 1918-1936*, Leipzig, 1940, p. 312.
[5] Seeckt's letter to Hasse of May 17, 1922 quoted Rabenau, op. cit., p. 313.
[6] Ibid., p. 312.

capacity as Chancellor, Wirth's main points in a very moderate
speech were the German fear of Article 116 and the fact that in
Rapallo there were no victors or vanquished—only equals.[1]
The other bourgeois speakers, whilst welcoming the Treaty, did
not all do so without qualifications. Hoetzsch, on behalf of the
Nationalist party, had reservations on the question of Russian
propaganda and compensation for the murder of Count Mirbach.[2]
Becker, speaking for the German People's Party, was hesitant over
Germany's cancellation of her claims on Russia.[3] These were the
snags; but they did not offset the general approval. This was best
summed up in the speech of Böhm, deputy of the Bavarian People's
Party. He called Rapallo a step towards 'an active foreign policy.'[4]

It was on the left-wing of German political life that the real
dissentients were to be found. Ebert, the Social-Democratic
President, was 'surprised and embittered' at the Treaty.[5] Hermann
Müller wanted it coupled with 'an attempted policy of fulfilment
towards the West'. He warned 'most emphatically' against over-
estimating its economic effects.[6] Crispien, for the Independent
Socialists, attacked the whole conception of a treaty between the
Bolsheviks and German 'heavy industry and finance capital'.
Such a 'capitalist orientated policy' was a betrayal of socialism.[7]
Frölich, the K.P.D. spokesman, was clearly in some embarassment.
He at first tried to soft-pedal the Treaty, calling it 'nothing more
than a confirmation of facts which have already been in existence
for some time'. He then said that Rapallo so far contained only
'fine phrases . . . which have no genuine content' and that
'influential forces' in the Government and the Foreign Office
were eager to sabotage it. Finally, he attacked Crispien, the
Independent Socialists and the Social-Democrats for the fact that
Russia was compelled at all to enter into agreement with a
bourgeois state.[8]

If the substance both of the German and of the Russian
approach to Rapallo is abstracted, it is clear that the Treaty meant
two very different things to its signatories. At the time, it is

[1] Reichstag Debates, Vol. 355, p. 7675.
[2] Ibid., pp. 7710-7711.
[3] Ibid., pp. 7720 ff.
[4] Ibid., p. 7734.
[5] F. Stampfer: Die Vierzehn Jahre der ersten deutschen Republik, Karlsbad, 1936, p. 250.
[6] Reichstag Debates, Vol. 355, p. 7680.
[7] Ibid., pp. 7716-7717.
[8] Ibid., pp. 7738-7740.

doubtful whether either side was aware of the real significance of its action. Certainly the formal terms offer little guidance. It was rather the future that defined the scope of Rapallo.

Even so, in 1922 two quite different evaluations of Rapallo are already discernible. To Germany the Treaty was a weapon of attack. If the Reichstag deputy's remark on Rapallo's significance for 'an active foreign policy' be translated into practical politics, it meant that Germany was taking up the fight against Versailles, or rather that she was now in a position to take up the fight against Versailles. Rapallo was a standing threat to the West that if Germany were not granted alleviation of Versailles, she could always turn Eastwards for support.

To Russia, on the other hand, Rapallo was primarily a defensive measure. It was what Chicherin had called 'a *point d'appui*', a foothold amongst the capitalist powers. It automatically prevented the formation of any capitalist united front, hostile to Soviet Russia. Come what may, Germany would always be the missing link in any such projected action. In other words Germany was neutralised. Beyond the western frontiers of Soviet Russia stretched a vast protective buffer of neutralised territory. After 1922 the Soviets never asked anything else of Germany than that she should be neutral. At all the crises in Russian foreign policy, notably in 1923, 1925, and 1927, it was always to German neutrality that the appeal was made.

But nothing can be had for nothing. The Soviets had to pay a price for German neutrality. They had to support the struggle of the German bourgeoisie against Versailles. To this extent the alarm of the Western Powers was justified. Within certain limits, the Soviets had hitched their star to the wagon of German nationalism. The bargain that was struck in Rapallo, whether or not Chicherin and Rathenau knew it, was this: Russia promised Germany her aid against Versailles and Germany promised Russia her neutrality.[1]

[1] There is one partial qualification to the distinction made above between the Russian defensive and the German offensive use of Rapallo. In the first few months following Rapallo, both Chicherin and Radek spoke to Seeckt of their aggressive aims against Poland; Radek even asked Seeckt for German co-operation in an attack on Poland (F. von Rabenau: *Seeckt—Aus Seinem Leben 1918-1936*, Leipzig, 1940, pp. 309 and 319). But although there may well have been plans in 1923 for joint Russo-German action against Poland, this was a response to the emergency created by the occupation of the Ruhr and does not contradict the general distinction established, as little as do the assertions of Radek and Chicherin.

CHAPTER IV

The Military Aspect of Rapallo

NOT content with supporting German nationalism, the Soviets also supplied the Reichswehr with arms and training facilities. Negotiations on this topic covered the whole period of the Rapallo negotiations. It was a little disingenuous, to put it no lower, for Chicherin to write to Barthou, the French delegate at Genoa, asserting: 'The Rapallo agreement contains no secret military or political clause and is accompanied by no such clause. . . . '[1] It is no less a reflection on Trotsky's conception of proletarian morality that, although he indignantly repudiated any thought of a Soviet-German political bloc, he, as Commissar for War at this time, was not above furnishing the Reichswehr with military equipment.

Although the message from Junkers taken by Enver Pasha to Moscow in 1919 shows the early German interest in Russian possibilities, it was not until after the Russo-Polish war in 1920-1921, that anything systematic was undertaken. It was then that Seeckt established 'Sondergruppe R' (Special Group R).[2] Sondergruppe R's first task was to dispatch to Moscow a three man mission consisting of Major Tschunke, General von Niedermayer, a Middle-East expert, and Lt. Col. von Schubert, the former German military attaché in Russia.[3]

Meanwhile, in Berlin, while Vigdor Kopp was negotiating the preliminaries to the trade treaty of May 1921 there took place talks aimed at circumventing the disarmament clauses of Versailles, on the establishment of a German arms industry in Russia and the

---

[1] Quoted in J. Saxon Mills: *The Genoa Conference*, London, 1922, p. 130.
[2] Major Tschunke, later intimately associated with the Red Army-Reichswehr contacts, states this in a letter dated February 13, 1939, addressed to von Rabenau. The letter was written in response to a request from von Rabenau—whilst engaged in writing his biography of von Seeckt—for more information concerning this side of his subject's activities. Enclosed with the letter was a document giving the information desired. The latter document is referred to above as 'Tschunke's Letter'. It is reproduced together with memoranda by Seeckt and Brockdorff-Rantzau in the German monthly magazine *Der Monat* 1 Jg, Nummer 2, November, 1948. The originals of all these documents are with the captured Potsdam Army Archives in Washington. The memoranda of Seeckt and Brockdorff-Rantzau are referred to subsequently by their dates. That of Seeckt is reproduced almost in its entirety in *Seeckt—Aus Seinem Leben 1918-1936*, Leipzig, 1940, pp. 315-318.
[3] 'Tschunke's Letter'.

neutral countries.[1] In September 1921 these talks were continued by Kopp and Krassin, representing the Russians, and General Hasse, representing the Reichswehr. The rendezvous of the negotiators was frequently the Berlin apartment of the then Major von Schleicher. Seeckt himself kept as much in the background as possible,[2] though he did on one occasion consent to discuss the matter with Radek, who for this purpose flew to Berlin, accompanied by Niedermayer, in January, 1922.[3] German officers were at work in Russia by April 1922[4] but not until the end of the year were the negotiations finally concluded.[5]

Two types of military collaboration emerged. The first comprised the erection of tank and aviation training schools with German participation. This was under the control of Niedermayer and Sondergruppe R. The second comprised the production of war materials on Russian territory. This was organised by a 'Gesellschaft zur Förderung gewerblicher Unternehmungen' (Society for the encouragement of industrial enterprises) usually known by its German initials as Gefu. Gefu had offices in Berlin and Moscow and its capital was supplied by Wirth, acting in his capacity as Finance Minister. It had three main functions: to direct a Junkers factory at Fili, near Moscow, producing all-metal aeroplanes for the Russian Government; to found a Russo-German limited company near Samara to produce poison gases (the company was known as Bersol); and thirdly, to produce 300,000 artillery shells for Germany with German technical aid. This took place at the Slatust works in Tula, at the former Putilov works in Leningrad and at Schlusselberg on Lake Ladoga. Only this last commission was satisfactorily fulfilled. In both the other cases the two manufacturers concerned—Professor Junkers and Dr Stolzenberg, the Hamburg chemist—were only unwilling collaborators of the Reichswehr. Russian economic conditions were also unfavourable.[6]

Seeckt's aims in Russia were very simple. 'We want two things; to strengthen Russia economically, politically and therefore militarily. We thereby strengthen ourselves by strengthening a

[1] F. von Rabenau: Seeckt—Aus Seinem Leben 1918-1936, Leipzig, 1940, p. 305.
[2] Rabenau, op. cit., p. 308.
[3] Journal of Modern History, Chicago, March, 1949, article by G. W. F. Hallgarten, p. 31.
[4] Rabenau, op. cit., pp. 309-310.
[5] Rabenau, op. cit., p. 319.
[6] All the foregoing is based on 'Tschunke's Letter'. Tschunke became one of the directors of Gefu.

possible ally of the future. Furthermore, we want to strengthen ourselves directly, at first carefully and gropingly by helping ourselves to build up a serviceable arms industry in Russia in case of necessity.'[1]

Under these circumstances, the replacement of Wiedenfeld and the nomination of an officially accredited German Ambassador to Moscow would clearly be of some importance. The choice at first fell on Nadolny.[2] He had been the pre-war Consul-General at St Petersburg and was at this time German Ambassador to Turkey. But eventually Count Ulrich Brockdorff-Rantzau was chosen. This highly displeased Seeckt who had quarrelled with Rantzau at Versailles and even gone so far as to challenge him to a duel.[3] But he was powerless to prevent the nomination.

The new Ambassador had been appointed by the Social-Democratic Government in 1919 to head the German delegation to receive the Versailles Treaty. He refused to sign the Treaty, resigned his post, and ever afterwards remembered the experience to which he had been exposed. On his death-bed he told his twin brother: 'I died long ago in Versailles. . . . It will be sad for me to leave you. The one thing that troubles me is how the British and French will rejoice over my death when I pass away.'[4]

Very early on he had become convinced of the need for a *rapprochement* with Russia as a means 'to correct the disaster of Versailles' and in 1920 was already in touch with Maltzan on this subject.[5] But he played no part, as far as is known, in the preliminaries to Rapallo. Not long after the signature of the Treaty however, he must have been sounded as to his views on policy, for on July 15, 1922 he sent to Ebert and Wirth a memorandum on the desiderata of German policy in Russia.

The memorandum is short but abundant in foresight. In 1922, Brockdorff-Rantzau foresaw, with some qualifications, the situation that arose in 1939—a France and Britain brought

[1] Seeckt's memorandum of September 11, 1922, reprinted in *Der Monat*, Jg. 1, Nummer 2, November, 1948. The origin of the military talks and their scope is confirmed in a somewhat sensationalised biography of Schleicher, based on the latter's papers, by H. R. Berndorff, entitled *General zwischen Ost und West*, Hamburg, 1951. Radek used to say of Schleicher and Seeckt respectively that the first was 'ein kluger Mensch' and the second 'ein kluger General' (Berndorff, op. cit., p. 90).

[2] F. von Rabenau *Seeckt—Aus Seinem Leben 1918-1936*, Leipzig, 1940, p. 314.

[3] Rabenau, op. cit., p. 179, n.1.

[4] Edgar Stern-Rubarth *Graf Brockdorff-Rantzau*. Berlin, 1929, p. 156.

[5] Stern-Rubarth, op. cit., pp. 123, 141.

together by a Russo-German bloc: 'at the present level of armaments technique England is no longer an island; the threat from
France follows for this very reason. England must therefore seek
an ally and one thing is certain; she will always seek this ally
against France so long as combinations do not develop which hold
France and England together or drive them together again.
Such a combination would be represented by a German-Russian
alliance. In the military field we should therefore plan our tactics
so that England seeks and must seek our alliance.' From this
standpoint Brockdorff-Rantzau went on to argue vigorously
against any one-sided Eastern orientation which would destroy
Germany's chances of exploiting Anglo-French differences.[1]

Between Brockdorff-Rantzau and Chicherin a deep friendship
developed. Both men were aware of the incongruity of their
position—two aristocrats, one representing the interests of a
bourgeois-democratic republic and the other the interests of a
Soviet republic. When Brockdorff-Rantzau handed over his
credentials, Chicherin pointed out: 'We were at first hesitant to
welcome here as German representative a Count and a former
Imperial diplomat.' To this the Count replied: 'Before I arrived
here, Mr Chicherin, I occupied myself to some small extent with
the history of your house. A descendant of the Narishkin's and
thereby of the House of Rurik does not seem to me quite the
person to reproach me with my feudal origin.'[2]

[1] *Der Monat*, 1 Jg, Nummer 2, November, 1948.
[2] Edgar Stern-Rubarth: *Graf Brockdorff-Rantzau*, Berlin, 1929, pp. 125-126.

CHAPTER V

Rapallo versus Revolution (1923)

WHEN the Russians signed the Treaty of Rapallo they had little inkling, doubtless, of what it would entail in the way of Comintern policy in Germany. It had been no part of their original purpose to sign treaties with the bourgeois world. It had, on the contrary, been very much to their purpose to overthrow the bourgeois world. Over a short period the two aims could be reconciled, but in the last resort they were contradictory. Beyond a certain point, the aims of overthrowing a government and of retaining a vested interest in that government's continued existence could not be *simultaneously* entertained. One or the other had to give way. Precisely which would be the first to succumb depended on the circumstances of the case.

The gravity of the problem bore on all the foreign relations of the Soviets. But to Germany the application was special. Not only was it the Treaty of Rapallo with Germany that guaranteed Russia against isolation, but it was on the same Germany that hopes of revolution had traditionally rested, and in which there existed the largest Communist party outside Russia. It was characteristic of the fluctuating nature of Russia's foreign relations at this time that in 1923 both courses were tried. The year began with the emphasis on Rapallo and ended with the emphasis on revolution.

When French troops, at Poincaré's order, occupied the Ruhr in January, 1923, the signal was given for events of the first international magnitude. The French action struck at an area containing 80 per cent of Germany's coal production, 80 per cent of her steel and 10 per cent of her population. It was these that were Poincaré's concern—not the few sacks of reparations coal or bundles of telegraph poles on which Germany had defaulted. His intention was to sever, in the form of a Rhineland buffer-state, the Ruhr from the rest of Germany. The French move was a confirmation of Seeckt's prophecy made a few months previously. The French aimed at 'the complete, not yet completed destruction of Germany'.[1] Had the plan succeeded, French hegemony on the continent would have been sealed. France would have made herself the dominant factor in the coal and iron production of the Ruhr, Luxemburg and Belgium and the Little Entente. Germany would have been virtually eliminated as a power-political factor and British influence on the Continent would have been severely limited. By the same token the Russian position would have been equally jeopardised. The Ruhr occupation threatened Russia with the loss of what Radek had called her 'counter-balance against the supremacy of the Allies'. Russia required Germany, not only as a source of industrial aid but also in order to continue as a great power. Without Germany, Russia would for all practical purposes have been isolated in a hostile capitalist world. Once she had hitched her wagon to the star of the German bourgeoisie, she had a very powerful vested interest in the continued power of that bourgeoisie. Thus the Ruhr occupation was a blow no less at Russia than at Germany. The natural result of this was to throw both countries closer together than at any time before or afterwards. Bukharin said later: 'this was a period of the maximum flirtation between the German bourgeoisie and a state alien to it in its social structure'.[2]

The tension was heightened in Eastern Europe by German rumours of impending Polish and Czech mobilisation. The detachment of Upper Silesia at the hands of Poland was thought to be an additional French aim. Point was given to this alarm when Marshal Foch paid a visit to Warsaw in May 1923.[3] This threat in the East, combined with the French threat in the West, immediately raised the price that Russia had to pay for Rapallo. The German proverb has it: 'The person who says "A" must also say "B".' It is not impossible that in 1923 plans existed for joint Russo-German military action.

Ironically enough, it was at the Fourth World Congress of the Communist International in November-December 1922 that this topic first came up. On this occasion Radek had already described in unambiguous terms the existence of a Soviet-bourgeois bloc. Bukharin, a more important figure than Radek by virtue of his membership of the Politburo, now supplied the theoretical basis

[1] See Seeckt's memorandum of September 11, 1922, quoted above p. 62, note 1.
[2] See below p. 67.
[3] F. von Rabenau: *Seeckt—Aus Seinem Leben 1918-1936*, Leipzig, 1940, p. 328, *Die Weltbühne*, No. 6, February 8, 1923. The ostensible reason for Foch's visit was the inauguration of a monument to Joseph Poniatovski.

E

for such a bloc. He too, it may be assumed, felt the Ruhr occupation to be in the air and, as a renowned theoretician, no doubt felt it his duty to trundle along the ideological super-structure to accord with the material sub-structure.

So long as the party was not in power, Bukharin maintained, it was wrong to accept money from bourgeois sources. But from the Marxist-dialectic viewpoint, this position underwent a change once power was achieved. What had hitherto been wrong, now became permissible. From this it was but one step further to holding that a military alliance between a proletarian and a bourgeois state was equally legitimate. 'May proletarian states', Bukharin asked, 'on the basis of strategic expediency for the whole proletariat, conclude military alliances with bourgeois states? Here there is no difference in principle between a loan and a military alliance, and I maintain that we have already grown so strong that we may conclude a military alliance with the bour-geoisie of one country in order with its help to crush the bour-geoisie of another country. . . .

In this kind of defence and military alliance with bourgeois states, our comrades in every country are obliged to further the victory of such a bloc. If, later on, the bourgeoisie of such an allied country is conquered, then other tasks will arise [laughter]. But I do not need to explain them here; you will easily understand them for yourselves.'[1]

The theme of this speech was given additional publicity of an unusual kind when Bukharin wrote an open letter to *Izvestya*. (This was in reply to a request from Boris Souvarine, a French Communist who had been present at the Congress and who, on his return to France, had been attacked for the 'opportunistic' tone of Bukharin's speech. He had therefore asked Bukharin to clarify his views.) This letter amplified the speech considerably by relating it to various examples, both potential and actual, of Soviet-bourgeois blocs. The dominating fact, wrote Bukharin, was the delay in the social revolution. This will stretch over many decades and during that interval many proletarian states will be obliged to conclude temporary agreements with oppressed or semi-oppressed bourgeois states. The whole International is obliged to support such agreements. One example was the Russo-Turkish

---

[1] *IV Vsyemirni Kongress Kommunisticheskovo Internatsionala, Izbranniye Dokladi, ryechi i rezolyutzii (4th World Congress of the Communist International—Selected reports, speeches and resolutions)*, Moscow and Petrograd, 1923, pp. 195-196. This speech is further referred to in its implications for the policy of the K.P.D. in 1923; see below p. 74.

Treaty. Bukharin went on: 'if a revolution were to break out in Germany and Poland struck at Germany from the East then revolutionary Russia would probably be obliged to attack Poland. And in this case the revolutionary workers of the whole world would be obliged to support both the German revolution and Russia's war against Poland.' Furthermore, if petty-bourgeois Lithuania were to use the opportunity to attack Poland, Russia would be justified in signing a military-political agreement with Lithuania.[1]

This made no mention of the most important Soviet agreement with an oppressed bourgeois state—the Treaty of Rapallo. Nor, although its implications are clear enough, did it make any mention of Soviet policy *vis-à-vis* a non-revolutionary Germany, or of how the K.P.D. as a member of the International was to express its support of any temporary agreement between Russia and an oppressed bourgeois state. The omission was made good in another speech by Bukharin some three years later: 'When Germany was crushed, was enslaved, when she was in the position of a semi-colony, and when in this capacity she offered a certain resistance to the victorious imperialism of the Entente, then even the highest organs of the Soviet power in their manifestos, declarations and so on, expressed their open sympathy for her. Then the German communist party posed the question in such a way that the possibility of defending the German Fatherland against victorious Entente imperialism . . . was not excluded. Germany's social role had changed from being imperialist into becoming a certain force serving as an objective obstacle to capitalism and into a force which, to a certain extent, was directly aimed against an imperialist Entente State. At the same time this was a period of the maximum flirtation between the German bourgeoisie and a state alien to it in its social structure.'[2]

Thus, when the Ruhr was occupied, the Russian line was clear. Unqualified support was given to the German bourgeoisie. 'The highest organs of the Soviet power', as Bukharin had called them, rallied to the support of the oppressed German capitalists who now played, *vis-à-vis* French imperialism, a quasi-revolutionary role in defending the Soviet Union. On January 13, 1923 the Central Committee published a protest at 'the mad policy of

---

[1] *Izvestya*, January 11, 1923.
[2] *XV Konferentsiya V.K.P. (b) Stenographicheski otchet (15th Conference of the All-Unio Communist Party (b) stenographic report)* Moscow & Leningrad, 1927, p. 30.

imperialist France and her allies' and at 'the suppression of the German people's right to self-determination'.[1] Both Chicherin and Litvinov backed this up with expressions of sympathy for Germany.[2] In his editorials in *Izvestya*, Steklov put the Russian view very forcefully, all the more so as he spoke in power-political terms and disregarded Bukharin's ideological trappings. He wrote that Germany's 'final subjugation would constitute a very grave threat to Soviet Russia'. French imperialism, through its control of Poland, would then become the direct neighbour of Russia and a new armed intervention would be possible.[3] A day or two later Steklov repeated his fear: 'It is quite obvious that the toiling masses of Soviet Russia have no special sympathy for the bourgeois governments of Germany, still less for her reactionary, imperialist elements. Nevertheless, Soviet Russia, *in her own vital interests,* cannot allow the final subjugation and destruction of Germany by an alliance of France and her vassals, of which Poland is the first. . . .

A Polish attack on Germany at the present moment is a direct blow at Soviet Russia.'[4]

These warnings to Poland were re-inforced 'by the tacit threat of moving the Red Army . . . the Bolsheviks saved the situation for Germany by keeping her eastern neighbour in inactivity'.[5] Seeckt was also counting on aid from 'Russian delivery depots' should an armed conflict with France materialise.[6] He had, furthermore, been considering a plan whereby Russia would guard the German rear should France advance further into Germany and should Poland attack in the East.[7] But there was no question of the 'Utopia' of a joint Russo-German offensive against France.[8]

There was no significant change in the Russian position until

[1] *Izvestya*, January 14, 1923.
[2] For Chicherin, see *Izvestya*, February 15, 1923; for Litvinov, *Manchester Guardian*, January 27, 1923.
[3] *Izvestya*, January 21, 1923.
[4] Ibid., January 24, 1923; italics in original.
[5] Louis Fischer: *The Soviets in World Affairs*, London, 1930, p. 452.
[6] F. von Rabenau: *Seeckt—Aus Seinem Leben 1918-1936*, Leipzig, 1940, p. 330.
[7] Edgar von Schmidt-Pauli: *General von Seeckt*, Berlin, 1937, p. 124.
[8] Ibid. Stresemann's threat to Lord d'Abernon on this point was pure bluff: 'Stresemann broke in to say that he fully recognised that without England's assistance, Germany would have lost the Rhineland. He added, however, that if Poincaré had carried through his policy, Germany would have formed a coalition with Russia and together they would have swept over Europe' (Lord d'Abernon: *An Ambassador of Peace*, Vol. III, London, 1929, pp. 145-146). This is a good example of the kind of pressure exercised by Stresemann on d'Abernon, and one to which the latter was very susceptible.

July—diplomatic and military support continued to be given to Germany, and Poland continued to be neutralised as a military factor. It is an interesting example of a country finding itself on the brink of aggressive war in order to safeguard a defensive position. In all other respects normality prevailed in Russo-German relations. Josef Wirth, for example, no longer in the German Government, visited Moscow as representative of a group of Bavarian manufacturers seeking timber concessions in Russia, eventually signing the required agreement.[1]

Inside Germany meanwhile, the Cuno government took office. The new Chancellor was, although a director of the Hamburg-Amerika Line, non-party. The members of his cabinet were divided amongst similar non-party representatives of big business and members of the right-wing Centre, Democratic and People's Parties. All in all, it was the most right-wing government Germany had seen since the war. Nevertheless it enjoyed the support of all parties including the Social-Democrats but excluding the K.P.D. A political truce was declared immediately Poincaré marched into the Ruhr. To this all parties subscribed, again with the exception of the K.P.D. Barring the Communists there was a resurrection of the mood of August, 1914.

On this basis a secret Seeckt-Severing agreement was signed on February 7th, 1923. The other signatories were Ebert, Cuno and Otto Braun. The purpose of the agreement was to secure the co-operation of the Government of the Reich and of the Government of the Prussian Landtag, headed by the Social Democrats Braun and Severing, in the formation of para-military forces.[2] Ludendorff was also in touch with Seeckt, with a view to putting at the latter's disposal the aid of the various underground nationalist organisations with which he was connected.[3] Another plan formulated by Ludendorff called for a *levée en masse* against the French.[4] It was in conjunction with such people that Ebert, Severing and Otto Braun hoped to save the Republic. It was the same sort of trap as that into which the Bolsheviks fell in signing Rapallo. Beelzebub would be used to cast out the devil.

[1] *Morning Post*, August 17 and September 22, 1923.
[2] Edgar von Schmidt-Pauli: *General von Seeckt*, Berlin, 1937, p. 116. The existence of the Seeckt-Severing agreement was revealed to the Reichstag on December 17, 1926 by Hermann Müller (Reichstag Debates, Vol. 391, p. 8623).
[3] Ibid.
[4] F. Thyssen: *I Paid Hitler*, London, 1941, pp. 109-110.

Ever since his experiences in the Baltic and the Kapp Putsch, Seeckt had fought shy of the extreme, anti-Russian right and their terror-tactics. In 1923 he must have judged the situation to be so critical as to leave him no choice. In any event, the political truce, plus the fact that the Control Commission had temporarily to suspend its activities[1] led to Seeckt being in a position where he could develop a shadow Reichswehr or 'Schwarze Reichswehr' to be used against the French should they attempt to march further East into the German interior.[2] The main centre of these shadow troops was Wehrkreis III (military district III) covering the area to the East of Berlin. By the beginning of September 1923 some 18,000 auxiliary troops had been assembled and organised into regiments.[3] All over the Reich there was also a rapid growth of illegal military formations, with the connivance of the Government.

These quasi-military preparations were one aspect of Cuno's policy. The other aspect was the declaration of passive resistance. Reparations deliveries to France ceased entirely and the population of the Ruhr were forbidden to co-operate in any way with the invader. In the early part of the year Reichswehr leaders and Ruhr industrialists discussed a plan for the invasion of Czechoslovakia; and the Reichswehr considered staging a 'Saint Bartholomew' against the French occupying forces.[4] Very soon however it became clear that through the inflation, Germany was in no position to wage any kind of struggle at all. The mark had been falling steadily since the end of the war, but from the beginning of 1923 the steady drop turned into a headlong descent until the currency lost its value entirely. The result was unprecedented suffering and distress amongst the workers and middle classes. Over a period of a few months the inflation made the K.P.D. into a political factor of the first importance, creating at the same time a potentially revolutionary situation.

[1] J. H. Morgan: *Assize of Arms*, Vol. 1, London, 1945, p. 213. The reason given was representations made by the German Government on the difficulty of protecting the members of the Commission from the German civilian population. These representations 'found, unfortunately, a credulous and sympathetic British ear in Lord d'Abernon' (Morgan, ibid.).

[2] A. François-Poncet: *De Versailles à Potsdam*, Paris, 1948, p. 107.

[3] Major Buchrucker: *Im Schatten Seeckts*, Berlin, 1928, p. 32. Buchrucker, a retired regular officer and a veteran of the Freikorps, was in command of these troops.

[4] *Journal of Modern History*, Chicago, March, 1949, p. 33 n. 29, article by G. W. F. Hallgarten. This article is based on Seeckt's papers now in Washington; see also F. von Rabenau: *Seeckt—Aus Seinem Leben 1918-1936*, Leipzig, 1940, p. 326, n.1. and p. 330, n.1.

At the beginning of 1923 the party had a membership of 218,555 throughout the Reich with ninety-seven representatives in the Landtage of the various states and thirteen representatives in the Reichstag. The membership was organised into trade-union, municipal, co-operative, youth, women's, student and agricultural branches.[1] It constituted a far more formidable force than the chance collection of utopian sympathisers of 1919.

Its policy was quite different. It was no longer committed to the direct struggle for power but to the tactic of the indirect struggle for power via the achievement of a united front with the Social-Democrats and the formation of a Workers' Government. This policy had first made its appearance in January, 1921, when Radek and Levi had addressed an open letter to all working class organisations and parties in Germany, inviting them to co-operate with the young K.P.D. in agitation for immediate working-class demands. The background to this change is to be explained by the internal dynamics of Communist policy. It was a response to the fact that the K.P.D. acting on its own had produced no enduring result. Consequently, the alternative method of enlisting the co-operation of the Social-Democrats as a temporary strate-gem was attempted.

Zinoviev, the Comintern's President, opposed from the start Radek's initiative and only through Lenin's intervention was the open letter policy put on the agenda of the Third World Congress of the Communist International in June 1921.[2] After thorough discussion at the Congress the new policy was concretised in the slogan 'To The Masses'. In December 1921 tactics were worked out for its application. In December 1922, at the Fourth World Congress, the policy was re-affirmed.

An enormous amount of controversy, both in Russia and Germany, developed around the definition and practical appli-cation of the policy. In essence, the plan was to separate the social-democratic and trade-unionist masses from their leaders by putting forward non-political, purely economic demands. This confronted the reformist leaders with two choices; they could either accept the demands, in which case they would have allied themselves, for all practical purposes, with the Communists and

[1] *Bericht über die Verhandlungen des III (8) Parteitags der K.P.D.*, Leipzig, pp. 51, 63, 73, Berlin, 1923.
[2] *V Vsyemirni Kongress Kommunisticheskovo Internatsionala—Stenographicheskii otchet* (*Fifth World Congress of the Communist International—Stenographic Report*), Moscow & Leningrad, 1925, p. 146 and pp. 449-451.

the way would be prepared for a joint Social-Democratic-Communist workers' Government; or on the other hand, the reformist leaders could reject the demands, in which case they would have unmasked themselves in the eyes of their followers as being unable to defend the interests of the working classes. The Communists would then be in a position to exploit the resulting disillusionment.

The danger in the tactic lay in the fact that by putting transitional economic demands, the Communists might encourage reformist illusions amongst the masses. They might give colour to the illusion that there was an easy way to socialism without the intervening stage of a civil war and the dictatorship of the proletariat. The strength of the tactic lay in the fact that it offered access to the majority of the working class at a time when this was indifferent, if not hostile, to the straightforward Communist appeal.

In Germany, from the very first promulgation of the United Front policy, a section of the K.P.D. had emphasised its possible dangers rather than its possible strength. By the time of the Leipzig Congress, in January 1923, the K.P.D. within the limits of the binding decisions of the Comintern, was split into a left-wing which discounted as futile any attempt to win influence amongst the Social-Democrats, and a right wing which stressed the danger of moving without the masses. The left was led by Ruth Fischer and Maslow, with its popular base in the ports and towns of the German North Sea and Baltic coasts, and in the Ruhr and Berlin-Brandenburg. Heinrich Brandler and August Thalheimer were the leaders of the right-wing. It was this group that enjoyed majority support. Brandler remained loyal to the most conservative interpretation of the theses on the united front and the workers' Government. His whole policy was pivoted on joint action with the Social-Democrats. On this score he did not hesitate to differ publicly from Zinoviev. The latter had once called a workers' Government 'a synonym for the dictatorship of the proletariat'.[1] To this Brandler retorted that Zinoviev was 3,000 kilometres away from 'the complicated and difficult situation' in Germany. 'We have no lords and masters and therefore we do not hold with the personal views of Comrade Zinoviev.'[2]

[1] *Pravda*, November 14, 1922.
[2] *Bericht über die Verhandlungen des III (8) Parteitags der K.P.D.*, Leipzig, p. 373, Berlin, 1923.

Brandler's intention was to wait until 'the social-democratic leaders, under the pressure of the masses, have at least got so far that they cease to be the left wing of the bourgeoisie and become the right wing of the workers'.[1]

Maslow, on the other hand, maintained that the S.P.D. would always be 'the party of the bourgeoisie'. To this Fischer added: 'if we do not bring up the question of power, we may nourish dangerous illusions in the masses . . . we do not see any genuine possibility of a workers' government in the present situation. . . .'[2]

On this issue between the right and left-wings of the K.P.D., Radek was an unqualified supporter of the right wing, the moderates. He discussed the party's policy in *Izvestya* on the formation of the Cuno Government. He described the latter as a Stinnes regime without Stinnes. 'The task of the K.P.D. in this position does not of course consist in restraining the workers from attacking the capitalists, or from the struggle against the high cost of living. The task of the Communist Party consists in giving this movement as much of an organised character as possible, in order that the Whites should not be able to divert this movement into massacres and armed conflicts which would end with the victory of a White dictatorship.' The K.P.D. must remember that it was not yet a majority. It must avoid being provoked and steer a middle way between passivity and recklessness. The tactic of the United Front was more than ever necessary if the K.P.D. was to win control of the Social-Democratic masses.[3]

The same divergence that existed between the two wings of the K.P.D. on internal policy also existed on foreign policy. The occupation of the Ruhr took place while the party congress at Leipzig was actually in session. This led to the left-wing demanding a separate debate on 'The political situation and the tasks of the K.P.D.' to deal with the new position. But the proposal was rejected by the narrow majority of 122 votes to 189.[4] The party's foreign policy was summed up by Klara Zetkin, a fervent member of the right wing and opponent of Ruth Fischer, as unrestricted class struggle on both sides of the Rhine. 'Poincaré—on this point we must be clear—must be beaten on the Ruhr but he can only be beaten there if Cuno is beaten on the Spree. And Cuno can only

[1] Ibid., p. 328.
[2] Ibid., pp. 335, 354.
[3] *Pravda*, November 24, 1922.
[4] *Bericht über die Verhandlungen des III (8) Parteitags der K.P.D.*, Leipzig, p. 187, Berlin, 1923.

be beaten on the Spree if the German workers beat Poincaré on the Ruhr.'[1]

The significance of this declaration lay in the fact that it exactly conformed to the views of Basil Kolarov, Zinoviev's emissary to the congress. Kolarov, a Bulgarian, was present at Leipzig in his capacity as the representative of E.C.C.I. in Moscow. He saw the Ruhr conflict as a clash between German heavy industry and le Comité des Forges. The K.P.D. had no reason to favour either one side or the other. The party's duty was to combat both.[2]

There was thus no question of the K.P.D. adhering to the political truce. The party, in fact, opposed every government of the Weimar Republic with the exception of the Wirth-Rathenau régime. Subject to certain reservations, it also opposed Cuno, and then Stresemann during 1923. But owing to the fact that the party was committed to the policy of winning the co-operation of the Social-Democrats this opposition never made itself effective: that is, until objective circumstances forced the issue in July and August. In the interval, the non-effectiveness of Communist policy was all the greater because of the Social-Democratic move to the right in signing the Seeckt-Severing agreement. Brandler would not move without the Social-Democrats and the Social-Democrats would not move without Seeckt.

It is not entirely accidental that the party was for all practical purposes diverted into a blind alley. In 1923 the K.P.D. was not purely and simply carrying on a policy that had originally been initiated in 1921. Brandler's good faith is not in doubt.[3] That of Radek is. During a large part of 1923 he worked hand in hand with Brandler, supporting the same policy of Communist-Social-Democrat co-operation, but with entirely different aims. Radek's aim was to render the K.P.D. as harmless as possible in order that it should not upset the equilibrium in Germany. Had not Bukharin, a member of the Politburo, affirmed that Soviet-bourgeois blocs must be supported by the whole International? Had he not also said that in 1923 'the German Communist Party posed the question in such a way that the possibility of defending the German Fatherland against victorious Entente imperialism . . .

[1] Ibid., p. 178.
[2] Ibid., pp. 188-190.
[3] For example, the worst accusation brought against him by a political opponent such as Ruth Fischer is timidity, cowardice even, but not deliberate treachery to the party (cf. Ruth Fischer: *Stalin and German Communism*, Harvard, 1948 pp. 252 ff).

was not excluded?' Thus Radek and Brandler, from entirely different premises, came to the same conclusion—the direct revolutionary struggle for power was to be diverted into the search for co-operation with the Social-Democrats.

This could not, of course, be put over to the K.P.D. in such a crude manner. It *was* possible to tell the Turkish Communists, for example, that they were obliged to support the Russo-Turkish agreement—for the simple reason that the Turkish Communist Party was a well-nigh non-existent force. Radek could tell *them* to line up behind their own bourgeoisie and he did so, quoting Marx himself: 'In 1847 Marx in the Communist Manifesto expressed himself in favour of supporting not only the German bourgeoisie, in so far as it was playing a revolutionary role, but also the group of powerful land-owning Polish nobility, which occupied a revolutionary position in the peasant question. Marx knew very well of course that the young workers' movement would have to wage a class war both against the German bourgeoisie and the Polish nobility. Marx was only showing within what limits the interests of this class war, the interests of the future development of the proletariat require that support be given to the struggle of the bourgeoisie at this lower level of development.'[1]

This could be said to the Turks. But the Germans were in a very different category. For them Radek applied, or rather abused, the policy of the United Front. As far as Radek was concerned, this was a synthesis of the requirements of Russian foreign policy, with its pro-German slant, and the requirements of the Communist International. The synthesis was plausible and impressive. Its only opponents were the left-wing of the K.P.D. —Ruth Fischer and Maslow. This opposition at the beginning of 1923 was very weak in relation to the forces arrayed against it. It was this weakness which was the condition of the policy being applied at all in the way it was. As Kolarov's remarks at Leipzig show, Zinoviev was unaware that the Ruhr occupation would produce a revolutionary situation in Germany. Nor did his views change until August. Earlier awareness of the developing crisis in Germany would certainly have led to a change in Zinoviev's attitude towards the united front policy; all the more so as he had disliked it intensely from the start and, even while accepting it, had constantly striven to emphasise its revolutionary aspect, no

---

[1] Radek's speech at the Fourth World Congress of the Communist International, reported in *Pravda*, November 24, 1922.

less than the fact that it could not eliminate the need for the dictatorship of the proletariat and a civil war.[1] The policy of the United Front originated at a time when the K.P.D. was weak in the absence of mass support. It was specifically designed to counter such a situation. Had Zinoviev realised in time that this situation would change in a matter of months, he would never have acquiesced in the continuance of the policy.

As it was, however, Zinoviev's failure to realise the revolutionary possibilities in Germany enabled Radek and Brandler to continue pursuing the lost hope of co-operation with the Social-Democrats. Unlike the latter the K.P.D. attacked the Cuno government, but it refrained from making its attacks as fully effective as they might have been by making the pre-condition of action unity of movement with the Social-Democrats. On some other points also, this lack of unity was made the threadbare excuse for conniving at the Government's secret military preparations. The *Rote Fahne* once wrote: 'The Government knows that the K.P.D. out of consideration for the danger from French imperialism has kept silent on many things that would make this government unfit for any international intercourse. So long as the Social-Democratic workers do not fight together with us for a workers' government, the K.P.D. is indifferent as to whether another bourgeois government replaces the present leaderless one.'[2] In this way the K.P.D. came to be more anti-Poincaré than anti-Cuno.

There was no fundamental change in this situation until July. But in the interval a number of significant meetings took place in Russia and in Germany. The first of these was an international conference at Frankfort-on-Main in March. It was attended by Lozovsky, the head of the Red Trade Union International, who re-affirmed the need for a united front and a workers' government.[3] In May, as the crisis inside Germany deepened, the differences between the left and the right wing of the K.P.D. were intensified and a special conciliation conference had to be held in Moscow. Its principal result was to secure the admission of four additional members of the German left wing to the Central Committee of the K.P.D.[4] The overall division between the two wings remained.

[1] See in particular Zinoviev's remarks at the Fourth World Congress of the Communist International reported in *Pravda*, November 11 and 14, 1922.

[2] *Rote Fahne*, May 27, 1923, quoted by Dr Schwarz in the Reichstag, December 17, 1926 (Reichstag Debates, Vol. 391, p. 8638).

[3] *Protokol der Verhandlungen der Internationalen Konferenz in Frankfurt am Main*, Berlin 1923, pp. 4, 20.

[4] Ruth Fischer: *Stalin and German Communism*, Harvard, 1948, p. 260.

The following month, June, a far more significant meeting of
E.C.C.I. was held in Moscow. There was no consideration at this
meeting of the question of power or the immediate organising of
a German revolution.[1] What was discussed was the national
question, *i.e.* the conquest of the German petty-bourgeoisie,
proletarianised by the inflation.[2] The two principal speeches
were both made by Radek. On June 15, he spoke on 'The
International Outlook'. The main theme of this speech was an
attack on the German bourgeoisie which, by inflating the currency,
had thrown the whole burden of resistance to the French on to the
workers. The aim of the German bourgeoisie was thereby to
provoke the workers into a revolt and then call in Poincaré to
crush the K.P.D. The party however had refused to play into the
hands of its enemies and had avoided being provoked in this way.
Its task was to continue to defend the living standards of the workers,
thereby giving an example of patriotism to the bourgeoisie.[3]

Radek's second speech was made five days later and concentrated on the same theme. It was the famous 'Schlageter speech'.
Albert Leo Schlageter was a nationalist lout, a proto-Nazi, who
was shot by the French after sabotaging railway lines in the Ruhr.
Radek now made him a symbol of the kind of people he was
trying to rally behind the Communist ranks. He asked the
Schlageters, 'the honest, patriotic masses', who were the true
German nationalists? The Communist party, defending the living
standards of the workers, or the forces of capital, responsible for the
inflation? Schlageter, said Radek, would have died in vain if the
nationalists of Germany did not align themselves with the K.P.D.

Following up this speech, Radek opened the columns of the
Rote Fahne to a public discussion of the feasibility of a Communist-
led nationalist bloc. Such a well-known nationalist as Count
Ernst Reventlow became a contributor to the K.P.D's. daily.[4]

[1] *The Errors of Trotskyism*, London, 1925, p. 345.

[2] *Die Lehren der deutschen Ereignisse*, Hamburg, 1924, p. 18. This is a record of
the post-mortem held in Moscow in January 1924 on the events of the preceding
year. It was presided over by Zinoviev and attended by representatives of all sections
of the K.P.D.

[3] *The International Outlook—Radek's Report to E.C.C.I. at the 6th Session on June 15, 1923*,
Eng. trans., London, 1922.

[4] For the text of the 'Schlageter Speech' and the subsequent discussion, see *Leo
Schlageter—Kommunismus und Nationale Bewegung*, 3rd. ed., Berlin, 1923. Radek's
discussions with Reventlow and other right wing publicists and politicians were
nothing new. For confirmation of their previous existence see Graf Ernst Reventlow:
Völkisch—Kommunistiche Einigung?, Leipzig, 1924, p. 44; and Ernst Troeltsch
Spektator—Briefe, Tübingen, 1924, pp. 269-270.

Furthermore, just before the Ruhr occupation, Radek had discussed with Seeckt what was in effect the Schlageter line. On December 19, 1922, at Schleicher's flat, he spoke to the Reichswehr Chief of 'the possibilities of an amalgamation of the most heterogeneous elements of the whole world in favour of Russia and Germany'.[1] The programme that emerged some six months later was, although it may well have had the aim of causing confusion and dissension in the enemy's ranks, certainly not revolutionary in intent. Radek, as the protagonist *par excellence* of Rapallo, was the last person to wish for a German revolution. It would have meant at the very least an added factor in the disruption of Germany, and possibly the occupation of the whole of Germany, by French troops—a prospect to which alarmed expression had already been given by Steklov. Radek himself had already written in 1919 that 'the German bourgeoisie would doubtless prefer even an open occupation by the Entente to a dictatorship of Soviets. From this it follows that the German working class can in no circumstances count on the aid of the German bourgeoisie in its fight against Entente Capital.'[2] What applied in 1919 applied with redoubled force in 1923: not only was the K.P.D. immeasurably stronger, but the French were actually in the Ruhr, and no longer merely in the Rhineland. This was the point of Radek's earlier praise of the K.P.D. for not allowing itself to be provoked into forcing the German bourgeoisie to call in the French. It was also the reason why he and the right wing prevented the K.P.D. from exploiting the situation, especially in the Ruhr where the miners were solidly behind Ruth Fischer and the left wing.[3]

The Schlageter line was not, it would seem, welcomed in the K.P.D. The only member of any eminence at all to join Radek in his discussions with the nationalists was Paul Frölich. Neither the Brandler-led right wing nor the Fischer-led left wing participated.

---

[1] F. von Rabenau: *Seeckt—Aus Seinem Leben 1918-1936*, Leipzig, 1940, p. 319. There is no indication of Seeckt's response.

[2] *Die Auswärtige Politik des deutschen Kommunismus und der Hamburger National-Bolschewismus*, first published December 20, 1919, in *Die Internationale*, Jg. I, Heft 17-18, p. 16. Radek's warning is repeated later in the same pamphlet (p. 17): 'The path that the German proletariat will have to take in its struggle against Entente capital, on the day after its victory, after the erection of the dictatorship of the proletariat, cannot be foreseen at the moment. It will depend on the concrete world situation which is today changing quicker than ever before. One thing is certain: it will fight together with the proletariat of the whole world—not with the German bourgeoisie.'

[3] For this latter point see Ruth Fischer: *Stalin and German Communism*, Harvard, 1948, pp. 254-259.

It is evident that the situation with which the Politburo was confronted in 1923 would have taxed the most skilful political tactician. Both as regards place and time, the situation was extremely awkward. The place factor willed it that it had to be in Germany, the signatory of Rapallo, where a crisis was arising. An attempt has been made to show how the contradictory requirements of Soviet foreign policy and of the Communist International were synthesised and to some extent overcome. The time factor, 1923, meant that Lenin was absent through illness from the meetings of the Politburo. The effect of this may be judged from certain of Zinoviev's remarks to the 13th Party Conference in January 1924: 'I must tell you, comrades, that for our views, especially in the German question, the responsibility is really borne by the whole Central Committee of the Russian Communist Party, and above all by the Politburo. This question touched Russia too closely. For this reason alone the representatives of our party in the Comintern were obliged to discuss every question in the Politburo, and afterwards, comrades, through force of circumstances, in the party. While comrade Lenin worked directly with us, it went like this—we, the workers of the Comintern, worked out policy of our own accord and consulted comrade Lenin personally. This was enough and the whole Central Committee knew therefore that matters were on the right lines. When this became impossible . . . it was necessary to replace Ilyich's leadership by the leadership of a collective. That is why the representatives of the Central Committee in the Comintern had to discuss the question of the German revolution in all its details in the Politburo—which is what we did.'[1]

During the transition period from Lenin's leadership to the leadership of a collective, unity, let alone unanimity, was lacking. Of the five members of the Politburo who play any part at all in the events of 1923—Zinoviev, Kamenev, Stalin, Trotsky and Bukharin—the first three were at loggerheads with Trotsky, while Bukharin occupied an intermediate position. The struggle for succession was under way. Under these conditions the crisis in Germany got involved in the crisis inside the Politburo. During the first half of 1923 this, as far as can be perceived, was not of much moment.

---

[1] *Pravda*, January 25, 1924. Part of Zinoviev's assertions concerning the responsibility of others has probably to be discounted. His aim was to clear his own name from responsibility for the defeat in Germany and to saddle others with the blame.

But in July 1923, only two or three weeks after Radek had initiated the Schlageter campaign, the German situation began to get out of hand. Without anyone being aware of it, the crisis was approaching. There was no stopping the mark's headlong descent. All over the Reich the increasing misery of the workers was expressed in ever more numerous demonstrations, strikes, food riots and clashes with the police. The K.P.D. rapidly grew to become the centre of the workers' hopes. It may even have had the support of the majority of the workers. In the first half of July it began to enjoy a mass influence such as it had never before, or would have again.[1]

Yet how little the Politburo understood what was happening is shown by one illuminating fact—at this time three of its leading members, Zinoviev, Trotsky and Bukharin, were on holiday in the Caucasus.[2]

In Germany, meanwhile, the *Rote Fahne* of July 12 devoted its entire front page to an appeal for an 'Anti-Fascist Day' to be held on Sunday, July 29. The appeal was couched in highly militant terms. Zinoviev and Bukharin had advised street demonstrations against the fascists.[3] This was presumably the response of the K.P.D., or rather the response of those sections of the K.P.D. who were opposed to Radek's 'Schlageter policy,' for the policy of wooing the fascists and at the same time of demonstrating against them, overlapped.[4] Zinoviev and Bukharin heartily welcomed the proposed demonstration and congratulated the K.P.D. on its struggle. Radek, on the other hand, in charge in Moscow during the absence of Zinoviev and Bukharin, sent the latter a telegram on July 12—the very same day that the appeal appeared in the *Rote Fahne*—warning them that their championship of the demonstration would force the party into a crushing defeat. Trotsky, when consulted, refrained from committing himself on the grounds that he had not enough evidence on which to base a judgement. In the end Radek sent through the Presidium of the Comintern a telegram to the K.P.D. on July 26 in which he

[1] Ossip K. Flechtheim: *Die K.P.D. in der Weimarer Republik*, Offenbach am Main, 1948, pp. 90-91, examines the results of various trade union, shop-steward and local elections at this period. He comes to the general conclusion: 'It can probably be definitely concluded that in 1923 the K.P.D. had behind it a strong minority of those workers organised in trade unions and perhaps even a majority of the unorganised workers.'

[2] *The Errors of Trotskyism*, London, 1925, p. 346.

[3] Ruth Fischer: *Stalin and German Communism*, Harvard, 1948, p. 305.

[4] In a letter (see below) Stalin took Brandler to be the originator of the proposed demonstration, his aim being to 'educate the masses'.

entirely misrepresented Zinoviev's views. The telegram read: 'The Presidium of the Comintern advises you to abandon the street demonstrations of July 29. . . . We fear a trap.' In this Radek was supported by 'other comrades'.[1]

Stalin was almost certainly one of those 'other comrades'. In his first overt intervention in the discussion, he also opposed the anti-Fascist Day. He sent to the absent Bukharin and Zinoviev a letter in which he argued that the Communists should not attempt to seize power without the Social-Democrats. It was of advantage to avoid a provocative 'demonstration', let the Fascists attack first, and thereby 'rally the entire working-class around the Communists'. The letter concluded: 'In my opinion the Germans should be restrained and not spurred on.'[2]

In the actual event, the K.P.D. disregarded Radek's advice. On the other hand the Anti-Fascist Day, in the form originally conceived, of mass street-demonstrations did not take place owing to police prohibition. It remained, as Brandler had wished, within the legal limits of interior demonstrations inside halls and the like. Even so, it was an undeniable success. In Berlin alone a quarter of a million people demonstrated with the K.P.D. The numbers were comparable throughout the rest of the Reich. A week later, on August 5 and 6, the Central Committee of the K.P.D. met to discuss the position. Once again there was no agreement between the Right and Left wings. Brandler agreed that the conditions were already those of civil war, but he argued that the slogan of a worker's government must still be retained

[1] All the foregoing is based on Zionviev's speech to the 13th Conference of the Party, reported in *Pravda*, January 25, 1924. The views of the personalities involved are fully confirmed elsewhere. (See *The Errors of Trotskyism*, London, 1925, p. 346).

[2] Quoted in Leon Trotsky: *Stalin*, London, 1947, pp. 368-369. Although its authenticity is unquestioned, the date of this letter has been the subject of much controversy. Trotskyists, and Stalin's opponents generally, assume it to refer to the question of a communist-led German Revolution and on this basis accuse Stalin of stabbing the K.P.D. in the back, or, at the very least, of nipping in the bud a promising revolutionary opportunity; c.f. C. L. R. James: *World Revolution 1917-1936*, London, 1937, pp. 181 ff.; Ruth Fischer: *Stalin and German Communism*, Harvard, 1948, p. 306. In Trotsky's biography of Stalin and in Ruth Fischer's book the letter is referred to August. In Trotsky's *L'International Communiste après Lénine*, Paris, 1930, p. 428, it is dated August 7. One thing is certain; the letter does not refer to the situation after the middle of August for at that time Zinoviev and Bukharin returned to Moscow and Stalin had, therefore, no need to write to them. Moreover, at that time there was no question of the German Government 'toppling over' but of its overthrow being organised jointly by the K.P.D. and the Politburo (see below p. 85). The letter must, therefore, refer either to the period between July 12 and 29, when the Anti-Fascist Day was first discussed, or to the first half of August. The reason why the earlier period has been tentatively identified here as the crucial one is Stalin's clear reference to 'the demonstration' of which the Anti-Fascist Day is the only outstanding example.

F

until more mass support was won. Fischer, on the other hand, argued that this was the very moment for the full-throated Communist appeal—'The dictatorship of the proletariat'. For the same reason the left wing opposed the support given by the K.P.D. faction in the Saxon Landtag to the left Social-Democratic Government of Dr Erich Zeigner.[1]

Events now took their own course. On August 10, intending to overthrow Cuno, the Berlin note-printers struck, paralysing the government in its most vulnerable point—its supply of paper money. On August 11, a general strike was called. On August 12, Cuno resigned. On August 13 and 14 the strike movement spread to Central Germany, the Rhineland, Thuringia and the Eastern Provinces. Everywhere the K.P.D. was carried on the crest of the wave. Never again was the party to find itself in such favourable circumstances.

Two of Lenin's three pre-conditions for successful revolutionary action were fulfilled: governmental authority no longer existed, and widespread discontent assailed the ruling classes. The third pre-condition—a united mass-party with a revolutionary leadership—was the missing factor. 'Seen from the inside . . . the Communists were an insufficiently organised group of panic-stricken people, torn by factional quarrels, unable to come to a decision and unclear about their own aims.'[2] On August 13 Brandler, despite the opposition of the K.P.D's. left wing, called off the strike on the grounds that it had succeeded in its aim of overthrowing Cuno.[3]

On the same day Stresemann replaced Cuno as Chancellor. He at once brought the Social-Democrats into the Cabinet. This split the nascent working-class front. In Stresemann's own words: it had 'the attraction of separating the moderate constitutional wing of the Social-Democrats from the Radicals'.[4] In foreign policy he immediately strove to come to terms with France, preparing to drop passive resistance. This, combined with the climax of the political crisis, was enough for the Russians. Not only were there unmistakable signs of revolution in Germany but

---

[1] *Izvestya*, August 15, 1923. This despatch from *Izvestya's* Berlin Correspondent did not appear until more than a week after the events it describes. The reason is probably that the editor wished to conceal from his public the truth about events in Germany.

[2] Ruth Fischer: *Stalin and German Communism*, Harvard, 1948, p. 338.

[3] Ibid., pp. 301-302.

[4] G. Stresemann: *Di   s, Letters and Speeches*, Vol. 1, London, 1935-1940, Eng. trans., pp. 78-79.

also, at the very same time, Rapallo expired. The German bourgeoisie were no longer serving as 'an objective obstacle to capitalism' or as 'a force . . . directly aimed at an imperialist Entente state'. Under Stresemann, the German bourgeoisie had abandoned their role as defenders of the Soviet Union. They had ganged up with imperialist France. They were no longer neutral. In other words, French imperialism—the conqueror of Germany, the ally of Poland—stood at the very gates of Soviet Russia.

In an article in *Izvestya,* entitled 'Hands Off Germany', Radek wrote: 'Soviet Russia is linked to the toiling masses of Germany by bonds of the deepest class solidarity. But more than that, she is bound to them by her fate. If Entente capital, having torn Germany to pieces, were to establish its hegemony over her, on the backs of the conquered German workers, this would signify the greatest danger for Soviet Russia. Soviet Russia succeeded in throwing back the intervention not only thanks to the enthusiasm of the Russian masses, not only thanks to the aid of the proletariat of the whole world, but also because the Allies had no immediate access to Russia through Germany, because they had to transport their armies and equipment through seas and whole continents. Had Germany been in Entente hands, this would have meant that the approach to Soviet Russia lay in the grasp of world capital.'[1]

In slightly different terms, Kamenev, a far more important figure than Radek by virtue of his membership of the Politburo, said the same thing. In a speech to the 2nd All-Union Congress of Soviets in January 1924 he drew a clear distinction between the sympathy of the Russian soviets for the German proletariat and 'other business-like considerations of state'. 'Comrades', he said, 'we are linked with Germany more closely than with any other state because of geography and our mutual economic interests. What also connects us is the fact that Germany, carved up by triumphant imperialism, found at one time sufficient courage and insight in its government to sign the Rapallo Treaty. In consequence the consolidation of our friendly relations with Germany, the strengthening of our economic ties, mutual encouragement in the development of these ties were pursued by us in the past as one of the bases of our policy—which they remain in the future. But during the period I am reviewing (*i.e.* 1923) this was not the only factor to show itself. The Soviet Government could not pass

[1] *Izvestya,* August 31, 1923.

by that October-November crisis which shook the whole of Germany. Not only because a proletarian conscience cannot regard with calm a situation anywhere in the world where the proletariat is exerting its strength to acquire improved conditions of existence, not only because our soviets are a trumpet for the moods and enthusiasm of the broad proletarian masses and cannot renounce their duty and their obligations to serve as this trumpet, but also, comrades, because of other, business-like considerations of state. Minister of Foreign Affairs Stresemann declared during the days of this October-November crisis that the fate of Soviet Russia was bound up with the fate of Germany, and this was the very point on which we were in absolute agreement with him. To us, as to Stresemann, it was perfectly clear that the victory of fascism, the victory of militarist-reactionary circles in Germany would mean that the door into the Soviet Republic was open for world imperialism. The advance of French troops from the Rhineland where they stand with their feet firmly planted on the shoulders of the triumphant German counter-revolution further into the interior of the country would denote the overturning of those bases of stability and balance in the world position on which stands the Soviet Republic.'[1]

This was the August reaction and analysis of the Politburo, made on Stresemann's assumption of power.[2] It shows that in the same way as the pre-August united front policy was a blend of the requirements of Rapallo and of the Communist International, there were also two factors conditioning the abandonment of this policy, and its replacement by revolution—first, Rapallo was dead; and secondly, the K.P.D. to all appearances stood on the threshold of power. As soon as Stresemann became Chancellor an electric shock went through the Kremlin. On August 14, the day following Stresemann's ascent to power, *Izvestya* headlined the news of Cuno's fall: 'Germany on the eve of Revolution'. It carried a leader, signed 'Non-Diplomat', terming Germany 'The second wave of World Revolution'. The first wave had submerged

---

[1] *Pravda*, February 1, 1924. It has not been possible to trace the speech of Stresemann referred to by Kamenev.

[2] Although Kamenev did not specifically say so, there is no doubt that his analysis does refer to August; for later in the same speech Kamenev mentions that 'during these months' Vigdor Kopp was sent to Latvia, Lithuania and Poland—and the Kopp visit took place in August (Louis Fischer: *The Soviets in World Affairs*, London, 1930, p. 459). The Kopp episode is dealt with below where further reference is made to Kamenev's speech.

Russia and then ebbed. But the tide had risen again and the second would submerge Germany. Nothing like this had appeared in *Izvestya* since November 1918. Even in the far-off Caucasus Zinoviev was galvanised into activity. He rapidly drew up new theses: 'The crisis is approaching, decisive events are at the gate. A new and decisive chapter is beginning in the activity of the German Communist Party and with this in the whole Comintern. The Communist Party of Germany shapes its course rapidly and decisively in view of the impending revolutionary crisis.' Zinoviev, Trotsky and Bukharin interrupted their holidays to return to Moscow whither the German leaders were summoned to receive strategical advice.[1]

It was on August 23 that the Politburo first discussed the possibility of a German revolution. Trotsky was all for pushing ahead. To this, for some unknown reason, Zinoviev retorted that the revolution was not a matter of weeks, as Trotsky claimed, but of months. Stalin, sceptical as ever, said that it was not yet time to speak of a revolution in Germany. Perhaps one could not speak of it at all.[2]

Eventually however the decision was taken to go ahead, for it was at about this time that Kopp was sent to Latvia, Lithuania and Poland. 'What was the purpose of Comrade Kopp's journey?' Kamenev asked. 'What did we attain? Two things. We endeavoured to make sure, we demanded from our neighbours guarantees of non-intervention in German affairs; secondly, we endeavoured to make sure, we demanded such agreements as would secure us unhindered transit between the U.S.S.R. and Central Europe, independently of the political changes, and changes in the social order, which might take place there.'[3]

The right of 'unhindered transit' was to apply to grain.[4] The Russians apparently expected that a Soviet Germany would be blockaded in the same way as they themselves had been blockaded from 1918-1920. Germany, a densely populated and highly industrialised country, would obviously be in a far weaker position to withstand such pressure than Russia had been. Kopp's demand for guarantees of non-intervention in German affairs was

[1] *The Errors of Trotskyism*, London, 1925, pp. 347-348.
[2] Boris Bajanov: *Stalin-der rote Diktator*, Berlin, 1931, pp. 122-125. Bajanov, as Stalin's secretary in the Politburo, was an eye-witness of these debates.
[3] *Pravda*, February 1, 1924.
[4] Louis Fischer: *The Soviets in World Affairs*, London, 1930, p. 459; see also Gregoire Bessedovsky: *Oui, j'accuse!*, Paris, 1930, pp. 47-48 and 61-62. Bessedovsky was a member of the Soviet diplomatic service and head of the Ukrainian Mission in Warsaw.

reinforced with the threat of force. Radek's article 'Hands off Germany' made this quite clear: 'Soviet diplomacy will do everything to suggest to all concerned that the best thing for the capitalist world will be to leave the decision on Germany's fate to the German popular masses, and not to try to hurl a sword on to the scales of history, for there is a sword not only in the hands of the capitalist powers but also in the hands of the first proletarian state—Soviet Russia.'[1]

Kopp's journey was the first concrete step taken by the Politburo. The second was a series of strategical conferences with the K.P.D. delegation to Moscow. Brandler arrived at the end of August and the left-wing leaders a little later. They found the capital gay with slogans welcoming the German revolution—'Russian Youth —Learn German—the German October is approaching'. Pictures of Clara Zetkin, Luxemburg and Liebknecht were in every shop window.[2] The capital was in a ferment. Students were preparing to abandon their studies to rush to the barricades in Berlin.[3]

Behind closed doors, Trotsky and Zinoviev debated the strategic position with the K.P.D. delegation. Not only had two such experienced revolutionaries deprived the German party of its leaders; not only were they going to organise a revolution in Berlin from Moscow, a distance of some 800 miles, but they also concentrated their attention solely on the military aspect, leaving the political side to look after itself. It was one more example of the fatal Russian habit of transferring to the international sphere precedents drawn from Russian experience. The Russian revolution had largely depended on the timing and planning of a well-organised *coup*. Therefore the German revolution would be on the same lines. It was only later that Zinoviev began to realise the difficulties the Comintern was up against in Germany. In 1925, he correctly attributed the repeated failure of revolution in Germany to the fact that the German bourgeoisie was not led by Rasputins, and to the strength of German Social-Democracy.[4] The discussions between Zinoviev, Trotsky and the K.P.D. delegation lasted roughly five weeks from the beginning of

---

[1] *Izvestya*, August 31, 1923.
[2] Ruth Fischer: *Stalin and German Communism*, Harvard, 1948, p. 312.
[3] Gregoire Bessedovsky: *Oui, j'accuse!*, Paris, 1930, p. 60; J. Stalin: *Leninism*, Vol. I, Eng. trans., London, 1928, p. 302.
[4] *XIV Syezd V.K.P.* (*b*) *Stenographicheskii otchet* (*14th Congress of the All-Union Communist Party* (*b*) *Stenographic Report*), 2nd ed., Moscow, 1926, pp. 660-661.

September to the first week in October. The first issue concerned
the date of the projected revolution. Trotsky wanted a timetable
of events reaching their climax on November 7 or 9. It was a
grandiose image—they would be celebrating the anniversary of
the Russian revolution in Moscow to the sound of the 'Red Flag'
in Berlin. Brandler however, as reluctant as ever to abandon his
moderation, and desirous of having as much elbow-room as
possible, refused to be tied down in this way. Zinoviev arranged
a compromise whereby no definite date was fixed.[1] Instead,
'an orientating interval' was laid down, with the decisive moment
to be determined on the spot.[2]

It was further agreed that the military force was to be composed
of a nucleus of Red Hundreds (Hundertschaften). These were
to be organised by the K.P.D. out of its own membership and
sympathisers. Red Army Intelligence men and strategical
advisers were to supplement this force. The whole would constitute the skeleton of a regular army.[3]

The overall strategic plan was as follows: 'The proletariat rises
in Saxony, goes beyond the defence of the workers' government
in which we enter, and it will try in Saxony to use governmental
power to arm itself and to form, in this closely-knit proletarian
area of Central Germany, a bulwark between the counter-
revolution in Bavaria and Fascism in the North. At the same
time the party intervenes all over Germany and mobilises the
masses.'[4]

By the end of September, the Russians and the K.P.D. were
ready to go ahead. *Izvestya* which had largely refrained from
editorial comment during September, came out at the end of
the month with a very vigorous leader: 'We have never renounced our idea of furthering by all means the development
of the international revolution, which will lead us to final
victory.

We are on the threshold of great events and we must be ready
for them in time. The present political situation . . . is more
favourable.'[5] The next day Trotsky gave an interview to U.S. Sen-
ator King in which he promised all aid short of war to the German

---

[1] Ruth Fischer: *Stalin and German Communism*, Harvard, 1948, pp. 316-317.
[2] Bukharin at the 13th Congress of the Russian Communist Party May, 1924
(*XIII Syezd R.K.P. (b) Stenographicheskii otchet*), Moscow, 1924, p. 374.
[3] Ruth Fischer: *Stalin and German Communism*, Harvard, 1948, pp. 319-321.
[4] *Die Lehren der deutschen Ereignisse*, Hamburg, 1924, p. 5.
[5] *Izvestya*, September 29, 1923.

revolution: 'With all our soul we are on the side of the German working class in its struggle against exploitation internally and externally. And at the same time we are wholly for peace.'[1]

But events in Germany were not marking time. The K.P.D. had lost the initiative at the end of July when it refused to give the Anti-Fascist Day a sufficiently aggressive character. Its prestige had then made a partial recovery through the party's decisive role in overthrowing Cuno a fortnight later. But the August strike movement had petered out for lack of an organising power. It was with Stresemann that the initiative now lay and he fought hard to retain it. On September 26 he finally declared an end to passive resistance in the Ruhr. The same night he proclaimed martial law throughout the Reich whereby executive power was transferred to Gessler, the Reichswehr minister, and through him to Seeckt and through Seeckt to the Wehrkreis commanders. In Saxony, where attention was soon to be centred, this was General Müller. Governmental power in Saxony was held by Dr Zeigner, a left-wing Social-Democrat. He had no Communists in his Cabinet, but was dependent on their support in the Saxon Landtag.

On September 27 and again on September 30, the K.P.D.'s Central Committee met to discuss the new situation. A general strike was called in the Ruhr, but a proposal to prepare for an armed rising in Saxony was rejected. The next day, however, October 1, Zinoviev sent a telegram to the K.P.D. instructing the party to enter Dr Zeigner's government in Saxony: 'We interpret the situation thus, the decisive moment will come in four, five or six weeks. We consider it necessary to occupy at once every position which can be of direct aid. On the basis of the situation the question of our entry into the Saxon government must be posed in practice. On condition that the Zeigner people are genuinely ready to defend Saxony against Bavaria and the Fascists we must enter. Push through immediate arming of 50,000 to 60,000 men. Ignore General Müller. Same for Thuringia.'[2]

Brandler, still in Moscow, objected to the telegram but eventually yielded to Zinoviev's pressure.[3] This was not the only last-minute dispute. Trotsky, who had great confidence in Brandler, wanted to detain Fischer in Moscow where she would not hamper

[1] *Izvestya*, September 30, 1923.
[2] *Die Lehren der deutschen Ereignisse*, Hamburg, 1924, p. 60.
[3] Ibid., pp. 24-25.

Brandler's revolutionary task. But Zinoviev defeated this proposition.[1]

On October 8, the German delegation left Moscow. Trotsky accompanied Brandler to the Kremlin gates. 'There they stood in the sharp light of an autumn afternoon', writes an eye-witness, 'the stocky Brandler, in his unpressed civilian suit, and the elegant Trotsky in his well-cut Red Army uniform. After the last words, Trotsky kissed Brandler tenderly on both cheeks in the usual Russian manner. Knowing both men well, I could see that Trotsky was really moved; he felt he was wishing well the leader of the German revolution on the eve of great events.'[2]

Two days later, Brandler and two other members of the K.P.D. became members of Zeigner's new Cabinet in Saxony. On October 16, three other Communists similarly entered the left Social-Democrat Cabinet in Thuringia. But already on October 13 General Müller, who did not allow himself to be ignored, decreed the dissolution of the Red Hundreds. This Zeigner refused, since they were behaving in perfect accord with the law. What is more, in the Saxon Landtag, Zeigner delivered a slashing attack on the Reichswehr and the Reich Government, for their toleration and encouragement of illegal militarist formations.[3]

This obliged Ebert, one of the signatories of the Seeckt-Severing agreement, to issue, on the basis of Article 48 of the Constitution a 'Reichsexekutive' against Zeigner, a fellow Social-Democrat. Müller was thereby entitled to supplant the Zeigner régime on the grounds of its refusal to comply with the Constitution.[4] As early as September, when there were no Communists in the Saxon Cabinet, Gessler, the Reichswehr Minister, had wanted to arrest Zeigner for high treason.[5] When the Communists did enter, the situation was exploited to get rid of Zeigner and keep his mouth shut.

While Müller, armed with the 'Reichsexekutive', was assembling his troops, preparatory to moving against the government, an interlude took place at Chemnitz. At a conference there of

[1] *The Errors of Trotskyism*, London, 1925, pp. 350-351.
[2] Ruth Fischer: *Stalin and German Communism*, Harvard, 1948, p. 323.
[3] This speech is quoted in Kurt Caro and Walter Oehme: *Schleichers Aufstieg*, Berlin, 1933, pp. 161 ff.
[4] This precedent was drawn on by Hindenburg in July, 1932, to dismiss the Social-Democratic Government of Prussia (Otto Braun: *Von Weimar zu Hitler*, 2nd ed., New York, 1940, p. 133).
[5] *Manchester Guardian*, September 8, 1923; see also Toni Sender: *The Autobiography of a German Rebel*, London, 1940, p. 207.

co-operatives, trade-unions and all working-class political parties Brandler, the chief Communist delegate, made a half-hearted proposal to call a general strike. Under the circumstances this would have been a certain prelude to civil war. No positive response was made. A committee was elected to discuss the proposal.[1] Through an error couriers left Chemnitz for Hamburg with orders to rise. The isolated Communists there fought for three days before giving in. This was the end of the German revolution—it ended 'not with a bang but with a whimper'. Two speeches by Trotsky show how much the Russians were out of touch with the situation: on October 20 and 22 he spoke in Moscow confidently prophesying victory.[2]

General Müller was not impressed with Trotsky's speeches. On the 23rd he began to move his troops into Saxony, encountering scattered working-class resistance. On the 27th Stresemann called on Zeigner to resign. This he refused to do, having come to power in a perfectly legal way and still enjoying the confidence of the Landtag. Moreover, although this was not what Zinoviev had wanted, Brandler remained within the best tradition of bourgeois democracy. The Times correspondent reported from Dresden: 'No revolutionary programme has been adopted. The most radical measure passed was one which made the burgo-master an elective representative instead of a state official. . . . '[3]

But the mere existence of Communists in the Cabinet in con-junction with Zeigner's disclosures of the Reichswehr's illegal auxiliaries was enough. When Stresemann called on Zeigner to resign, Stresemann's Social-Democratic colleagues in the Reich Cabinet tried to mediate between the two premiers.[4] But Stresemann did not wait. On October 29, after Müller had deposed Zeigner by force, he installed Heinze of the People's Party as Reich Commissioner for the province. Even for the long-suffering Social-Democratic ministers this was too much. They resigned on November 3. The Moor had done his duty; the Moor could go. As Stresemann said: 'If we were able to march into Saxony and Thuringia without bloodshed, then perhaps the reason was that the Social-Democrats were won over to support the invasion and that therefore the Communists stood alone against us.'[5]

[1] Ruth Fischer: Stalin and German Communism, Harvard, 1948, pp. 336-337.
[2] These speeches are reported in Izvestya, October 21 and 23, 1923.
[3] The Times, October 22, 1923.
[4] F. Stampfer: Die Vierzehn Jahre der ersten deutschen Republik, Karlsbad, 1936, pp.335-336.
[5] Quoted by Koenen in the Reichstag (Reichstag Debates, Vol. 391, p. 8502).

CHAPTER VI

The German Balance between Rapallo and Locarno (1925-1926)

NEITHER in Germany nor in Russia was the extent of the defeat at first clear. Steklov's leader in *Izvestya*, a week after the Hamburg rising, treated it as of no significance. Early in November he again wrote as if the German Revolution were imminent.[1] But as November passed into December and 1923 into 1924, the truth about a cruel defeat became apparent. Not even Zinoviev, a congenital optimist, could delude himself any longer.

There was at once a furious and unedifying outburst of public polemics and recriminations. Zinoviev, his prestige as Comintern President severely discredited by the defeat, was foremost in putting the blame on others. Brandler was one obvious scapegoat.[2] With more justice perhaps, Zinoviev also attacked Radek. At the 13th Party Conference in January 1924 he accused him of 'holding the party back by the coat-tails when it should have been urged into battle';[3] and at the 5th World Congress of the Comintern later the same year he repeatedly assailed Radek of wilfully misleading the K.P.D. and of watering-down the slogan of a 'Workers' Government'.[4]

Radek in his turn, blamed E.C.C.I. and Bukharin.[5] Trotsky blamed the K.P.D. for failing to correct its tactics in time and not turning to good account an objectively revolutionary situation.[6]

In the end there were two fall-guys for the German revolution. In Germany Brandler took the rap; and in Russia, Radek. Radek never again played any part in the formation of policy and was transferred to the post of rector of the Sun-Yat-Sen University in Moscow. Brandler suffered a less spectacular eclipse. He lost the

[1] *Izvestya*, November 1 and 3, 1923.
[2] See Zinoviev's speech at the 13th Party Conference reported in *Pravda*, January 25, 1924.
[3] *Pravda*, January 25, 1924.
[4] See especially *V Vseymirni Kongress Kommunisticheskovo Internatsionala—Stenographicheskii Otchet* (*5th All-World Congress of the Communist International—Stenographic Report*), Moscow & Leningrad, 1925, pp. 75 ff.
[5] *XIII Syezd R.K.P.* (*b*)—*Stenographicheskii Otchet* (*13th Congress of the Russian Communist Party* (*b*)—*Stenographic Report*), Moscow, 1924, pp. 351-374.
[6] L. Trotsky: *The First Five Years of the Communist International*, New York, 1945, pp. 2-5.

leadership of the K.P.D. which fell into the hands of the left-wing—Fischer, Maslow, and Thälmann.

One name was conspicuous by its absence from the polemics. It was that of General-Secretary Stalin. In later years he came under much obloquy for allegedly sabotaging the German Revolution. But at the time there was no hint of this. Stalin's attitude had been reserved with a tendency towards pessimism. What emerged as significant in this pessimistic evaluation was its accuracy. In the shifting struggle for power enveloping the Politburo in the winter of 1923-1924, Stalin was not associated with defeat in the same way as were Trotsky and Zinoviev. To say the least, his prestige was not tarnished by backing the wrong horse. This was not valid for any of his adversaries and especially, of course, for Trotsky and Zinoviev.

But the events of 1923 had an importance far transcending the personal element. The significance of the abortive German Revolution, coming as it did after so many earlier frustrated hopes, lay in the fact that it sealed Russia's isolation in the capitalist world. Henceforward there was to be no more sacrifice of foreign policy to the prospect of revolution, however alluring. As a consequence, such treaties as Rapallo became even more important in the fulfilment of their role as Russia's foothold in the capitalist world. In personal terms this meant that Chicherin's star would rise, whereas Zinoviev's would sink. The expression of this situation in political terms was Stalin's doctrine of 'socialism in one country'. It was a theoretical adjustment rendered necessary by the circumstances of isolation in which Russia found herself. The theory was first enunciated in the Autumn of 1924. In March 1925 the Communist International proclaimed new theses on 'temporary stabilisation'; and at the end of the year the 14th Party Conference approved Stalin's theory—Russia had everything required to build socialism in one country.[1]

Bukharin replaced Zinoviev as President of the Comintern. A new conception of the revolutionary process became current. It was far more realistic, as events have shown, than the earlier one. Bukharin once expressed it with characteristic vigour. 'The international revolution will not only come but it *is* a fact. It is

[1] *XIV Syezd V.K.P.* (b)—*Stenographicheskii Otchet* (*14th Congress of the All-Union Communist Party* (b)—*Stenographic Report*), 2nd. ed., Moscow & Leningrad, 1926, p. 968.

absolutely untrue, naïve and stupid to imagine the international revolution as a single act, when simultaneously throughout the whole world, as if at the stroke of a clock, as if by command, a "world conflagration" will burst out. It is stupid to think that there exists a mystic, pre-determined "hour" when "His Highness —The Proletariat" will ascend to power.

The international revolution is a gigantic process to be calculated in decades. . . . The world revolution will only complete its course when it is enthroned in all countries. Then its circuit will be closed. . . . The international revolution appears in different forms, takes on different shapes. . . . But we stand in the very thick of international-revolutionary events and only thick-headed cranks, only the blind . . . can look round and ask: where is this elusive international revolution, anyway?'[1]

As for the K.P.D., having failed to seize its opportunity in the summer of 1923, it rapidly lost its mass influence. From 1924 to 1929 the party shared in the general stabilisation of German society. Simultaneously, it became weaker and weaker in relation to the Comintern, declining more and more into an institution for the defence of the Soviet Union.

But none of this was clear in 1924. Only in perspective does the significance of the abortive German Revolution become visible. For all that the world at large was aware, Soviet Russia might have continued on her revolutionary path.

There is thus something highly paradoxical in the complete lack of any perceptible influence on Rapallo of the German events of 1923. Through a supreme stroke of good luck the Russians were able to have their cake and eat it. Rapallo emerged unharmed from the Russian-sponsored German Revolution. In December 1923, for example, Stresemann wrote to Brockdorff-Rantzau in Moscow. His comment on the aid given by the Russians to the K.P.D. did not go beyond stating that it made Russo-German relations 'very difficult'.[2]

The reason for this is not, of course, that the German bourgeoisie were indifferent to the possibility of a Russian-promoted revolution. On the contrary, Stresemann's action in defence of their interests in Saxony and Thuringia lacked nothing in

---

[1] *Izvestya*, January 13, 1927.
[2] G. Stresemann: *Diaries and Papers*, Vol. I, Eng. trans., London, 1935-1940, pp. 255-256.

brutality and directness. No, the reason is that Germany in 1924 was still in far too weak an international position to cavil at the strange habits of her Bolshevik friends. She was forced to take the Russians at their word when they denied any connection between the Comintern and the Soviet Government. Germany, through weakness, had no choice but to overlook the connection. It was not until the international position of Germany had decisively improved, by 1930-1931, that Communism and Russia came to be identified. Until then, the fiction of their division was maintained —and with some success.

For their part, the Russians too suffered from no inhibition in evoking the memory of their support for Germany during the occupation of the Ruhr. It crops up again and again. In 1924 Chicherin spoke of how 'the Soviet Government appeared before all other Governments as the friend of the most oppressed country, Germany, whose very existence was gravely threatened'.[1] In 1927 Theodore Rothstein, at one time Soviet Ambassador to Persia and later chief of the Narkomindel Press Department, writes of how the Rapallo Treaty protected Germany's rear against possible Polish attacks in 1923.[2] And in June 1930, when the Rhineland was finally evacuated, a feature of Litvinov's congratulatory message to the German Government was a reminder of the original Soviet protest at the Ruhr occupation.[3] All in all, the pro-German stand of the Soviets during 1923 is a recurrent background theme to the Rapallo policy. The Soviets played it up for all they were worth. This, in conjunction with the German weakness at the time, had as a parodoxical consequence that on November 7, 1923 the anniversary of the Russian Revolution was celebrated at the Russian Embassy in Berlin by a mixed gathering of German bankers, industrialists and communists, and Russian officials.[4]

Even more paradoxical was the shape taken by 1924. Not for nothing has this become known in Soviet Russian history as 'The Year of Recognitions'. Just after having tried to pull off a revolution in one of the great powers of Europe, the Soviet Government all of a sudden received *de jure* recognition from a number of European powers. These included Great Britain, France, Italy,

---

[1] *Izvestya*, April 16, 1924.
[2] *Osteuropa*, Jg. 3, Heft 2, p. 131.
[3] Quoted below p. 147.
[4] Lyubov Krassin: *Leonid Krassin*, London, 1929, pp. 220-222; *The Daily Telegraph*, November 24, 1923.

Norway, Sweden, Denmark, Austria, Hungary and Greece. This was indeed a windfall.

To mar this spectacular improvement in the Soviet's international status an equally sudden storm blew up with Germany. In the Spring of 1924 it led to a virtual rupture of Russo-German diplomatic and commercial relations lasting almost three months. It was caused by a German police raid on the premises of the Soviet Trade Delegation in Berlin. During the morning of May 3 a German Communist named Bozenhard was being escorted across Berlin by two detectives from Wurttemberg. He suggested that the three of them enter a café for some refreshment. The unwitting Wurttembergers were then led to the Russian trading premises in the Lindentrasse where Bozenhard gave them the slip. On attempting to follow after him, the detectives were told that the building enjoyed extra-territorial rights. They then withdrew. But in the afternoon a detachment of Berlin police arrived and disregarding all the protests of the personnel employed in the Delegation carried out a thorough search.[1] The Russian reaction was immediate. Krestinski left Berlin in protest, leaving Bratman-Brodowski, the Counsellor of Embassy, in charge. All orders to German firms were cancelled and all negotiations on concessions suspended. Russian participation in the Cologne fair and the Leipzig fair auction was withdrawn. In Leipzig and Hamburg the Branch offices of the Trade Delegation were closed.[2] A very vigorous protest was also made by Krassin at the Thirteenth Party Congress in Moscow, which met shortly after the incident. He roundly accused the Germans of a breach of the 1921 trade agreement.[3]

It was never suggested that the German Government were behind the raid. But it is plausible to suppose that Stresemann expressly delayed the settlement of the dispute.[4] On May 23, the Nationalist organ, the *Deutsche Allgemeine Zeitung,* reported that the negotiations between Brockdorff-Rantzau and the Russian Foreign Office were on the verge of successful conclusion. Yet not until July 29 was the necessary protocol eventually signed. This belated date gains in significance in view of the fact that only a week later Stresemann went to London to participate in the

[1] Louis Fischer: *The Soviets in World Affairs,* London, 1930, p. 582.

[2] Ibid., p. 583; A. Erusalimski: *Germaniya, Antanta i S.S.S.R. (Germany, the Entente and the U.S.S.R.),* Moscow, 1928, p. 127.

[3] *XIII Syzed R.K.P. (b)—Stenographicheskii Otchet,* Moscow, 1924, pp. 146-151.

[4] See for example an article in *Die Weltbühne,* May 22, 1924, pp. 702-704.

closing stages of the Dawes Plan. This Plan, together with its political implications, was to strain Rapallo to the uttermost and Stresemann could not but have welcomed the opportunity to keep the Russians at bay, even if only temporarily. Moreover, the sequence of signing with the East and then, a few days later, of signing with the West was raised by Stresemann to a fine art. Exactly the same thing happened in 1925 and again in 1928.[1]

The Dawes Plan represented for Germany a substantial easing of reparations payments. It also opened the way to foreign credits, for the Plan itself assured Germany of a loan of 800 million gold marks. Germany's total liabilities were left blank but she was obliged to begin by making payments of between one and two and a half milliard gold marks. Guarantees for her creditors were provided by international control over the Reichsbank and the German Railway system. Foreign loans in ever-increasing quantities now began to flow into Germany. A turning point in the post-war history of Europe had been reached. The whole plan was the justification of a development foreseen by Stresemann at the end of 1922. He had then told the Reichstag: 'This feeling of solidarity in the fight against Bolshevism acts as an inducement to the economic forces of capitalism to co-operate in the reconstruction of Germany or at least to try to prevent her collapse. We ought to be glad of the fact. This is the only way, to my mind, in which we can extricate ourselves from the present situation.'[2]

But what Stresemann saw as a means to improve Germany's position, was seen by the Russians as a momentous threat to both Germany and to themselves. Chicherin for example, asserted that as a result of the Dawes Plan Germany had lost her freedom of action.[3] Rykov, the President of the Council of Peoples' Commissars, said that Germany had been turned into 'a colony of Western European capitalism', thereby forfeiting her political and economic independence.[4] This soon became the staple theme of Soviet propaganda—Germany had dwindled into a tool of the Western Powers.

As 1924 passed into 1925, this fear merged with another—that Britain was trying to draw Germany into an anti-Russian bloc,

---

[1] These cases are dealt with below pp. 108, 134.
[2] G. Stresemann: *Essays and Speeches on Various Subjects*, Eng. trans., London, 1930, p. 143.
[3] *Tsentralni Ispolnitelni Komitet 2 sozyv, 2 sessiya—Stenographicheskii Otchet (2nd Sitting, 2nd Session of the Central Executive Committee—Stenographic Report)*, Moscow, 1924, p. 65.
[4] *Izvestya*, November 28, 1924.

or at the very least to detach Germany from Russia, which would have had the effect of isolating Russia. This new fear was fore-shadowed in an *Izvestya* article by Steklov in which he prophesied a strengthening of international-reactionary pressure on the Soviet Union after the election victory of the British Conservatives.[1] Justification of this was soon seen in the German application for membership of the League of Nations, and in the proposed Locarno Treaty, sometimes known as the Security or Guarantee Pact.

In its simplest, most uncomplicated form, Locarno was a contractual arrangement whereby Great Britain and Italy guaranteed the Rhine frontier between Germany and Belgium and between Germany and France. Germany, Belgium and France also undertook never to resort to war. The demili-tarisation of the Rhineland enforced by Versailles was confirmed and Germany freely renounced any claims to Alsace-Lorraine. The whole was to enter into force on Germany's adherence to the League. At the same time Germany signed arbitration treaties with Czechoslovakia and Poland in which both parties undertook to settle any conflicts that might arise by peaceful means. Further-more, France signed treaties of mutual aid with her allies Poland and Czechoslovakia. These French treaties and Germany's treaties with her smaller Eastern neighbours were both indepen-dent of the Rhineland Pact proper. The net effect was therefore to create a frontier—the Franco-German—in which Britain declared her interest and a Polish-German frontier which Britain refrained from guaranteeing. Germany's frontier in the East did not enjoy the same unalterable status as did that in the West.

When, however, the implications of the Locarno Treaty are examined, this simple picture is obscured by divergent inter-pretations. Broadly speaking, two predominate. These are the German and the Anglo-Russian. The German viewpoint is simplicity itself. Stresemann could put it in one sentence: 'Our policy regarding the security offer was undoubtedly correct; it secured the Rhineland against a French policy of persecution, split the Entente and opened new prospects for the East.'[2] Germany in fact, had secured the assurance of British support should the French again occupy the Ruhr and had succeeded in

---

[1] *Izvestya*, November 5, 1924. The election victory referred to was that won on the 'Zinoviev letter'.

[2] G. Stresemann: *Diaries, Letters and Papers*, Vol. II, Eng. trans., London, 1935-1940, p. 263.

sealing off Eastern Europe from Western Europe. On this basis, Stresemann indulged in fanciful visions of the future—the end of reparations, the recovery of the Polish Corridor, the 'correction' of the frontier in Upper Silesia, the Anschluss with Austria and the end of the Allied occupation of the Rhineland. 'Moreover, all the questions that lie so close to German hearts, as for instance, War Guilt, General Disarmament, Danzig, the Saar, etc., are matters for the League of Nations and a skilful speaker at a plenary session of the League may make them very disagreeable for the Entente. France, indeed, is not very enthusiastic at the idea of Germany's entering the League, while England is anxious for it, in order to counteract France's hitherto predominant influence in that body.'[1]

There is a singular contrast between this view of Locarno and its potential consequences, and that of the British and the Russians. In the case of these two powers there was virtual unanimity. But what appeared to Lord D'Abernon, for example, as a source of hope, appeared to Chicherin as a source of alarm. To Lord D'Abernon, Locarno made Britain 'a dominating factor in European politics'.[2] It re-established the balance of power by using Germany as a counterweight to France. No one power would thus be in a position to dominate the Continent. Britain would hold the balance and be able to use her influence to favour whoever might at any moment be the weaker party.

But this was not all. 'A secondary effect of the (Locarno) Pact', writes Lord D'Abernon, 'will be to relieve Germany of the danger of being driven into the arms of Russia. I have never been an alarmist on this subject, believing the difference of political temper between Germany and Russia to be such that a close alliance between Soviet Russia and a fundamentally aristocratic Germany is hardly conceivable. Still, the circumstances of the Genoa Conference may recur, and another and worse Rapallo Treaty ensue. Under the Pact, Germany is accepted as an equal and as a co-partner with France and England in the maintenance of Western European conditions. As such the danger of her being attracted into the Russian communistic orbit is obviously diminished.'[3] Elsewhere Lord D'Abernon writes: 'It is clear that

[1] All the above is taken from Stresemann's letter of September 7, 1925 to the ex-Crown Prince of Germany (ibid., 503-505). Lord Acton's dictum that public reputations rarely survive the opening of private archives applies with particular force to Stresemann. It is undoubtedly hard luck to be singled out in this way.
[2] Lord d'Abernon: *An Ambassador of Peace*, Vol. III, London, 1929, p. 184.
[3] Ibid.

the entry of Germany into the League of Nations will have a decisive influence on the relations between Moscow and Berlin.'[1]

Sir Robert Hodgson, the British chargé d'affaires in Moscow, did not share Lord D'Abernon's optimism—or the latter's capacity for self-delusion. On the contrary, he told D'Abernon he did not think 'that Germany's joining the Pact of Security and entering the League would make any violent difference in Russo-German relations'.[2]

But in Moscow Hodgson's views were isolated. The Russians quickly came to see Locarno in the same light as Lord D'Abernon and British Conservative opinion generally. But where the British statesmen approved, the Russian statesmen naturally disapproved. Thus it was justifiably argued in the Russian press that Locarno and Germany's entry into the League denoted an attempt, first to isolate Russia by detaching Germany, and secondly to make England the dominant power on the Continent. The net result would be to deprive Russia of her *point d'appui* amongst the capitalist powers and thus deal a crippling blow at her diplomatic position.[3] It was further argued that Germany, by joining the League, was subordinating her policy to that of England and that this would oblige her to abrogate the Rapallo policy. 'Germany is subordinating herself to English policy. . . . Germany is necessary to England as a means of balance on the Continent and also as a *place d'armes* for future attacks against the Soviet Union.'[4] A less alarmist, though not fundamentally dissimilar point of view was once developed by Rakovsky, Soviet Ambassador to Great Britain. 'Is Locarno directed against the U.S.S.R.?' he asked. 'In spite of the assurances of Mr

[1] Lord D'Abernon: *An Ambassador of Peace*, Vol. III, London, 1929, p. 163. In some quarters the British Locarno policy towards Germany was identified with the defence of Western civilisation. Ormsby-Gore, for example, the Under-Secretary for Colonies at the time, asserted of Locarno: '. . . There was again a sense of security on either side of the Franco-Belgian frontier. Even more important was the drawing together of all the powers of Western Europe in defence of Western civilisation, which had been so rudely disturbed by the war. Things were not so secure as some were apt to think and the solidarity of Western civilisation was necessary to stem the most sinister force that had arisen not only in our lifetime but previously in European history. The question was: "is Germany going to regard her future as being bound up with the fate of the great Western powers or is she going to work with Russia for the destruction of Western civilisation?" . . . The significance of Locarno was tremendous. It meant that as far as the present government of Germany was concerned, it was detached from Russia and was throwing in its lot with the Western Party' (*The Times*, October 26, 1925).
[2] Lord D'Abernon: *An Ambassador of Peace*, Vol. III, London, 1929, p. 191. This is unfortunately the only expression of Sir Robert Hodgson's views to be available.
[3] *Izvestya*, June 11 and 21, 1925.
[4] Ibid., June 12, 1925; see also *Izvestya*, August 5, 1925.

Chamberlain, we have the assurances of other English ministers to the effect that the aim of English policy is to detach Germany from Russia and to create a European coalition against us. . . .

I wish to be moderate: I maintain that in Locarno there is no anti-Soviet bloc but that it contains the seed of one. Everything will depend on our relations to Europe, how they develop, and on the tempo of our economic development . . . we do not know whether this anti-Soviet bloc will be formed but there is a danger and we must take it into consideration.'[1]

In the discussion that raged round Locarno in the Soviet Press, one aspect of the Treaty was left largely unexamined. Whereas the British aim of detaching Germany from Russia was diagnosed correctly and debated *ad nauseam*, the heart of the Russian objection was left in the dark for the simple reason, no doubt, that it contradicted the soi-disant ideological purity of Soviet foreign policy. The fact is that in the same way as Britain relied on Germany for *her* balance of power, Russia also relied on Germany for *her* balance of power. Lord D'Abernon and Radek echo each other. Radek wrote: 'The policy of throttling Germany implied as a matter of fact the destruction of Russia as a great power, for no matter how Russia is governed it is always her interest to see that Germany exists. . . . A Russia which has been weakened to the utmost by the war could neither have continued as a great power nor acquired the economic and technical means for her industrial reconstruction unless she had in the existence of Germany a counter-balance against the supremacy of the Allies.'[2] Lord D'Abernon was no less precise: 'Regarding the whole position in Central Europe and the problem of what policy England should adopt, the clearest conclusion appears to be that the essential interest of England is to prevent the breaking up of Germany. . . . Directly Germany breaks up that balance [of power] disappears.'[3] Thus, in the same way as Rapallo seemed to threaten the British policy of balance, did Locarno seem similarly to threaten the Russian policy of balance. In the same way as Lloyd George in 1922 had seen the danger of 'a fierce friendship' between Germany and Russia as a result of Rapallo, did Chicherin in 1925 see the

[1] *Izvestya*, January 14, 1926. Rakovsky also wrote in his *Liga Natsii i S.S.S.R.* (*The League of Nations and the U.S.S.R.*), Moscow, 1926, 'They [the Locarno Treaties] certainly contain the seed of an anti-Soviet bloc but what will in fact emerge from these treaties will depend on circumstances which we cannot at the moment foresee' (p. 52).

[2] Quoted above pp. 55-6.

[3] Lord D'Abernon: *An Ambassador of Peace*, Vol. II, London, 1929, p. 238.

same possibility between Germany and the West as a result of Locarno. Chicherin called it 'an anti-Soviet bloc' but it came to the same thing. In reality, neither threat materialised. Stresemann was much too astute to line up with either one side or the other. He would use the Anglo-Russian struggle over Germany for his own purposes. In the last resort, the sole effect of the Dawes Plan and Locarno was to cause a slight swing away of Germany from Russia. In this it exactly parallelled the situation created in 1929-1930 when the Young Plan and the evacuation of the Rhineland were the next steps on the Locarno path, and the Munich situation of 1938-1939. In each of these cases, a swing back of Germany eastwards compensated the swing westwards; in 1926 there was the Berlin Treaty, in 1931 the renewal of the Berlin Treaty and in 1939 the Stalin-Hitler Pact. Chancellor Luther, on his return from Locarno, was able to speak in terms that anticipated Hitler: 'We had attained at Locarno a hundred per cent of what we had undertaken. Never had a delegation had such a success. We had been a nation of Helots and today we were a state of world importance.'[1]

The struggle opened at the end of 1924. In September, Germany, with certain reservations regarding Article 16 of the League Covenant, applied for membership of the League; in November Russo-German trade negotiations opened in Moscow; and in December the Russians sent to Stresemann proposals for closer political and economic co-operation between the two countries. But it was a time of governmental crisis in Germany and the proposals received scant attention.[2] This was nevertheless the first move towards what was to become the Russo-German Berlin Treaty of 1926. Early in 1925 German notes to the Western Powers laid the basis of the actual negotiations at Locarno at the end of the year.

Very soon, the Russo-German situation began to revolve round Article 16 of the League Covenant. This was the nodal point of the whole affair. Around it crystallised the fiercest conflict. The Article stipulated that members of the League were 'to take the necessary steps to afford passage through their territory to the forces of any members of the League which are co-operating to protect the Covenant of the League'. The case in everybody's

[1] G. Stresemann: *Diaries, Letters and Papers*, Vol. II, Eng. trans., London, 1935-1940, p. 192.
[2] Ibid., p. 467; *Osteuropa*, Jg. I, Heft 6, p. 338.

mind was a new Russo-Polish war. Were this to break out, with
Germany a member of the League, subject to the unrestricted
operation of Article 16, she might thereby have been obliged 'to
afford passage' to French troops coming to the aid of France's
Polish ally. This possibility was resisted to the utmost by both
Chicherin and Stresemann.

For Chicherin the matter was clear enough. Were Germany
to agree to such a procedure, she would have abandoned her
neutral status. It would have been equivalent to a jettisoning of
Rapallo. Germany would no longer be able to function as the
vast, neutral buffer, so essential to the Russians. She would no
longer be the one and only great power on whose neutrality
Russia could count, come what may. For Russia, Germany's
acceptance of the full obligations of Article 16 would indeed have
been tantamount to German submission to the Western Powers.

In 1923, it was Radek who had first voiced Soviet appreciation
of German neutrality in 1919. In 1925, when the crisis in Russo-
German relations was similar in nature and origin, he again
pointed out what this had meant to Russia: 'A considerable
part of the confusion that prevailed during the intervention from
1918 to 1920 lay in the fact that the Entente had to transport its
men and equipment by sea.'[1] Zinoviev was more specific and
went so far as to tell the 14th Party Congress in December 1925
that 'to a large extent the intervention against us did not succeed
because Germany did not participate in it. . . . The picture
might have changed decisively if our enemies had at that time
succeeded in drawing Germany on to their side, if Germany had
not been neutral, but had played an active part in the struggle
against us. . . . We must keep in mind that the Locarno decisions
are purely directed at making Germany in certain conditions, a
participant in future interventions against us.'[2]

Stresemann had as little desire to be committed to an anti-
Russian policy as Chicherin had to see him in such a position.[3]
For this reason he fought against Article 16 as vehemently as the
Russians. Despite the fact that Germany was joining the League
and signing a treaty with the Western powers, Stresemann
remained no less intent on preserving his country's full liberty of

[1] *Izvestya*, November 5, 1925.
[2] *XIV Syezd V.K.P.* (*b*)—*stenographicheskii otchet*, Moscow, 1927, pp. 652-653.
[3] See Stresemann's remarks to Krestinsky, Litvinov and Chicherin (G. Stresemann:
Diaries, Letters and Papers, Vol. II, Eng. trans., London, 1935-1940, pp. 473, 477, 479)

action. 'The question of a choice between East and West does not arise as the result of our joining the League. Such a choice can only be made when backed by military force. That, alas, we do not possess. We can neither become a continental spearhead for England, as some believe, nor can we involve ourselves in an alliance with Russia.'[1]

But it was of course not only for the *beaux yeux* of the Russians, important though these were to him, that Stresemann rejected Article 16. The 'new prospects in the East' of which he had spoken, the 'correction' of the Upper Silesian frontier, the recovery of Danzig and the Polish Corridor—these also required the elimination of any French right to march across Germany to Eastern Europe. The situation there must be kept as fluid and as uncertain as possible. It was for this reason that Stresemann termed the French desire to guarantee the arbitration treaties between Germany and Poland, and Germany and Czechoslovakia as 'wholly unacceptable'.[2]

The ideal Russian intention, as publicly expressed, was of course to prevent or persuade Germany from entering the League altogether. This was predominantly Chicherin's effort. But in 1925-1926 as in 1923, the unanimity of Soviet policy and propaganda was non-existent. Neither Stalin nor Litvinov altogether supported Chicherin in this. But the latter could produce quite a plausible argument and this he developed in a letter to Professor Ludwig Stein, a journalistic contact in Berlin. In 1922 he had already argued in a talk to the *Mittwochsgesellschaft* that 'after Rapallo it seemed ordained that Germany should not enter the League in isolation but only hand in hand with Russia'.[3] In September 1924 he now expanded these views and wrote to Stein that 'from the standpoint of German interests, entry into the League would signify a capitulation, a going to Canossa. . . . No formal reservation can get away from the fact that the League

---

[1] Ibid., p. 504. Stresemann told the Reichstag exactly the same thing: 'The task of German policy will always consist in harmonising its interests vis-à-vis the West and the East' (Reichstag Debates, Vol. 385 p. 1870).
[2] G. Stresemann: *Diaries, Letters and Papers*, Vol. I, Eng. trans., London, 1935-1940, p. 95. In the Reichstag Stresemann said: 'There is nobody in Germany who could acknowledge the frontier drawn in the East—in flagrant contradiction to the right of self-determination—as a once and for all unalterable fact' (Reichstag Debates, Vol. 1385, p. 1881).
[3] Professor Ludwig Stein: *Aus dem Leben eines Optimisten*, Berlin, 1930, p. 238. The *Mittwochsgesellschaft* was a club composed largely of journalists, diplomats—both German and foreign—and a few retired field-marshals. Stein himself was a leader-writer for several Berlin journals.

Covenant represents an international guarantee and a unification of existing frontiers, and particularly of the Versailles frontiers, raised to the heights of a system. . . . The League of Nations is a League of victors, a mutual insurance society of those who have gained something by it. . . . Through entry into the League Germany accedes to a definite coalition. Germany's policy thereby collides with the Rapallo policy. Against her own wish, through the power of facts, Germany will in this way be drawn into such combinations and actions as will lead her into conflict with us.'[1]

This was a threadbare thesis, however plausible. It neglected the realities of the situation, of which Stresemann had shown far more accurate awareness. Moreover, Litvinov took a view almost diametrically opposed to that of Chicherin. He foresaw, not that Locarno would tie Germany down and make her an instrument of the West but, on the contrary, that Germany might turn anti-Soviet as a result of increasing strength.[2] Stresemann in actual fact paid little attention to either position. As far as the Russians were concerned, he was playing from strength and could keep *them* waiting. To the West he was playing from weakness. To Britain and France he had to show himself much more complaisant. In comparison with what they could offer him, the Russians had practically nothing. It is pathetic to read Steklov on this point: 'In upholding and developing further the Rapallo Treaty', he writes, 'and in seeking in the East the satisfaction of her economic interests, whilst renouncing any aggressive intentions, even though of a purely economic character, Germany may find to the East of her frontiers a market for her manufactured products and an opportunity to employ her capital and the energy of her population'.[3]

Until March 1925 however, the Russians remained comparatively calm. Even Chicherin struck a moderate note. 'We may be certain', he told the Central Committee on March 4, 'that whatever waverings there are in German policy—and there have been, there remain and there will be such waverings—in the last

---

[1] Stein, op. cit., pp. 239-240. Substantially the same argument was once put forward by Rakovsky. Since politics are a continuation of war by other means, the League, which had its origin in the Allied victory in the Great War, was predestined to reinforce the position of the victors. It could not therefore be an impartial body (*passim* Kh. Rakovsky: *Liga Natsii i S.S.S.R.*, Moscow, 1926).

[2] See p. 104 below.

[3] *Izvestya*, May 24, 1925.

resort Germany will despite everything not break with us'.[1] Later that month the atmosphere took a turn for the worse when the League Council rejected Germany's application for membership of December 1924 on the grounds that modification of her status under Article 16 could only be introduced *after* her entry and not before. The Russians therefore saw the prospect opening up before them of Germany's joining the League without any pre-conditions at all. This fear was reflected in increased diplomatic activity in Berlin. It must also have been reinforced as Germany's negotiations with the Western powers made slow but steady progress.

Krestinsky now began to make repeated calls on Stresemann —on March 10, and April 15 and 25. Much the same ground was covered on each occasion. Time and again Stresemann assured Krestinsky that Germany maintained her unqualified objection to Article 16; that it was not Germany's intention to side with Poland against Russia; that Germany was determined to assert her freedom of action in the East; that the Locarno Pact was not an anti-Russian instrument; and that German policy could not be based *solely* on co-operation with Russia. In short, the simple German aim, he said, 'was to create a stable situation in the West while keeping a close watch on developments in the East and preserving our freedom of action'. On April 27, two days after the last of these interviews with Stresemann, Krestinsky left Berlin for Moscow.[2]

In the meantime, in mid-April, Brockdorff-Rantzau himself had arrived in Berlin. When he saw Stresemann he complained that Germany's negotiations with the West were endangering the Moscow negotiations with the Russians.[3] But there was more to Brockdorff-Rantzau's *démarche* than that. In concert with Chicherin he opposed *in toto* Stresemann's Locarno policy. He fully shared in the view of the Russian Commissar that it would inevitably lead to Germany's subordination to the West. During his stay of almost three months in Berlin—for he did not return till towards the end of June—his opposition on these grounds led him to offer his resignation. Only President Hindenburg

[1] *Tsentralni Ispolnitelni Komitet 2 sozyv, 3 sessiya—Stenographicheskii Otchet (Central Executive Committee 2nd sitting, 3rd session—stenographic report)*, Moscow, 1925, p. 33.
[2] G. Stresemann: *Diaries, Letters and Papers*, Vol. II, Eng. trans., London, 1935-1940, pp. 468-470.
[3] Ibid., p. 468.

persuaded him to withdraw it—and then with difficulty.[1] Like
the Bolsheviks, Brockdorff-Rantzau wanted a Russo-German
Treaty of the widest possible scope. The Bolsheviks had in mind
something on the lines of the Russo-Turkish Treaty of December
1925, which virtually precluded Turkey's adhesion to the League.[2]
It was too late for Germany to give any such comprehensive
undertaking—even if she had wanted to, which was not at all the
case. Instead, a treaty narrower in scope was drafted, corresponding far more to Stresemann's views than to Brockdorff-
Rantzau's. Brockdorff-Rantzau dissociated himself from this
draft as much as possible and more or less refused to take it back
to Moscow with him. He eventually agreed, however, to allow
Dirksen, at this time head of the Eastern Department, to accom-
pany him back to Moscow with a copy of the draft. They left
Berlin at the end of June.[3] Krestinsky, who had in the meantime
returned to Berlin, left again for Moscow on June 23. He was
preceded thither by Rakovsky and Krassin, Soviet Ambassadors
in London and Paris respectively.[4]

Krestinsky, it will be admitted, got a very queer send-off from
Stresemann. At an interview on June 10, Stresemann remembered
Bismarck's maxim—even a diplomatist should occasionally tell the
truth—and he told Krestinsky quite frankly that for the moment
all the German proposals to Russia were little more than eyewash.
Germany's real interest lay in the Western negotiations and until
these were settled, Russia would have to wait. Stresemann began
by explaining that it was a 'misunderstanding' to allege 'that he
had taken the view that negotiations with Russia were not
desirable, so long as negotiations with the Western Powers were
pending'. He went on: '*I did not say that we could not negotiate with
Russia* but I had said that *I would not care to conclude a treaty with
Russia so long as our political situation in the other direction was not
cleared up,* as I wanted to be able to answer the question whether
we had a treaty with Russia in the negative.' Stresemann ended
his remarks to Krestinsky with the hope that a *modus vivendi*

[1] Edgar Stern-Rubarth: *Graf Brockdorff-Rantzau*, Berlin, 1929, pp. 143-144 ; Louis
Fischer: *The Soviets in World Affairs*, London, 1930, p. 599.
[2] Ibid., p. 605. The relevant clause in the Russo-Turkish Treaty stipulated that
each party was 'not to participate in any union or agreement of a political nature
with one or several third parties directed against the other contracting party . . .
and not to participate in any hostile act on the part of one or several powers directed
against the other contracting party'.
[3] H. von Dirksen: *Moskau—Tokio—London*, Stuttgart, 1949, pp. 66-67; Louis
Fischer: *The Soviets in World Affairs*, London, 1930, p. 606.
[4] *The Times*, June 24, 1925.

might be discovered enabling Germany at the same time both to enter the League and to be free from the necessity of 'applying any coercive military measures against Russia. . . . '[1]

In substance, the remarks were an avowal that Stresemann was prepared to negotiate with the Russians *ad infinitum*. He would not sign any treaty with them until the Western pact was safely 'home'. It is not surprising therefore that the proposals taken by Dirksen to Moscow were found unsatisfactory. They were hardly meant to be anything else. After about six weeks Dirksen returned empty-handed to Berlin where there was not overmuch disappointment.[2] But Dirksen did succeed in laying the basis for a German loan to Russia of 100 million marks.[3]

This was the end of the first stage of the negotiations—if they deserve such a description—that were eventually to lead to the Russo-German Berlin Treaty. The next stage did not begin till the end of September. This interval of some two and a half months did not pass smoothly. In the background the Soviet Press continued to warn Germany that she was delivering herself into England's clutches and that all her hopes of escaping from Article 16 would prove a fond illusion.[4] In the foreground, two disputes between Russia and Germany suddenly arose. The first centred round two German students, named Kindermann and Wolscht, and an Esthonian, who were arrested in Russia on a charge of plotting to assassinate Stalin and Trotsky. The accused belonged to the same organisation as had the killers of Rathenau, so the charge was doubtless not without its foundation. In the event the three were sentenced to death, then reprieved and exchanged for 'General' Skobelevsky, similarly sentenced to death for his part in the abortive revolution of 1923.

The second subject of dispute was rather more serious. It concerned the trade talks which had opened at Moscow in November 1924. By approximately mid-July 1925 a trade treaty was almost ready for signature. A month earlier Stresemann had denied a suggestion by Litvinov that he was making the conclusion of the talks dependent on prior agreement over the Western Pact.[5] But there is no doubt that this was the case.

---

[1] G. Stresemann: *Diaries, Letters and Papers*, Vol. II, Eng. trans., London, 1935-1940, pp. 472-473. The italics have been added.
[2] H. von Dirksen: *Moskau—Tokio—London*, Stuttgart, 1949, p. 69.
[3] Louis Fischer: *The Soviets in World Affairs*, London, 1930, p. 606.
[4] *Izvestya*, June 12, July 23, September 24, 1925.
[5] G. Stresemann: *Diaries, Letters and Papers*, Vol. II, Eng. trans., London, 1935-1940, p. 474.

In fact, Ganetzky, one of the leading Soviet negotiators, gave an interview to *Izvestya* in which he openly accused the Germans of dragging out the settlement of the few remaining points at issue. This was, as he naïvely put it, despite the fact that 'the signature of the trade treaty with the Soviet Union would undoubtedly strengthen the position of the German Government in its present negotiations with the Entente'.[1] In August and early September it was reliably reported in Berlin that the treaty was due for early signature.[2] Not until September 26, however, did Stresemann give his consent. He told Litvinov that this would show the West that 'we intend to keep the economic way clear towards the East'.[3] The public announcement was made on October 2, a day or two before Stresemann left for Locarno, and on the 12th the Treaty was signed in Moscow. This went a long way towards calming Russian nervousness. Chicherin called it 'a clearly expressed demonstration in favour of the Rapallo line'.[4] Rakovsky saw in it 'a proof of the constancy of German feelings' towards the U.S.S.R.[5]

By now the climax was approaching in Germany's Western negotiations, for on September 15 the invitations were issued to the actual conference at Locarno. Chicherin at last played his trump-card to avert what in his heart of hearts he perhaps believed to be inevitable. He threatened Germany with a Russo-Polish non-aggression pact, or at the very least with a Russo-Polish *rapprochement*. Had this come about, it would have blocked all Stresemann's 'new prospects in the East' and would simultaneously have undermined Rapallo.

On September 25, Chicherin left Moscow on a much publicised visit to Western Europe. Warsaw was his first stop. His reception was very cordial, and on the 27th he saw Count Skrzynski, the Polish Foreign Minister. An official communiqué gave as the two main topics of conversation a Russo-Polish commercial treaty and the need for closer political relations in fulfilment of the Russo-Polish Treaty of Riga (1921).[6] To the press also Chicherin spoke of his desire for the development of friendly Russo-Polish relations.[7] For the moment this remained an empty threat. No

[1] *Izvestya*, July 19, 1925.
[2] See *D.A.Z.*, August 25, September 6, 1925.
[3] Stresemann, op. cit., p. 477.
[4] *Izvestya*, October 4, 1925.
[5] Kh. Rakovsky: *Liga Natsii i S.S.S.R.*, Moscow, 1926, p. 43.
[6] *Survey for 1925*, Vol. II, p. 65.
[7] *Izvestya*, October 1, 1925; see also *Izvestya*, September 27 and 30, 1925.

notice was taken of it in Germany. Not until 1931 did the question of a Russo-Polish *rapprochement* seriously disturb Rapallo—and then the Russian attempt was made in deadly earnest.

After the Warsaw interlude, Chicherin's next stop was at Berlin, where he arrived on September 29. He at once began holding press conferences, in order to denounce British policy. 'Germany is becoming a pawn in the anti-Soviet diplomacy of Britain. . . . By means of Article 16 Britain is forcing Germany to act against Russia.' 'Russia would never join the League.' The British guarantee pact is 'the main element in an English manoeuvre aiming at the unleashing of a world war against the Soviet Republic'.[1] As already mentioned the German announcement on October 2 of willingness to sign the trade treaty contributed to calming Chicherin's agitation. A social engagement, it may be assumed, which was at the same time a political demonstration, had the same effect; for on October 1 Chancellor Luther gave a luncheon in Chicherin's honour at which Krestinsky, Bratman-Brodowski, Stresemann, Seeckt, Gessler, von Schubert, (the State Secretary in the Auswärtiges Amt) and the old Prince Bülow were present,as well as various parliamentary personalities.[2]

More important than this was the fact of Chicherin's being in more or less constant touch with Stresemann. Their sessions were nocturnal in accordance with Chicherin's habit. They began at ten or eleven at night and lasted into the early morning. In this way the text of a Russo-German treaty was prepared, though it was not initialled.[3] Together with Krestinsky, the two Ministers also discussed the German attitude towards Article 16. Stresemann explained that the phrase 'formal liberation' from this Article, as contained in the draft taken to Moscow by Dirksen in the summer should not be misunderstood. Stresemann pointed out that there was a distinction between an 'unambiguous interpretation' and what that 'unambiguous interpretation' really meant. Germany distinguished between a *de jure* liberation from Article 16 carried through by a majority of the Members of the

---

[1] *Berliner Tageblatt*, October 2, 1925; *D.A.Z.*, October 3, 4, 1925. Chicherin also used to ask the Germans: 'Why play Marguerite to England's Faust?' (Lord D'Abernon: *An Ambassador of Peace*, Vol. III, London, 1929, p. 214). Another reference to Faust came from Rakovsky, who spoke of the two souls in the German breast—the Eastern and the Western (Rakovsky, op. cit., p. 44).

[2] *D.A.Z.*, October 2, 1925; F. von Rabenau: *Seeckt—Aus Seinem Leben 1918-1936*, Leipzig, 1940, p. 420.

[3] Louis Fischer: *The Soviets in World Affairs*, London, 1930, p. 606.

Assembly of the League and a *de facto* liberation. The latter 'consisted in the League of Nations giving to this Article, for example, an unambiguous interpretation, which in reality affirms Germany's right in the case of a decision by the League, to act according to her own discretion'.[1] Conversation on these lines continued until an hour before Stresemann's departure for Locarno. In the end, Chicherin extracted from Stresemann a pledge that he would neither accept Locarno nor enter the League without previous modification of Article 16.[2]

On the next day Chicherin was asked at a Berlin press conference whether his talks with Stresemann had not allayed his fears. He replied that though the talks had been thorough, it was not yet known what results Locarno would bring.[3] In any case Chicherin was taking no chances. He remained behind at Berlin while Stresemann went to Locarno, continuing his campaign against Article 16 and British policy via more interviews with the press. To such an extent was this the case that while actually at Locarno Stresemann was obliged to issue a statement denying Chicherin's allegations of German participation in an anti-Soviet Western bloc. The hand-out ended: 'For us there is no option between East and West policy. We wish to live on good terms with both sides.'[4] Whether Chicherin really expected his campaign to break up the Locarno Conference is an open question. But there can be no doubt that he enormously strengthened Stresemann's hand in dealing with France and Britain.

Of this Stresemann took full advantage. He was able to use the Russian card on several occasions. His wisdom in keeping Chicherin at arm's length, while not dropping him entirely, now showed itself. In the first place he secured a modification of Article 16 which, in Stresemann's own words, enabled Germany to reserve to herself 'the right of deciding as to the extent to which [she] would join in taking action against a disturber of the peace, even when a state was obviously and unmistakably in the wrong. . . . '[5] The actual formula ran: 'Each state member of the League is bound to co-operate loyally and effectively in support of the Covenant and in resistance to any act of aggression

---

[1] G. Stresemann: *Vermächtnis*, Vol. II, Berlin, 1932, p. 527.
[2] Louis Fischer: *The Soviets in World Affairs*, London, 1930, p. 606.
[3] G. Stresemann, op. cit. ibid.
[4] G. Stresemann, op. cit., pp. 527-528.
[5] G. Stresemann: *Essays and Speeches on Various Subjects*, Eng. trans., London, 1930, p. 237.

to an extent which is compatible with its military situation and takes its geographical position into account.' This formula was meaningless. It drove a horse and cart through the Covenant. Germany entered the League without undertaking any concrete obligation at all. She retained her full liberty of action. Even Chicherin was satisfied—the Article he said, was 'really emasculated'.[1]

In the second place Stresemann used Russia in order to break up any connection between the Locarno Pact proper and the French pacts of alliance with Poland and Czechoslovakia. If Germany were isolated in this way, Stresemann threatened to invite Russia to the Conference.[2] The mere prospect was enough to avert the threat—the two series of Pacts remained entirely separate.

Stresemann's last triumph in this line concerned the withdrawal of the Inter-Allied Military Control Commission. The Western Powers were so eager not to jeopardise the conclusion of the Security Pact or German entry into the League that the final report of the Commission, revealing the full extent to which Germany had thwarted its work, was hushed up by Chamberlain and Briand.[3] It was the climax to a process foreseen by Seeckt in January 1920: 'We are ready to form a bulwark against Bolshevism, in our own interest, which in this case is also the interest of the Entente. For this they should leave us the necessary weapons.'[4] Into the same framework fits Stresemann's request at Locarno that 35,000 police be allowed to be kept in barracks instead of 25,000. 'Chamberlain . . . showed, in particular, that

---

[1] Louis Fischer: *The Soviets in World Affairs*, London, 1930, p. 604.

[2] A. Erusalimski: *Germaniya, Antanta i S.S.S.R.*, Moscow, 1928, p. 150.

[3] General J. H. Morgan, K.C.: *Assize of Arms*, Vol. I, London, 1945, p. 240; see also A. Francois-Poncet: *De Versailles à Potsdam*, Paris, 1948, p. 146. For earlier British opposition to the work of the Control Commission on the grounds of its alleged encouragement to Communism see Général Nollet: *Une Expérience de Désarmement*, Paris, 1932, p. 29. Nollet was the head of the French section of the Commission.

[4] F. von Rabenau: *Seeckt—Aus Seinem Leben 1918-1936*, Leipzig, 1940, p. 252. On another occasion Seeckt wrote that if the Entente wanted to build up Germany as a bulwark against Bolshevism they would have 'in their own interest to make Germany capable of defending herself' [abwehrkräftig] (ibid., p. 318). Even Seeckt's biographer who shared his subject's opposition to Stresemann's Locarno policy—on the grounds of its unsettling effect on the Russians—was constrained to confess: 'On the whole it must nevertheless be admitted that with Locarno a certain *détente* set in generally and, in particular, also for the work of the military officials. It cannot be denied that Locarno has had useful consequences' (ibid., p. 423). Part of these 'useful consequences' was reflected in the sudden jump of almost 100 million marks in the Reichswehr budget for 1925-1926 as compared with that for 1924-1925 (*League of Nations Armaments Yearbook*, Third Year, Geneva, 1927, p. 480). This represented an increase of just under 20%.

he understood the police question when I represented it from the point of view of a struggle against Communism.'[1]

Stresemann's reputation has passed through various stages. To deliver a final verdict the evidence at present available does not allow. There can at least be no denying his masterly statesmanship. He was able to pose simultaneously as a Westerner and an Easterner. He was able to assure the Western statesmen that he was in reality on their side at the same time as he was able to assure the Eastern statesmen that he was in reality on *their* side. The fact is that he belonged to neither and was first and foremost concerned with Germany. But it was only by posing as the friend of both and by exploiting their differences that he was able to advance his German aim. In the military as in the political sphere he was equally successful. If Germany faced both ways politically, this applied no less to her military position. From the West Stresemann received tacit permission to re-arm at home; from the Russians he received actual deliveries of arms.

At Moscow in December 1925 Stalin, a statesman equally astute, delivered at the 14th Party Congress his maiden political report for the Central Committee. He concentrated in the main on the possibility of 'peaceful co-existence' between the two worlds of capitalism and socialism. This was based on temporary stabilisation in the capitalist world, with its corollary in an ebbing of the revolutionary movement. 'In general, the picture is such that the post-war economic crisis in Europe is being overcome; production and trade are approaching their pre-war level.'[2]

Later in the report, Stalin showed that he, like Stresemann, was playing from weakness, for he fell back on the identical strategem of exploiting differences. He enumerated five basic contradictions permeating the world; that between the bourgeoisie and the proletariat in the capitalist countries; that between the imperialist and the colonial countries; that amongst the victors and the vanquished in the Great War; that amongst the victorious countries themselves; and, lastly, that between the Soviets and the capitalist world as a whole. Our present concern is that between the victors and the vanquished, between Germany and the Entente. Stalin's general interpretation of Locarno

[1] G. Stresemann: *Diaries, Letters and Papers*, Vol. II, Eng. trans., London, 1935-1940, p. 185.
[2] *XIV Syezd V.K.P. (b)—Stenographicheskii Otchet*, 2nd ed., Moscow & Leningrad, 1926, pp. 8-10.

conformed to the run of Soviet comment, whilst differing from
t in one important particular—the German future. He emphasised to a greater extent that Locarno was 'only a continuation
of Versailles'. Germany still remained a defeated country and the
Entente a victorious alliance. Germany's territorial losses to
Poland and France remained unaltered. He went on to say that
this was a situation unstable in the extreme, as though he were
suggesting to Germany the advantages of a Russian-orientated
policy: 'To think that a growing and advancing Germany will
reconcile herself to this state of affairs [*i.e.* her post-Versailles
frontiers] is to count on a miracle. If previously, after the Franco-
Prussian war, the Alsace-Lorraine question . . . served as one of
the most important causes of the imperialist war, then what
guarantee is there that the Versailles Peace and its continuation—
Locarno, which legalises and juridically consecrates Germany's
loss of Silesia, the Danzig Corridor and Danzig, the loss of
Ukrainian Galicia and Western Volyhynia, the loss of the Western
part of Byelorussia—what guarantee is there that this Treaty
which has made mincemeat of a whole series of states and created
a whole series of knots of contradictions, will not share the fate of
the old Franco-Prussian Treaty which tore Alsace-Lorraine from
France after the Franco-Prussian war? There is not and there
cannot be any such guarantee.'[1]

Nevertheless, the task of Russian foreign policy was to struggle
for peace and 'the maintenance of so-called normal relations with
the capitalist countries'; to extend trading operations with the
outside world; and to seek '*rapprochement* with the countries
conquered in the imperialist war, with those countries which are
above all humiliated and, out of all the capitalist countries,
unfairly treated and which in consequence find themselves in
opposition to the prevailing union of great powers'.[2]

This last was a clear reference to Germany. As it happened,
leading Soviet statesmen were by no means unanimous on the
question of Germany's entry into the League. Some saw that
Germany, once inside, would be able to break up any incipient
anti-Soviet bloc and prevent unanimity at Geneva.[3] All Chicherin's actions and words suggest that he under-estimated this
factor. Indeed, it is impossible to reconcile Chicherin's view of

[1] Ibid., pp. 13-14.
[2] Ibid., pp. 26-27.
[3] Louis Fischer: *The Soviets in World Affairs*, London, 1930, p. 600.

Germany 'going to Canossa' with Stalin's view that Germany was 'growing and advancing.' Stalin certainly, and perhaps also Litvinov, argued that Russia would be in a stronger position if she were to have a friend in the League.[1] On one occasion, in fact, Stresemann told Litvinov that as any decision by the Council of the League required unanimity, Germany would be able to use her veto to protect Russia, should the necessity arise.[2]

On the other hand, to the advantage that a friendly Germany in the League would be able to bring Russia, there was a corresponding disadvantage. This also was discussed between Stresemann and Litvinov, when the latter showed acutely prophetic insight. Litvinov said it was not feared in Moscow that there would be an immediate German swing westwards away from Russia. But he foresaw that once Germany was in the League her claims in regard to Danzig, the Saar, etc., would be supported by a Britain, anxious to check French influence on the Continent; and as Britain was pursuing an anti-Russian policy, Germany would in this way drift into the anti-Russian camp.[3] In other words, a time might come when the Anglo-German contradiction, for all practical purposes, would have ceased to exist. Litvinov in 1925, so far as is known, did not think any further ahead. But some ten years later he must often have recalled this conversation with Stresemann. For Hitler consummated what Stresemann began. In the long run, Rapallo and a German *rapprochement* with the West were incompatible. The question was: how long would a short run be?

In 1925-1926 of course, there was no hint of this. A comment by Lord D'Abernon indicates this in a superficial but not unamusing way: 'I still hold that prolonged co-operation between the German Right and the Russian Left is unthinkable, but I must admit that the other night at the Russian Embassy, I was somewhat shaken to see how many gentlemen were with stiff military backs and breasts bedecked with iron crosses, all partaking freely of Soviet champagne.'[4]

This was written in November 1925. The following month saw further negotiations between Chicherin, Krestinsky and Stresemann. These were primarily concerned with defining the con-

[1] A. U. Pope: *Maxim Litvinoff*, New York, 1943, pp. 211-212.
[2] G. Stresemann: *Diaries, Letters and Papers*, Vol II, Eng. trans., London, 1935-1940, p. 474.
[3] Ibid., pp. 476-477.
[4] Lord D'Abernon: *An Ambassador of Peace*, Vol. III, London, 1929, p. 205.

ditions under which mutual neutrality would operate between the two countries, as far as the projected Russo-German Treaty was concerned. The Russian aim was to widen the concept of neutrality so that it would apply no matter in what kind of a conflict Russia were involved. Germany however, succeeded in narrowing this down to the obligation to exercise neutrality if Russia were attacked 'in spite of its peaceful attitude'.[1] It also appears that Germany refused to commit herself to make a declaration 'disavowing' any Russian aggressive action.[2] Brock-dorff-Rantzau again offered his resignation to Hindenburg before a formula satisfactory to the Russians was achieved.[3]

But by the end of December 1925 all was in order—even Chicherin was relieved. Stresemann 'had the impression that Chicherin was well satisfied with his Berlin impressions and that the nightmare of a continent arrayed against Russia was dispelled. . . . All the negotiations were carried on in a friendly fashion and there was every indication that the tension had been eased.'[4]

It was now Stresemann's intention to sign the Treaty with Russia after Germany's entry into the League, scheduled for March.[5] But the attempt failed. It provided the Russians with an opportunity to laugh at Stresemann's discomfiture on returning empty-handed from Geneva. A writer in *Mezhdunarodnaya Zhizn* termed it 'a sorry spectacle'.[6] It also gave Chicherin a good debating point—if the Western Powers could not even fix German entry to the League, how could Germany expect anything more serious from them?[7]

Stresemann still wished to delay signing until the League should have admitted Germany at its next session in September 1926. But he now came under heavy pressure from the Right Wing in Germany, as well as from Chicherin himself. The latter threatened to resume complete liberty of action *vis-à-vis* Germany if the Treaty were not signed at once;[8] and on March 11 *Izvestya* published an interview with Hoetzsch, Dr Scholtz of the German People's

[1] Louis Fischer: *The Soviets in World Affairs*, London, 1930, p. 608.
[2] G. Stresemann: *Diaries, Letters and Papers*, Vol. II, Eng. trans., London, 1935-1940, pp. 482-483.
[3] Ibid., pp. 486-487.
[4] Ibid., p. 489.
[5] A. Vallentin: *Gustav Stresemann*, Eng. trans., London, 1931, p. 207.
[6] *Mezhdunarodnaya Zhizn*, No. 4, 1926, p. 65.
[7] Chicherin in *Izvestya*, April 6, 1926.
[8] A. Vallentin, op. cit., pp. 207-208; see also Lord D'Abernon: *An Ambassador of Peace*, Vol. III, London, 1930, p. 246.

Party and Count Reventlow of the neo-Fascist Völkische group. They all called for a treaty with Russia, 'the best proof', said Dr Scholtz, 'that Germany is not obliged to choose between England and Russia'.[1]

All the same, how to break the news to the Western Powers that Germany was contemplating a Treaty with Russia was causing some concern to the Auswärtiges Amt.[2] Eventually a disclosure of the terms in *The Times* of April 14 solved the problem.[3]

The impending signature of a Russo-German Treaty was now inspiring some alarm in the Western camp. In the case of France particularly, this was reflected in a revival of plans to split Germany and Russia, isolate England and blunt the anti-French aspects of Locarno. As a result, France would regain her former position in Eastern Europe. These plans resulted in a partial success—the Polish-Rumanian pact of guarantee of March 26, 1926. But it defeated its own ends; for by Article II of this Pact both parties pledged each other their mutual aid if either were the victim of an unprovoked aggression by a third party. This endangered both the Russian claim to Bessarabia (seized by Rumania in 1918) and the German claim to recovery of the Polish Corridor. Thus the net effect was to underline the common interests of Germany and Russia. On April 24, 1926 the Berlin Treaty was finally signed.

The outstanding feature of the new Treaty was its re-iteration of Rapallo. It contributed no new element. The entire significance of the Treaty lay purely and simply in the fact that the pre-suppositions of Rapallo were made more precise. In concrete terms, this meant that the conditions of German neutrality were more fully outlined; for as far as Russian policy itself was concerned, the new Treaty meant no change.

Article I confirms that Russo-German relations shall continue to be based on Rapallo and that both governments 'shall remain in friendly touch in order to promote an understanding with regard to all political and economic questions jointly affecting their two countries'. Article II stipulates that if either Party be attacked 'despite its peaceful attitude' the other is to remain neutral. Article III obliges each Party not to take part in any

[1] *Izvestya*, March 11, 1926.
[2] H. von Dirksen: *Moskau—Tokio—London*, Stuttgart, 1949, p. 78.
[3] *Osteuropa*, Jg. 1, Heft 6, p. 339.

economic or financial boycott of the other. By Article IV the Treaty was to remain in force for five years.

In notes exchanged with Krestinski, Stresemann dealt with Germany's position as a future member of the League and of the compatibility of League membership with German freedom of action *vis-à-vis* Russia. In the first place, 'the German Government is convinced that Germany's membership of the League cannot constitute an obstacle to the friendly development of the relations between Germany and the Union of Socialist Soviet Republics. . . . If, however, though the German Government does not anticipate this, there should at any time take shape within the League . . . any efforts directed exclusively against the Union of Socialist Soviet Republics, Germany would most energetically oppose such efforts.'

In the second place, Stresemann explained that 'the application of sanctions against the Union of Socialist Soviet Republics would come into consideration, in the absence of other causes, only if the Union of Socialist Soviet Republics entered upon a war of aggression against a third state'. But the identification of the aggressor in such a conflict 'would only be determined with binding force for Germany with her own consent'. Thus, if Germany regarded any accusation of Russian aggression as 'unjustified' this 'would not oblige Germany to take part in measures of any kind instituted on the authority of Article 16'.

In a final re-assurance to Russia, Stresemann referred to the Allied interpretation of Article 16 as to whether Germany would be able to apply any sanctions at all against Russia.[1]

In a formal, diplomatic communication Stresemann could not, of course, state that he was totally uncommitted in any eventuality to any action at all hostile to Russia. In a speech already quoted he had no such inhibition.[2] Nor to Krestinski was he uncommunicative. He emphasised to the Russian Ambassador that even if Germany considered Russia guilty of aggression, she was still, despite her membership of the League, absolutely free to decide for herself the extent of her co-operation with the League.[3] Thus German membership of the League would in no way conflict with her obligation to preserve towards Russia the strictest neutrality. Russia could not have asked for more. Rapallo was confirmed and

[1] L.N.T.S., Vol. 53, pp. 387 ff.
[2] See p. 110 above.
[3] G. Stresemann: *Diaries, Letters and Papers*, Vol. II, Eng. trans., London, 1935-1940, p. 483.

defined anew. Germany remained Russia's vast neutral buffer against Europe.

In the same way as Rapallo had signified something different to Germany and to Russia, did the new Treaty receive a similarly divided reception in each country.

The theme of Litvinov's speech to the Central Committee, introducing the Treaty, was its defensive and peace-like character. In contrast to such military groupings as the Polish-Rumanian pact of alliance, the Berlin Treaty not only assured peace between 'two great peoples' but also restricted any area of possible conflict. It was, furthermore, a measure of defence against Locarno. 'If Locarno, as its authors try to convince us, is aimed at the pacification of Europe . . . then it would seem that the supporters of Locarno would have to give a cordial welcome to the Soviet-German Treaty, as a new step to the consolidation of friendship between two great peoples. If, however, Locarno, as we have always suspected, has as one of its aims the formation of a united anti-Soviet bloc and the isolation of our Union—then in that case it must be acknowledged that the Treaty signed today in fact contradicts the spirit of Locarno and we may rejoice that to some extent we have succeeded in extracting the anti-Soviet sting from Locarno.'[1]

The German emphasis was different. Far from considering the Berlin Treaty as in any way opposed to Locarno, the tone of most comment was to interpret the two Treaties as complementary. Locarno settled Germany's relations with the West; Berlin those with the East. The necessary balance had been maintained. 'The Treaties of Locarno and that of Berlin are not mutually destructive instruments but are complementary to one another.'[2] With both sets of Treaties in her pocket Germany was in a very strong position.

The Berlin Treaty was very much more popular in Germany than was Locarno. The Foreign Affairs Committee of the Reichstag approved it unanimously—an unprecedented event in the history of that body;[3] and in the Reichstag itself, only the three-man dissident group of 'International Communists' voted against it. Against Locarno, on the other hand, the combined opposition of

---

[1] *Izvestya*, April 25, 1926.

[2] G. Stresemann: *Essays and Speeches on Various Subjects*, Eng. trans., London, 1930, p. 263. The extract is quoted from a speech made on May 1, 1926.

[3] Lord D'Abernon: *An Ambassador of Peace*, Vol. III, London, 1929, p. 252.

Nationalists and Communists had resulted in 174 votes being cast. Chancellor Marx in deed, in introducing the Treaty, explained that as Berlin only re-affirmed Rapallo it was not constitutionally necessary to have it ratified by the Reichstag at all. He was, however, taking this step in view of the Treaty's 'special political importance'. Later in his speech he said that the Berlin Treaty 'does not create a new political situation, but clarifies the existing situation. It represents only the contractual expression of the attitude which the German Government has always expressed.'[1] In the rest of the debate, the usual party lines were followed. Dernburg of the German Democrats, on behalf of his own party, the German People's Party, the Centre and the Bavarian People's Party gave Berlin an unqualified welcome. Breitscheid of the Social-Democrats saw it as a step on Russia's path towards the League. Hoetzsch, on the other hand, speaking for the Nationalists, emphasised that as Germany was not yet in the League and as Locarno was therefore not yet in force, the Berlin Treaty was quite independent of any arrangements Germany might make with the West.

Korsch, leader of the 'International Communists', quoted Rosa Luxemburg's 11th Spartakusbrief of September 1918: 'and the Bolsheviks, at the terminus of their thorny path, are threatened with the most awful thing of all; like some eerie ghost, an alliance between the Bolsheviks and Germany approaches. That, of course, would be the final link of the fatal chain that the war has slung round the neck of the Russian Revolution—first retreat, then capitulation, and finally an alliance with German imperialism. . . . Socialist revolution sitting on German bayonets, proletarian dictatorship under the tutelage of German imperialism —that would be the most monstrous thing that we could experience.'[2]

Like the personification of this 'eerie ghost' General von Seeckt greeted 'with gratification' the Berlin Treaty. On April 22, 1926 he had celebrated his sixtieth birthday. The signature two days afterwards was, albeit slightly belated, a none the less welcome gift.[3]

---

[1] Reichstag Debates, Vol. 390, pp. 7434 ff.
[2] All the above speeches are taken from Reichstag Debates, Vol. 390, pp. 7435 ff.
[3] F. von Rabenau: *Seeckt—Aus Seinem Leben 1918-1936*, Leipzig, 1940, p. 443.

CHAPTER VII

The Heyday of Rapallo (1926-1929)

IN the event Locarno justified neither extreme Russian fears nor extreme British hopes. It definitely did not succeed in detaching Germany from Russia. It did, nevertheless, considerably weaken the basis of Rapallo. By sheer force of circumstances any improvement in Germany's relations with the West could not but weaken her hitherto exclusive dependence on Russia. Germany was now able to play ball with both sides. She was in the position of a man who has regained the use of an arm of which he had temporarily been deprived. Thus, the value of the one arm on which he has been able to rely all along decreases automatically, both absolutely and relatively. To this extent Russian alarm was justified. Rapallo lost what one German diplomat called 'its romantic nimbus'.[1] No longer would Germany and Russia appear as the two outcasts of Europe. The first had moved up in the world to become a member of decent society.

This contrast was accentuated when Germany eventually joined the League in September 1926. An editorial in *Izvestya* revealed, despite all Germany's assurances, an under-current of apprehension. 'We, for our part, can only express the hope that German participation in the League of Nations will not prevent her fulfilling to the letter all the obligations she has assumed in relation to the U.S.S.R. We would also like to count on Germany —despite her participation in the League—continuing to live in peace and friendship with our country.'[2]

Soviet diplomacy did not limit itself to the expression of pious hopes. From the end of 1925 there began to develop the conception of a Moscow-centred security system which would counteract that centred on Geneva. It was pre-eminently defensive in character and all the contractual obligations undertaken by the adherents of the system were negative. They undertook to *hold aloof* from any coalitions or actions hostile to the other party, and to *remain neutral* if either became the victim of an unprovoked attack. In broad terms, the effect was to create

[1] H. von Dirksen: *Moskau—Tokio—London*, Stuttgart, 1949, p. 75.
[2] *Izvestya*, September 11, 1926.

a belt of neutralised territory all round the borders of the Soviet Union.[1]

The actual links of the belt were formed of non-aggression pacts between Russia and her neighbours. The first such pact was that with Turkey. It was signed in December 1925 after the League Council, in accordance with British wishes, had awarded the disputed Mosul area to Iraq. The Berlin Treaty with Germany was the second such pact. It was also, of course, the most important. In March 1926 negotiations were opened with the Baltic States; and renewed efforts were also made to settle the question of debts and credits with France.

By the end of the year two minor but by no means negligible results had been achieved. Litvinov secured the signature of a Russo-Lithuanian Pact and Chicherin a Russo-Afghan Pact. These were signed in August and September respectively. In December Chicherin was able to tell the *Berliner Tageblatt* quite justifiably; 'Step by step we are realising our programme of direct pacts with the other powers individually.'[2]

Despite Chicherin's air of quiet confidence, in marked contrast to his agitation of the previous year, a troubled note suddenly came to disturb the atmosphere. The principal cause of this were Scheidemann's revelations to the Reichstag, on December 16, 1926, of certain aspects of the Russo-German military collaboration. Despite many previous rumours of this activity, the news did not break on a large scale until publicised by the *Manchester Guardian*. Its issue of December 3 contained a despatch from Berlin giving details of the Junkers factory in Russia. The story was then taken up by the Social-Democratic *Vorwärts* of December 5. Five days later it reached the Reichstag. Creutzberg, a Communist deputy, accused the Social-Democrats of trying to curry favour with Britain. 'Come what may', he told them, 'you want to bring about a breach between Germany and Russia'. Creutzburg's speech ended with a sarcastic reminder of the time when the Social-Democrats, far from being the enemies of the Reichwehr, had willingly used its services against the working class.[3]

When Scheidemann spoke on the 16th the ground was thus well prepared. He largely justified Creutzburg's accusation, for the brunt of his attack bore on the foreign-political implications

[1] For an interesting account from the Soviet angle of the genesis of this policy see the article by Theodore Rothstein in *Osteuropa*, Jg. 3, Heft 2, pp. 126 ff.

[2] *Berliner Tageblatt*, December 7, 1926.

[3] Reichstag Debates, Vol. 391, pp. 8424-8425.

of the factories. The Reichwehr was sabotaging German foreign policy by concluding secret agreements with Russia behind the back of the Government.[1]

After calling Scheidemann 'a traitor to the Fatherland' most of the right-wing deputies now left the Reichstag. The rest of the debate degenerated into a slanging-match between the two left-wing parties. The 'Left-Communist' Dr Schwarz castigated both sides with equal venom. If the Social-Democrats were a pack of hypocrites, then the Communists were guilty of collusion with the Reichwehr.[2]

By a strange coincidence, on the very same day that Scheidemann spoke to the Reichstag, both *Pravda* and *Izvestya* carried leading articles admitting the existence of German arms factories in Russia. *Pravda* wrote: 'It appears that within the boundaries of our Union, by agreement between our military authorities and those of Germany, certain German firms several years ago erected three factories, for the production of material necessary to our defence. In this material are included aeroplanes, gases, shells, etc. We are not initiated into the secrets of our military authorities and do not know whether or not these reports correspond to the facts. If we suppose that they do not lie, then they mean nothing at all. If we grant to foreigners concessions for the erection of factories and workshops for the production of material necessary to our consumers' market, then why should we forbid them, or even not encourage them, to open factories and workshops necessary to our defence?'

It was denied of course, that any arms had been supplied to the Reichswehr—as though Seeckt were philanthropist enough to arm the Russians and not himself. A final thrust at the Social-Democrats ended the article—they had earned their bread from the Entente and now deserved the Nobel Peace Prize.[3]

The article in *Izvestya* was contributed by Radek. After reference to Noske's friendship for the Reichswehr and to Social-Democratic support for the war-credits in 1914, he too admitted the Junkers story. 'The U.S.S.R. does not refuse the use of foreign technicians in order to strengthen its defences against foreign imperialists.'[4]

In connection with the German factories Bukharin made a

[1] Ibid., pp. 8577 ff.
[2] Ibid., pp. 8636-8637.
[3] *Pravda*, December 16, 1926.
[4] *Izvestya*, December 16, 1926.

remarkably frank speech in Moscow which might have come from the lips of any bourgeois statesman. He began by stigmatising the publicity given to the arms factories as part of a campaign of 'moral mobilisation' of the masses against the Soviet Union. He justified them on the grounds of Russia's defence requirements. 'We have had and continue to have a contract with the firm of Junkers which, as *Pravda* correctly wrote a few days ago, is concerned with the manufacture of aeroplanes and not boiled sausages. We do not, nor have we ever hidden the fact that there *was* a contract with Junkers, they did and do build aeroplanes; and we may declare with perfect candour that we will not refuse to use any capitalist state whatever that will send us instructors and which, for appropriate payment, will produce on our territory aeroplanes and other weapons of war for the defence of the country. Although we are arming proportionately much less than any other powerful state, we are certainly not such fools, at a time when all countries are re-arming, as to disarm or to allow ourselves to be taken by the nose and shown that sort of 'socialist reconstruction' which we would never forget.' Nevertheless, Bukharin explained in all sincerity, 'our whole policy, every diplomatic move we make, every diplomatic note we send must be permeated with the thirst for peace'.[1]

The episode constituted one more item to be chalked up against the Social-Democrats. Russian resentment on this score was to find its most mature expression in the decisions of the Sixth World Congress of the Comintern in the summer of 1928.

As far as the military collaboration itself was concerned, this continued as before. It did not cease until Hitler came to power. The indications of this are however of the most fragmentary kind. In March and April 1929, for example, the German pacifist Carl von Ossietzky published in *Die Weltbühne* details of a Reichswehr subsidy of 27 million marks, part of which was to be devoted to the construction of Junkers factories in Russia. In 1930, a Lieutenant-Colonel Amlinger was accidentally killed while on duty in Russia, his widow subsequently committing suicide by jumping out of an aeroplane flying from Frankfurt to Berlin.[2]

Further evidence, concerning the period 1932-1934, came to

[1] *Izvestya*, January 13, 1927. It seems that the publicity given to the factorie caught the Soviets unprepared. In that same month when Bukharin congratulate *Pravda* on its accuracy, *Mezhdunarodnaya Zhizn* (No. 1, 1927) describes Scheidemann's speech as 'a vile slanderous campaign'.
[2] This case is reported in the *Manchester Guardian* of August 30, 1930.

light during Krupp's trial on charges of war-crimes. One witness, Hugo Seligman, a submarine expert, stated that as an employee of Krupps he visited Leningrad in 1934 to instruct the Russians in submarine construction.[1] Another witness, Johann Hofmann, mechanical engineer and designer by profession, stated that in 1932 and 1933 he instructed Russian officers at Kazan in the manufacture of tanks. German officers were also present to study the performance of the tanks. Hofmann added that apart from the Krupps installation at Kazan, the firms of Rheinmetall and Daimler also had installations in the town.[2]

During 1927 the contrast between German and Russian policy became more and more marked. The first, directed by Stresemann, smoothly pursued its campaign for the gradual revision of Versailles. The second suffered blow upon blow. In Asia and in Europe the whole structure of the Soviet's foreign relations seemed suddenly to be placed in jeopardy. In March, after a visit by Chamberlain and Churchill to Italy, the Italian Government ratified the Bessarabian Convention of 1920. This sanctioned the Rumanian seizure of Bessarabia in 1919. The Italian move was made despite warning by Chicherin to Mussolini that Russia had never recognised the validity of the Convention and would consider its ratification by Italy an unfriendly act. The next blow was far more severe. In April and May Chiang-Kai-Shek turned on the Communists in the Kuomintang, destroying much Communist influence in China for more than twenty years. It was also in May that a long period of Anglo-Russian friction culminated in the Arcos raid and led to the British rupture of diplomatic relations with Russia. Finally, in June, Voykov, the Soviet Ambassador in Warsaw, was killed by an emigré Russian monarchist. A little later in 1927 the laboriously erected Anglo-Russian Trade Union Committee was dissolved by the Trades Union Congress. On almost all fronts, with the single exception of Germany, a heightened tension characterised the relations between Russia and the bourgeois world. It was openly admitted by Theodore Rothstein, chief of the Narkomindel Press Department, that the end of the first decade of the Soviet Union's existence found the country in a far worse international position

[1] Official Transcript of the American Military Tribunal No. III—A in the matter of the United States of America against Alfred Krupp von Bohlen und Halbach et al.

[2] Official Transcript etc., pp. 455, 475-477 and 486-488.

than that enjoyed in 1924. In retrospect, the latter year was seen to be the high-spot of the Union's diplomatic prestige.[1]

Far more important, the blows concentrated in the first half of 1927 gave rise to a genuine Russian fear of war. Two independent observers both testify to this. The French Ambassador speaks of 'the incredible intensity of this obsession'.[2] Artur Just, for many years the *Kölnische Zeitung* correspondent in Russia, noted a similar mood.[3]

Inside the party the Soviet defeat in China gave a new handle to the Trotskyist opposition, which now alleged that Stalin had bungled the Chinese as well as the German Revolution. It was at this moment that Stalin, under fire at home and abroad, came out with a characteristically phrased article: 'The task of the Soviet Government', he wrote, 'is to pursue in the future firmly and unshakeably a policy of peace, a policy of peaceful relationships, despite the provocative actions of our enemies, despite the pin-pricks in our prestige. Provocators from the enemy camp are teasing us and will continue to do so, saying that our peaceful policy is explained by our weakness, by the weakness of our army. This occasionally aggravates some of our comrades, who are inclined to succumb to provocation and to demand that we take "decisive" measures. This is a weakness of nerve. This shows an absence of endurance. We cannot and must not dance to our enemies' tune. We must continue on our way, defending the cause of peace, demonstrating our will to peace, unmasking the predatory aims of our enemies and showing them up as the instigators of war.'[4]

At the same time, the critical tension of the war-scare was artificially screwed-up by Stalin as a weapon against Trotsky. The crisis was a boon to Stalin, enabling him, as it did, to reinforce his position at home. If Trotsky could claim that the worsening position of the Soviet Union was due to the defective Stalinist leadership, Stalin could equally well argue that this was no time for internal polemics and recriminations. The hour demanded unity. His article ended: 'What are we to say of this very opposition that finds the threat of war a suitable moment to strengthen

---

[1] See Rothstein's article in *Osteuropa*, Jg. 3, Heft 2.
[2] J. Herbette: *Un Diplomate français parle du péril bolchévique*, Paris, 1943, p. 52. This volume consists of despatches sent by Herbette from Moscow to Paris. They were published by the Nazis during the occupation of France. They are clearly incomplete and are in some cases truncated.
[3] Arthur Just: *The Red Army*, Eng. trans., London, 1936, pp. 105-106.
[4] *Izvestya*, July 28, 1927.

its attacks on the party? What good can there be in finding it appropriate to use the difficulties of the position of the U.S.S.R. for new attacks on the party, instead of rallying round the party against the foreign threat?'[1]

In the circumstances, Russian foreign policy was reduced to 'sitting tight' while parrying the blows. Also, as so often before in Russian history, the complete collapse of the position in Asia was reflected in increased activity in Europe.

The first step in the direction of Geneva was taken in April 1927. It was then that Krestinsky and the Swiss Ambassador in Berlin signed a convention settling the Russo-Swiss dispute, originally evoked by the murder of Vorovsky, the Russian ambassador to Berne, in 1923. Shortly afterwards it was announced that Russia would attend the impending International Economic Conference at Geneva, held under the auspices of the International Labour Office.

Her delegation was led by the former Prince Obolensky-Ossinsky. The main item in his programme was the Russian need for a loan or credits from the capitalist powers and the desirability of the maximum economic contact between Russia and the rest of the world. To this end he succeeded in securing the adoption of the following resolution: 'The Conference—recognising the importance of a renewal of World trade; refraining absolutely from infringing upon political questions, regards the participation of all the countries present, irrespective of differences in their economic systems, as a happy augury for the pacific co-operation of all nations.'[2]

But naturally enough, Soviet eyes were fixed on Germany. Would Germany follow the British lead in breaking off diplomatic relations, or would she remain neutral? This was the *point névralgique* of the Soviet foreign system. So long as Germany held firm, so long as what Chicherin had called his '*point d'appui*' did not give way, complete isolation would be impossible. It was little enough to ask. All that was required of Germany was her neutrality, but as 1919, 1920 and 1925 had already shown, this was equivalent to a pro-Russian stand.

The auguries were favourable. In March when the Anglo-Russian breach was clearly in the air, *Izvestya* quoted with approval

[1] Ibid.
[2] *Verlauf und Ergebnis der internationalen Wirtschaftskonferenze zu Genf*, ed. Konsul Dr E. Respondek, Berlin, 1927, p. 320.

an article in the semi-official *Deutsche Diplomatisch—Politische Korrespondenz:* 'Germany will in no way allow herself to be dragged off that path of absolute neutrality which she has unshakeably followed up till now.'[1] The following day *Izvestya* replied editorially: 'For our part, we also assert that the political and economic value for Germany of her relations with the U.S.S.R. which have become closer and closer from 1921 onwards, is a factor which cannot be so easily erased from the post-war history of Germany.'[2] A few weeks later, a frequent spokesman for Stresemann in the Reichstag, von Rheinbaben, added his authoritative voice. 'We remain', he said, 'loyal to Rapallo and Berlin. The Anglo-Russian conflict only arouses in us the desire to remain outside and not to be dragged in.'[3] On April 16, the telegrams exchanged by Stresemann and Litvinov on the fifth anniversary of Rapallo confirmed their mutual attachment to the provisions of the Treaty—in the future no less than in the past.[4]

When the Anglo-Russian rupture passed from threat to actuality —on May 25, 1927—Chicherin was in Paris. He left at once for Frankfurt. Thence he drove over to Baden-Baden to see Stresemann. Two days later the two Foreign Ministers met again when Chicherin gave a dinner in honour of Stresemann at the Russian Embassy in Berlin.[5] What was discussed at these meetings has not been disclosed. But it can only have been the German attitude *vis-à-vis* the Anglo-Russian situation. Chicherin always attributed to British policy the worst possible motives. On this occasion all his actions suggest the conviction that Britain would exert pressure on Germany, also to break with Russia. Chicherin wanted at all costs to ensure that, at the imminent June session of the League, Germany would remain neutral. Thus, when Stresemann left for Geneva, Chicherin remained behind in Berlin, in constant touch with German governmental circles. Brockdorff-Rantzau was also in Berlin at this time,[6] no doubt adding his own influence to that of Chicherin. This juxtaposition of personalities is an almost exact parallel to what happened in 1925. Then Chicherin had remained in Berlin when Stresemann had gone to Locarno. Now Stresemann went to Geneva. That was the only difference. On both occasions,

---

[1] *Izvestya*, March 8, 1927.
[2] Ibid., March 9, 1927; see also *Izvestya*, March 17, 1927.
[3] Reichstag Debates, Vol. 392, p. 9848.
[4] *Izvestya*, April 19, 1927.
[5] *The Times*, May 28 and June 10, 1927; *F.Z.*, June 8, 1927.
[6] Ibid., June 17, 1927.

under the anxious supervision of Chicherin, he defended Russian interests as well as his own.

By now Sir Austen Chamberlain had become the *bête noire* of the Soviets. In March 1927, it is true, he had complained to Stresemann that German credits to Russia were releasing funds for propagandist purposes.[1] But in June when the two men met again, and the Anglo-Russian breach was discussed, Chamberlain expressly disclaimed any notion of exerting pressure on Germany. He told Stresemann: 'I have no intention of undertaking a crusade against Russia. . . . Apart from what we have now done in the matter of a breach in relations, we shall do nothing, and have no objection to a continuance of legal trade with Russia.' Stresemann was even more forthright: 'We are convinced that it is necessary to combat the Bolshevist agitation inside Germany and we have done so. But we think it is a wrong policy deliberately to isolate Russia by any common action and provoke an internal crisis. . . . Any idea of a crusade against Russia I conceive as foolish and meaningless.'[2] This was on June 15. On June 17 Chicherin left Berlin for Moscow,[3] doubtless a much relieved man.

On his return from Geneva, Stresemann told the Reichstag, in rather circuitous language, why he had acted as he did. 'Our position requires economic relations with every country. We could have no security for the obligations which rest on us if we had to reckon with a large and powerful economic area being cut off from general economic intercourse, if that which binds us in this matter to Soviet Russia should perhaps yield to a condition excluding such intercourse.'[4]

Izvestya welcomed Germany's attitude. 'There is no doubt', wrote the paper, 'that leading circles in Germany have grasped the whole importance of a policy of strict neutrality. . . . Deviation aside from this policy and inclusion in the orbit of English influence would inevitably deprive German foreign policy of an indispensable factor of balance, so necessary to it in the East. . . .'[5]

Once a continuance of German neutrality was assured, the critical point was surmounted. The worst could not happen. Complete isolation would be an impossibility. But only in retrospect

[1] G. Stresemann, *Diaries, Letters and Papers*, Vol. III, Eng. trans., London, 1935-1940, p.122.
[2] Ibid, pp. 161-163.
[3] *The Times*, June 17, 1927.
[4] Reichstag Debates, Vol. 393, pp. 11002-11003.
[5] *Izvestya*, June 25, 1927.

is this clear. At the time it could not have been known. Who knew what further blows might not be on the way? In October 1927 a sympathetic observer, Professor Hoetszch, drew up a balance sheet of Russia's foreign relations that lacked nothing in dismal precision. 'The position in the Far East is lost. The position in the Near East is of little or no help. Hostility with England continues. There is no positive progress in relations with the border states. There was the Rakovsky conflict with France, America holds aloof. So there only remains the link with Germany.'[1]

The 'link with Germany' was an indispensable factor in largely nullifying the effects of Russia's diplomatic reverses. But it could not erase the fact that they had taken place. The impact of the first half of 1927 therefore gave rise to a complete revaluation of the whole political and economic context in which Soviet foreign policy operated. A thesis was enumerated which was to have the most momentous consequences, especially in Comintern affairs. The first hint of the new analysis came in a leader in *Izvestya*. 'At the present moment the period of the breathing-space which our Union has enjoyed since 1921 is clearly coming to an end.'[2]

The same theme, embroidered with the usual ideological trimmings, formed the *leitmotiv* of Stalin's report to the 15th Party Congress at the end of 1927. 'We are living on the eve of a new revolutionary upheaval both in the colonial and imperialist countries. If two years ago it was necessary and possible to speak of an ebb in the revolutionary wave in Europe, then today we have every ground for claiming that Europe is definitely entering on a phase of new revolutionary upheaval. I am not speaking here of the colonial countries where the situation of the imperialists is daily becoming more catastrophic.' Stalin then enumerated pell-mell all the recent steps taken by the Union in an effort to preserve friendly relations with the rest of the world. A non-aggression treaty with Turkey; guarantee treaty with Germany; credit agreement with Germany; customs agreement with Greece; recognition agreement with Uruguay; guarantee treaty with Afghanistan and Lithuania; trade treaty with Turkey; settlement of Russo-Swiss conflict; neutrality treaty with Persia; improve-

---

[1] *Osteuropa*, Jg. 3, Heft 1, p. 15. The 'Rakovsky conflict' with France refers to the French demand for Rakovsky's recall from France where he was Ambassador. He was a Trotskyist, who in 1927 signed a manifesto calling for 'the defeat of all the bourgeois states which carry on war against the Soviet Union'.

[2] *Izvestya*, August 10, 1927.

I

ment of Russo-Japanese relations; and growing business relations with America and Italy. He went on: 'If it was possible and necessary two years ago to speak of a period of a certain balance and "peaceful co-existence" between the U.S.S.R. and the capitalist states then today we have every reason to affirm that the period of peaceful co-existence is receding into the past, giving way to a period of imperialist attacks and of the preparation of intervention against the U.S.S.R.'

Under these circumstances the over-all task was 'to take into account the contradictions in the imperialist camp in order to put off war, to ransom ourselves from the capitalists and to take all measures for the preservation of peaceful relations'. There was, said Stalin, 'a certain opportunity for the U.S.S.R. to utilise for the preservation of peace' two contradictory tendencies in the capitalist world. The first were 'interventionist tendencies in one section of the capitalist world headed by Great Britain, and reluctance on the part of another section of the capitalist world to get entangled in a war with the U.S.S.R. preferring the establishment of business relations with it'.[1]

In the programme, as distinct from the analysis, there was nothing new. Exploiting the differences between the capitalist powers had been the mainstay of Soviet foreign policy since 1920. Equally so had been the Soviet effort to normalise its relations with capitalism as a whole. *Au fond* of course these two principles were incompatible. The Russians would be in no position to back one group of capitalists against another group, were they to enjoy equally amicable relations with both groups. But the dilemma never arose in this stark form. The Soviets never attained to a working arrangement with France and Britain in the same way as they did with Germany. Consequently, they were enabled to continue backing German nationalism without overmuch thought for its effect on their relations with the West.

Stalin's programme of peaceful relations with capitalism was pushed ahead with all the greater urgency in view of the alleged greater imminence of imperialist attacks. By a policy of conciliation he helped to buy as much time as possible. From now on peace and security are the constant cries of Soviet diplomacy. What Boris Stein, the chief of the Central European department of Narkomindel, wrote on the tenth anniversary of the Revolution

[1] *XV Syezd V.K.P. (b)—Stenographicheskii Otchet*, Moscow & Leningrad, 1928, pp. 49-50.

was echoed a hundred times: 'The watchword of our foreign policy is, as before, peace. The aim of this policy will be, as before, to guarantee to the Soviet Union those conditions which are most favourable to the accomplishment of the grandiose task set before us by history—the task of the construction of socialism.'[1]

In particular, it became a settled principle of Narkomindel to break out of isolation by seizing every possible opportunity of playing a part on the European stage, be it the Preparatory Commission of the Disarmament Conference, the Kellogg Pact or the Briand Pan-Europa plan. This was Litvinov's forte. It is connected with Chicherin's gradual withdrawal into the background and with Litvinov's rise to sole power in Narkomindel. The heart of Chicherin's approach was hostility to England and the League.[2] He also disapproved of such of Litvinov's ventures into Western Europe as the Disarmament Conference and the Kellogg Pact.[3] As for Russia and the League he once wrote to Louis Fischer: 'I am and always have been an absolutely un-diluted, unmixed, unwavering, unswerving enemy of our joining the League of Nations.'[4]

Litvinov's first venture on the grand scale into Western Europe was at the Preparatory Commission of the Disarmament Conference sitting at Geneva. It was there that he startled the world with sensational proposals for complete and immediate disarmament. These proposals were worked out at the highest level.[5] None of those concerned, and least of all such a hard-boiled diplomat as Litvinov himself, were sufficiently un-marxist and naïve to suppose that they stood any chance of success. As Bukharin had obligingly explained, although the Soviets strove for peace, they also prepared for war. No, in November 1927, in what seemed an increasingly threatening situation for the Soviet Union, the paramount need for the U.S.S.R. was to appear as the peace-lover par excellence. By an air of transcendent innocence it would render impossible the moral position of any potential aggressor. The propagandist aspect should also not be neglected. Here was the one socialist state in the world prepared to disarm down to the last man and the last gun, whereas the serried ranks of capitalism clung desperately to their weapons. Not that

[1] *Izvestya*, November 6-7, 1927.
[2] For a discussion of this point see *Osteuropa*, Jg. 3, Heft 6, pp. 435-436.
[3] Louis Fischer: *Men and Politics*, London, 1941, p. 125.
[4] Ibid, p. 143.
[5] J. Herbette, op. cit., pp. 79-80.

any converts to Communism were necessarily made by Litvinov. It was rather a question of creating a public opinion sympathetic to the Soviets.

This does not exhaust the many-faceted merits of the Soviets' disarmament proposals. They also allowed scope for co-operation with Germany, for Count Bernstorff, the German delegate, also defended the cause of disarmament. He took the line that security could not be assured except by prior disarmament. (This was principally aimed at France, reluctant to jeopardise her superior military position). Should this prior disarmament not be achieved, Germany herself would then automatically acquire the right to re-arm.

In their insistence on disarmament there was a great deal of common ground between Litvinov and Bernstorff. By entirely different paths they came to the same destination. 'Even if the Treaties of Berlin or Rapallo had not existed', writes Count Bernstorff, 'the German attitude at Geneva would have been the same'.[1]

This cannot be said to the same extent of Russian policy. Litvinov entirely pulled his punches as far as Germany was concerned and never exposed Bernstorff's hypocrisy as he did that of the other capitalist representatives. In consequence between Litvinov and Bernstorff there developed a certain degree of tactical co-operation. The pattern was for Litvinov to set the pace and for Bernstorff to follow him up. 'Do what you can to support the Soviet Russian attitude' was the advice Bernstorff received from Brockdorff-Rantzau in Moscow.[2] The advice was faithfully followed. After Litvinov had made his sensational speech, Bernstorff was the only delegate to give it a sympathetic reception. 'It is true that the speech of M. Litvinov was extremely severe, and that his proposals were very radical, but I would like to remind you . . . among other things, that in the Fourteen Points of President Wilson the same idea was expressed. It was said that complete disarmament was necessary, a disarmament which only left states the forces necessary for domestic security.'[3]

The procedure was repeated at the 5th Session in March-April 1928. When Litvinov produced a plan for gradual disarmament,

---

[1] Count Bernstoff: *Memoirs*, Eng. trans., London, 1936, p. 304.
[2] See a letter from Brockdorff-Rantzau to Bernstorff, dated February 2, 1928 (Bernstorff, op. cit., pp. 223-224. The two men were distantly related); see also E. von Weizsäcker: *Erinnerungen*, Munich, 1950, p. 77.
[3] Documents of the P.C.D.C., Series V, Minutes of the 4th Session, pp. 14-15.

Bernstorff commented: 'I give the most cordial welcome to these proposals. . . . I must confess that I have found in the Soviet proposal some very interesting ideas which appear to me deserving of our most careful attention and which may in my view be perfectly useful for the purpose of our work.'[1]

And at the beginning of the 6th Session, April 1929, when Litvonov's draft convention was again discussed, Bernstorff again commented: 'I cannot but feel that the aim to which the Soviet proposals are directed is identical with that which the Commission ought to hold up as its own aim.'[2]

Litvinov himself once mentioned the common ground between Germany and Russia on the disarmament question: 'from motives different from ours, the German delegation is also interested in a rapid solution of the disarmament question. Disarmed by the Versailles Treaty Germany bases her demand for the disarmament of other countries on one of the Articles of the Covenant of the League. Should this article not be fulfilled there may arise for Germany the right to demand rearmament for herself.'[3]

Litvinov's first trip to Geneva did not only bring to light an additional subject of Russo-German agreement, it also brought to light a topic that was to engender the most explosive disagreement—the Polish question. Litvinov discussed with Briand, in tentative terms, the possibility of an Eastern Locarno, *i.e.* an arrangement which would ensure the *status quo* in Eastern Europe in the same way as the Locarno Treaty of 1925 had done in the West. The effect of this would have been to exclude the prospect of any revision of Germany's Eastern frontier, or at the very least to render it much more difficult. At the end of 1927, the matter did not go beyond the discussion stage. But the mere suggestion of such a Franco-Russian-Polish understanding was seen by Hoetzsch as 'fantastic'. He at once interpreted it as questioning the special position enjoyed by Germany *vis-à-vis* Russia.[4]

However slight, this was the first explicit admission that the Rapallo policy, from the German angle, was incompatible with friendly Russo-Polish relations. Furthermore, even before Litvinov broached the subject, note how Stresemann viewed an Eastern Locarno. In a letter to Chancellor Marx in September 1927, he wrote: 'Briand, in spite of a good deal of opposition in

---

[1] Ibid., Series VI Minutes of the 5th Session, p. 242.
[2] Ibid., Series VIII Minutes of the 6th Session, 1st Part, p. 25.
[3] *Izvestya*, December 15, 1927.
[4] *Osteuropa*, Jg. 3, Heft 4, pp. 252-253.

the French delegation, equally adopted the attitude (as well as Chamberlain) that he would in no circumstances agree to an extension of the Locarno treaties to Eastern Europe. . . . We may, I think, be well satisfied with the outcome of the dispute. The proposal of the Poles for an Eastern Locarno is rejected. The collaboration between the great Locarno powers has proved steady and secure.'[1]

This remained, of course, a ripple on the surface, and it soon died away. But by 1931, when the question of a Russo-Polish *rapprochement* had, after many ups and downs, at last become practical politics, the ripple had grown to a powerful current seeping at the already shaken foundations of Rapallo.

All this lay in the future. Of more immediate moment during the first half of 1928 was the detention of five German engineers, who were amongst a group of fifty technicians arrested on charges of economic espionage and sabotage. Two of the Germans were at once released; two more were acquitted after the trial in May-June 1928, and the fifth received a year's imprisonment with reprieve. President Kalinin explained that the goodwill of German industry as such was not in question; only that of some of its members.[2]

In itself the incident was unimportant. But it was used by Germany as an excuse to delay the granting of further credits at a time when this would have prejudiced an anticipated scaling-down of reparation payments to the West. A visit by Brockdorff-Rantzau and Litvinov to Berlin in July to discuss the resumption of credit negotiations[3] led to no immediate results. Stresemann did not signify German willingness to re-open the talks until the day he left for Paris to sign the Kellogg Pact.[4] This was in accord with the pattern established by Stresemann in 1924 and 1925—one step East, one step West.

In all other respects, harmony prevailed. The Kellogg Pact for the outlawing of war was a clear indication of this. Russia was not among the invited and the press viewed the fact as the seed of an anti-Soviet bloc. *Pravda* denounced it as 'conceived without the participation of and against the U.S.S.R.' Protests were also made at the initial exclusion of Turkey, Afghanistan and China.

[1] G. Stresemann: *Diaries, Letters and Papers*, Vol. III, Eng. trans., London, 1935-1940, p. 209.
[2] *F.Z.*, June 3, 1928.
[3] *The Times*, July 30, 1928.
[4] Louis Fischer: *The Soviets in World Affairs*, London, 1930, p. 781.

Social-Democracy and the 2nd International were the object of special attacks for the welcome they gave to Kellogg's proposals. They were participating in 'a pacifist trick', to deceive the masses.[1] None the less, through German mediation, Litvinov was provided with another opportunity to stride the European stage and to demonstrate the Soviet's will to peace.[2]

On this note, one of the main German protagonists of the Rapallo policy—Count Brockdorff-Rantzau—died suddenly in Berlin. Ever mindful of the Fatherland, on his actual death-bed he dictated a letter to Chicherin and Litvinov exhorting them to uphold Rapallo, and making his last confession of Russo-German friendship.[3] Chicherin came to Berlin for the funeral to pay his last respects to his old friend.

As successor to Brockdorff-Rantzau, Dirksen, until now head of the Eastern Department of the Auswärtiges Amt, was chosen. This was a compromise between the choices of Hindenburg and Stresemann.[4]

In a sense Chicherin had also been attending his own funeral. The announcement of the tenth anniversary of his position as Commissar for Foreign Affairs was relegated to an inside page of *Izvestya*. Ten years of hard work brought him no public greetings from any Soviet notabilities. These only came from foreign representatives in Moscow and such collaborators abroad as Stresemann and von Schubert.[5] It was strongly rumoured, in fact, that he wanted to settle permanently in Germany and entirely to sever his connection with the U.S.S.R.[6] Although it was not until the summer of 1930 that Litvinov displaced him, for all practical purposes Chicherin's day was over in 1928. He was to spend the last years of his life in a shabby Moscow apartment sustained by devotion to Mozart whose arias he played to himself on the piano and in meditation on 'the whirligig of time'.[7] He died in 1936, unhonoured and unsung.

Litvinov's report to the Central Committee at the end of 1928 was as uncertain in tone as had been Stalin's report to the party

[1] *Pravda*, June 28 and September 1, 1928.
[2] Louis Fischer: *The Soviets in World Affairs*, London, 1930, pp. 774-780; see also H. von Dirksen: *Moskau—Tokio—London*, Stuttgart, 1949, pp. 82-83.
[3] Dirksen, op. cit., p. 86; Peter Laukhard: *Brockdorff-Rantzau Contra Versailles*, Berlin, 1934, p. 62.
[4] Dirksen, op. cit., p. 88.
[5] *Izvestya*, June 2, 1928.
[6] Dirksen, op. cit., pp. 94-95; Bessedovsky, op. cit., p. 92.
[7] Louis Fischer: *Men and Politics*, London, 1941, pp. 142-143; Dirksen, ibid.

a year before. Russia, he emphasised, was completely absorbed in internal reconstruction and held herself aloof from all warlike combinations and enterprises. Nevertheless, all along her Western frontiers were armed states able to count on French military aid; and the British Conservatives were still trying to complete the isolation of Russia that they had initiated in 1925. 'The struggle against our Union has never stopped. It has only taken on different forms according to changing circumstances. Yesterday it was intervention and complete blockade; today it is the attempt at a boycott and isolation; tomorrow it will perhaps again be intervention or war.' His remarks on Germany warned her that no permanent gains could be expected from the Locarno orientation, and he protested against the accession of certain German banks to an International Union of Russian creditors. But he closed on an optimistic note: 'This collaboration [*i.e.* with Germany] has a solid base in the treaties of Rapallo and Berlin.'[1]

The following day *Izvestya* confirmed the overall Russian satisfaction with Germany: 'The relations between the U.S.S.R. and Germany, despite temporary misunderstandings on certain concrete questions, are a model connection, corresponding to the correctly understood interests of both countries, as much in the political as in the economic field.'[2]

There was soon confirmation of this from the German side. Relations with Russia were so harmonious that Stresemann required to make no mention at all of them in a review of foreign policy to the Reichstag.[3] The question was raised a little later by the K.P.D. deputy Willi Münzenberg. He protested that those German banks who had joined the Union of Russian creditors had violated Article II of Rapallo, by which Germany had renounced all claims on Russia. Von Rheinbaben replied to the effect that German policy towards Russia had undergone no change.[4]

In fact, very shortly after this debate a Russo-German conciliation agreement was signed in Moscow—one of the very few agreements of its kind ever to have been signed by Soviet Russia. It admitted the principle of conciliation as between a proletarian and a bourgeois state. A commission of two members of each

---

[1] M. Litvinov: *Mirnaya Politika Sovietov* (*The Peace Policy of the Soviets*), Moscow & Leningrad, 1929, pp. 7-26. This is a reprint of Litvinov's report to the Central Committee 4th sitting, 4th session.
[2] *Izvestya*, December 11, 1928.
[3] Reichstag Debates, Vol. 423, pp. 414 ff.
[4] Ibid., pp. 447-448 and 453-454.

party was to meet at least once yearly for the purpose of settling, as they arose, any disputes arising out of the interpretation of the economic and political treaties between Russia and Germany. The commission could also be summoned at any other time if requested by either party. The agreement was to remain in force for three years.

At the same time, Litvinov gave a jerk forward to the stagnant relations with the border states. In February, he secured the signature of the so-called 'Litvinov Protocol' whereby Russia and her Western neighbours, as well as Turkey and Persia, all renounced war as an instrument of policy. With Germany, the only passing flurry on an even surface took place in May when Marshal Voroshilov made a speech on May Day attacking the German Government, and when popular processions paraded before the astonished German ambassador, bearing caricatures of German statesmen.[1] This was an indiscreet throwback to that day in 1918 when Count Mirbach had been exhorted to overthrow his own government.

As a result of all these exertions it might fairly be said that the diplomatic position of 1923, after its near-collapse in 1927, was largely re-established. There was hardly a country in the world with which Russia had not some kind of co-operating agreement. Narkomindel had successfully performed its task of keeping the 'warmongers' at bay. Yet all this was but the lull before the storm. Only a few months later Germany, the linch-pin of the whole system, began her second swing westwards. After a short recovery in 1930, the final collapse of Rapallo was not to be long delayed.

[1] Dirksen, op. cit. p. 98.

CHAPTER VIII

The First Breach (1929-1931)

DURING 1924-1929 the K.P.D. shared in the general stabilisation of German and European society. Its Reichstag membership remained at an average of fifty and the party membership at around a hundred and fifty thousand. In policy matters the great change introduced at the 6th World Congress of the Communist International in July-August 1928 was heralded in Russia.

Although the Comintern had a reputation for swift and sudden reversals of policy, observation shows that it required approximately a year to inaugurate a change. Before the slogan 'To the Masses' was formulated in December 1921, it had been foreshadowed in the Radek-Levi Open Letter of January 1921. Similarly, the upheavals of all kinds prophesied in August 1928 made their original appearance in August 1927 and were a response to purely Russian experience. When *Izvestya* wrote: 'at the present moment the period of breathing-space which our Union has enjoyed since 1921 is clearly coming to an end'[1] it was basing its analysis on Russian experience. On this followed Stalin's prophecy of a collapse in partial capitalist stabilisation at the 15th Party Congress in December 1927.[2] To this the corollary was a directly revolutionary period with the necessity for intensified attacks on Social Democracy. 'On the basis of the beginning of the revolutionary rise of the Labour movement, the most important tasks of the Communist International are to accentuate the international struggle against reformism.'[3]

Some six months later the new analysis was carried into the Comintern. There it ran: 'The upheavals in the international position which have taken place since the 5th Congress [in 1924] are characterised by an enormous sharpening of all the contradictions of capitalism, by the tremendous economic and political strengthening of the Soviet Union, by the swift growth of the national-revolutionary movement in the colonies and

---

[1] *Izvestya*, August 10, 1927.
[2] See above, pp. 129-30.
[3] *XV Syezd V.K.P. (b)—Stenographicheskii Otchet*, Moscow & Leningrad, 1928, p. 1289.

semi-colonies, especially in China, and a sharpening of the class struggle in the capitalist countries.'[1]

At the same time the Social-Democrats were stigmatised as Social-Fascists. This analysis had first been put forward by Zinoviev in 1924.[2] It was based on the Social-Democrats' support for Stresemann rather than Brandler. It had then been discarded, only to return with redoubled force in 1928.

Although it cannot be proved, it is likely that the all-out attack on the German Social-Democrats was a response to the demands of Russian foreign policy. Ever since 1918 they had been the *bête noire* of the Russians. Not only inside Germany were they the resolute opponents of the K.P.D. but the Social-Democrats were also the greatest enemies of Rapallo and the foremost supporters of Locarno. Entirely apart from this, their action in drawing public attention to the Reichswehr-Red Army contacts had drawn venomous Russian attacks. An article in *Mezhdunarodnaya Zhizn* (the organ of Narkomindel) in discussing the foreign policies of the various German political parties showed that the Social-Democratic Party was characterised by its single-minded Western orientation. 'Social-Democracy, in contrast to the Western parties, knows no wavering. It treads the Western path, without looking round and without re-insuring itself. If it does make gestures of conciliation towards the Soviet Union, this is only under pressure and to sooth its working masses, and after every such gesture there follows necessarily some shocking and repulsive act.'[3]

Attacks of this kind were linked with fears for the Russian position in Germany when the Social-Democrats re-entered the Government under Hermann Müller in May 1928. (Although they had supported Stresemann, they had been out of the Government ever since the Autumn of 1923.) *Izvestya* wrote of the election results: 'If we turn to the foreign-political perspectives we can hardly expect any direct and sharp changes in German foreign policy in so far as . . . the policy of Stresemann was supported and publicised by the Social Democrats, who were formerly in opposition, to a greater extent than by the Nationalists who were formerly in power. However, it is essential to bear in

---

[1] *Kommunisticheskii Internatsional v Dokumentakh* (*The Communist International in Documents*), ed. Bela Kun, Moscow, 1933, p. 793.

[2] *V Vseymirni Kongress Kommunisticheskovo Internatsionsala*, Pt. I, Moscow, 1925, p. 61; *XIII Syezd R.K.P.* (*b*)—*Stenographicheskii Otchet*, Moscow, 1924, p. 62.

[3] *Mezhdunarodnaya Zhizn*, No. 12, 1927.

mind that the influence of the Social-Democrats cannot but express itself in a strengthening of the so-called Western orientation in Germany.

. . . For German Social Democracy the question of the propagandising and realisation of the *rapprochement* of Germany with other capitalist countries is the central point of its programme and practical activity. Moreover, Social-Democracy, as is well known, has always adopted the viewpoint that the liquidation of the peace treaties, with their burdensome consequences for Germany, is only possible as a result of a policy of concessions and agreements with the former Entente countries.'[1]

Whether the policy of attacking the Social-Democrats was really expected to produce a German revolution is an open question. It would seem doubtful that this could be seriously expected after so many disappointments. In any event, to all appearances, the K.P.D. went from strength to strength from about 1930 onwards. This was not due to the new line but to the Great Depression.

This did not show itself for a year or two. If the middle of 1929 marked the high-spot of Russo-German harmony, then the following months marked the beginning of the second swing by Germany westwards. The first such swing took place in 1925-1926. It had been very slight in extent and was, as far as Russia was concerned, largely compensated for by the Berlin Treaty of 1926. Exactly the same procedure was now repeated, although on a larger scale. In the same way as the first swing was associated with, if not occasioned by the Dawes Plan and Locarno, the second swing bore the same relationship to the Young Plan and the evacuation of the Rhineland. For about a year, from the middle of 1929 until the middle of 1930, German policy hardly concerned itself with Russia and concentrated on the achievement of its western aims.

It was in February 1929 that a Committee of Experts met in Paris to study the Reparations problem. By June, the result of their work—the Young Plan—was ready. The principal advantage of the Plan to Germany lay in the fact that it at last fixed the full total due from Germany. At the same time the annuities under the Young Plan were approximately £35 million less than those under Dawes, and international control over such institutions as

[1] *Izvestya*, May 23, 1928.

the Reichsbank and the German Railways, originally established as a guarantee for the payment of the annuities, was totally abolished. Finally, the German price for the acceptance of the Plan was the evacuation of the Allied-occupied Rhineland five years before the date foreseen by the Treaty of Versailles. For Stresemann the Paris negotiations were not unnaturally 'the most important factor in German foreign policy'. In the same Reichstag speech, significantly enough, he made no mention of Russia.[1] It was the beginning of the second swing. Locarno was going to be repeated—though on a larger scale. For the moment German attention was concentrated on her Western aims and the Russians would have to take a back seat. Following on Stresemann's speech, the German Nationalist Freiherr von Freytagh-Loringhoven complained of this in somewhat exaggerated but not entirely unjustified terms: 'I cannot rid myself of the impression', he said, 'that today Russia is hardly any longer a card in our diplomatic game, that because of Locarno, because of our membership of the League and in spite of the Berlin Treaty of 1926, we have undertaken commitments towards the West that no longer leave us a free choice to the degree that German foreign policy requires'.[2] Stresemann made no comment on this.

Soviet opinion remained relatively quiescent. In the press there was none of the alarm that had accompanied the pre-Locarno negotiations. None the less, at the end of 1929 Litvinov showed that he saw the way the wind was blowing. His survey of relations with Germany was by no means as confident as the previous year. For the first time he openly envisaged the possibility that the Russians, in supporting Rapallo, might actually be cutting their own throats. He saw that a position might arise when Germany might be so successful in freeing herself from Versailles as no longer to require the Rapallo lever. He told the Central Committee that Russia followed 'with great sympathy' all Germany's efforts to free herself from Versailles. 'We would', he continued, 'cordially welcome the result of these efforts if they really led to the liquidation or even to a weakening of the fetters of Versailles. Our interests are not in conflict with the efforts of Germany to settle her relations with other countries, but of course only in those cases when this settlement of relations does not draw Germany into anti-Soviet campaigns and does not lead her away

[1] Reichstag Debates, Vol. 425, pp. 2810-2811.
[2] Ibid., p. 2871.

from the Rapallo Treaty, which has had such beneficial results both for Germany and for our Union.'[1]

This was an entirely new note. Its nearest approach till now had been Litvinov's remarks to Stresemann in 1925 that Germany might drift into the anti-Soviet camp as a result of receiving continual concessions from Britain, anxious to restrict French influence on the Continent. Hitherto however the question of Soviet reservations in supporting the German struggle against Versailles had never been raised—openly, at least. That Germany might find a one-sided Western orientation more congenial than a pro-Soviet neutrality was of course a commonplace. But that Russian policy, via Rapallo, might itself be contributing to making Germany so strong as to put her perhaps in a position where she would no longer need Russia at all—this was an unprecedented thought. The near future justified *in toto* the Soviet fear.

The Reichstag, in March 1930, ratified the Young Plan. At the same time it was announced that in June 1930 the Allies would evacuate the Rhineland. Under these circumstances, where lay the need for further *rapprochement* with Russia? During the first half of 1930, Germany suddenly turned away from Russia. It seemed that Rapallo had already paid all the dividends that could be expected of it and that there was no point in continuing an association the yield of which was exhausted. An article in *Der Börsenkurier*, a liberal journal expressing, as the name implies, the views of stock-exchange and financial circles, was symptomatic of this state of mind: 'The time is past when harmony between East and West was necessary. We can now settle our relations with Russia independently of all tactical considerations. The time is past when there existed friendship for Russia, when Moscow was the only active post in the foreign policy of the Reich. The Rhineland is evacuated and there is no longer any need to fear complications in the West. Our sovereignty as a great European power is re-established. Russia must ask herself if she is willing to do all that is necessary in order that our position in regard to her may remain the same as before.'[2]

In the Reichstag in June, Curtius, Stresemann's successor as Foreign Minister, confirmed that during the previous six months

---

[1] *Pravda*, December 5, 1929.
[2] *Der Börsenkurier*, May 1930, quoted in P. Milyukov: *La Politique Extérieure des Soviets*, Paris, 1936, p. 220.

'a radical change of mood' had threatened to take place *vis-à-vis* Russia.[1] Even Hoetzsch had to admit that as a result of German pre-occupation with western questions, relations with Russia had stagnated.[2]

None of this went unremarked in Russia. Both *Izvestya* and *Pravda* of March 15, 1930 spoke nervously of an anti-Soviet wave sweeping the German bourgeoisie after The Hague Conference and the Young Plan. *Izvestya* went so far as to demand of the German Government that it openly show its policy towards Russia had undergone no change;[3] and Molotov a little later noted to his 'deepest regret' that the German attitude was 'a threat to the cause of consolidating Soviet-German relations'.[4] While the crisis was still on, *Izvestya* came out with a slashing attack on Germany. It began by complaining of the anti-Russian views being expressed in Germany with which it accused the government of sympathising. 'Neither the Herman Müller government nor the present Brüning régime have done anything to create that sole pre-supposition which was and is the essential condition for any kind of Soviet-German negotiations. On the contrary, the whole tactics of the German Government amount to the accumulation of claims having as their aim a belated justification of the malice of the German press. . . . These tactics try to create the impression that the U.S.S.R. must expiate "her crimes" and at the price of "repentance" purchase Germany's return to the path of Rapallo and Berlin. Only after this and depending on the price offered by the U.S.S.R., will Germany be ready to determine her new political line with regard to the Soviet Union. Such is the sum total of recent Soviet German relations.' The article went on to warn Germany, in more familiar terms, against imagining that 'the weakening of Rapallo could strengthen and not weaken Germany's position face to face with Anglo-French imperialism'. Russia, *Izvestya* ended, remained faithful to Rapallo but would not pay a higher price for its maintenance than her interests required.[5]

In both camps voices were raised to heal the breach. In Germany Hoetzsch argued that whatever misgivings might be felt about Rapallo, at the very least Russia was not a participant in the Versailles system and that German vital interests demanded

[1] Reichstag Debates, Vol. 428, p. 5817.
[2] *Jahrbuch für Auswärtige Politik*, p. 22. Berlin, 1931.
[3] It was at the Hague Conference that the evacuation of the Rhineland was arranged.
[4] Quoted below p. 150.
[5] *Izvestya*, April 24, 1930.

that Russia be not brought into this system.[1] In the Reichstag too, he argued that Germany should continue on her path as the mediator between Moscow and Geneva and not throw in her lot with any anti-Soviet system: 'We would be mad were we to join that sort of combination which would be borne on our backs, from which we would get nothing at all and which would end with a total defeat in Russia itself.'[2] These remarks alone indicate the atmosphere in Germany. In the analogous circumstances five years previously, during Locarno, such outspokenness would have been quite out of place and unnecessary.

On the Russian side there was a similar frankness in probing the German *malaise*. At the beginning of 1929 a pseudonymous article signed Politicus in *Mezhdunarodnaya Zhizn* had examined 'The Paths of German Economic Expansion'. It was based largely on German published sources and statistics and came to the general conclusion that after the setbacks to German imperialism—it got off to a late start in the pre-1914 race for colonies and after 1918 suffered from the loss of its fleet and overseas possessions at Versailles—it was once more expanding. This was all the more the case owing to the rationalisation of German production after the inflation. 'Objectively, Germany is once again being pushed into an activisation of her foreign policy with the aim of consolidating favourable conditions for the expansion in every way of her industrial exports and for the resumption of the export of capital.' Hence arose German trade treaties with, and large scale investments in such territories as Rumania, Bulgaria, Turkey, Persia, South America, Greece, Jugo-Slavia, China and Siam. Politicus even spoke of a 'Drang Nach Osten'—'only of course in other forms'.[3]

Just over a year later, an article by N. Kornev in the same authoritative journal applied this analysis to the special case of German relations with Russia. The article bore the title 'Rapallo Crisis?' and differed from most of the matter of *Mezhdunarodnaya Zhizn* in being devoted to a topical subject and in not being a background study. It frankly admitted the existence of a crisis in Russo-German relations whose cause it identified quite correctly with the changed position of the two countries. In 1922 both Germany and Russia had been oppressed by the imperialist West;

[1] *Osteuropa*, Jg. 5, Heft 6, pp. 380-382.
[2] Reichstag Debates, Vol. 428, p. 5866.
[3] *Mezhdunarodnaya Zhizn*, No. 3, 1929, pp. 37-50.

and Russia had been unable to refuse Germany her sympathy, especially during the occupation of the Ruhr. Although Russia knew that gratitude had no place in politics she saw no reason for not reminding Germany of her pro-German stand on that occasion. But by 1930, Kornev went on, the paths of the once oppressed Germans and Russians had diverged considerably. The latter through the Five Year Plan had initiated the socialisation of their economy; the former, on the other hand, had developed neo-imperialist tendencies, albeit hampered by Versailles. Kornev now asked the really crucial question; had the time come for Russia to cease making a distinction between German neo-imperialism and Western imperialism? The answer was a qualified no: 'the opportuneness of the question seems to us doubtful'. On this note he ended. The air had been cleared.[1]

There was one thing, however, that all the exchanges of this type could do nothing to eliminate—and that was the K.P.D. From now on this must be accounted a factor jeopardising Rapallo. At this point a comparison with 1923-1924 is instructive. Then, the abortive German revolution had left no impress on Rapallo owing to the fact that the German bourgeoisie was not in a strong enough position to dispense with Russian diplomatic support. In consequence it refrained from identifying Russia and Communism. Through weakness it had no choice but to do this.

But in 1930 Germany was in a very much stronger position and could afford to be more discriminating in her choice of friends. With the Rhineland evacuated and reparations scaled down, Germany was now emancipated from exclusive reliance on the Soviets and no longer required to turn a blind eye to some of the strange habits of her Bolshevist friends. This was all the more the case as the K.P.D., with the onset of the depression in 1929, grew daily stronger. In September 1930, for example, the party won seventy-seven seats in the Reichstag, a gain of twenty-three over the previous election results in 1928. Four and a half million voters supported Communist candidates.

From now on, in relation to Germany, Stalin was less the master of a situation than mastered by a situation. It is doubtful whether the K.P.D. was expected to achieve its aim of a German revolution. It is even more doubtful whether its policy was formed with

[1] *Mezhdunarodnaya Zhizn*, No. 3, 1930. This article in view of its importance, was reproduced, apart from insignificant omissions, in the German political monthly *Zeitschrift für Politik*, July, 1930.

K

this end in view. But what did this matter to a German bourgeois? He could not be expected to know this. He could not be blamed if, confronted with the K.P.D's growing strength, he drew the conclusion that the party might, in the not so distant future, become the ultimate threat to his position. By a stroke of grotesque irony Stalin was credited with revolutionary intentions at the very time when his attention was concentrated more and more on the paramount needs of Russian industrialisation. *Die Reichspost* wrote: 'A glance at the French, German, English, and even at the small American Communist Party, at the Communist organis-isations in the Balkans, at the Russian move in Manchuria, and at Communist subversive activity in the colonial countries is enough to show that Bolshevism is in bitter earnest with the World Revolution. It is thought that the situation here [*i.e.* in Germany] can be made ripe for revolution before anywhere else by a sharp-ening of the contradictions caused by unemployment and economic collapse. . . . For Communism world revolution is no longer, as it was only a short time ago, a theory of the future, but a real development of the present, and one that is already beginning.'[1] In the Reichstag Curtius gave as one of the reasons for the diplomatic crisis over Rapallo 'above all an accentuation of the revolutionary will of the whole of Communism';[2] and at the beginning of 1931, the *Frankfurter Zeitung* began a leading article with the menacing words: 'Since Bolshevism in Russia opened its Communist attack against the whole of the rest of the world. . . .'[3]

This was a mistaken analysis. But what helped to render the mistake less harmful was the fact that, although Germany could afford to take up a more independent attitude towards Russia, she could still not afford to deprive herself entirely of Russian diplomatic support. Despite everything, Germany still needed Rapallo to support her in her struggle against the Allies. The right to equality of armaments had not yet been obtained; reparations had not yet been finally annulled. The Polish Corridor and Upper Silesia were not yet incorporated in the Reich. There was the Anschluss with Austria. . . . Many of the items on the agenda submitted by Stresemann to the ex-Crown Prince in 1925 were still outstanding. The reasons dictating the

[1] *Die Reichspost*, February 4, 1930; see also *F.Z.*, March 13, 1930.
[2] Reichstag Debates, Vol. 428, p. 5817.
[3] *F.Z.*, February 2, 1931.

maintenance of Rapallo were of a strength equal to those dictating its abandonment. The pull was both ways. In consequence, German policy from now on wavered between these two extremes. At one time it appeared wiser to play the Russian card; at another, it appeared wiser to hide it from sight.

By the middle of 1930 the immediate crisis was largely over. After special negotiations a joint Russo-German communiqué was issued in Berlin. It stated that both Governments 'were determined to uphold their mutual relations and to approach the tasks still lying before them, whether these tasks concerned the direct relationship between the two countries or other questions affecting their interests' on the basis of the Treaties of Rapallo and Berlin.[1]

That these were not entirely empty words was shown by the cordial greetings exchanged between Litvinov and Curtius when the last Allied troops left the Rhineland in June 1930. Litvinov wrote to Curtius: 'In the name of the government of the Union, I request you, Mr Minister, to accept and to transmit to the German Government, our congratulations on the occasion of the ending of the occupation régime by foreign troops of part of German territory and the restoration of the sovereignty of the German people. The government of the Union, which on January 13, 1923 protested before the whole world against the occupation of German territory, notes with particular satisfaction the restoration of the rights of the German people in the Rhineland.' Curtius replied: 'I request you, Mr People's Commissar of the U.S.S.R., to accept the gratitude of the German Government for the congratulations which you offered in the name of the government of the U.S.S.R. on the occasion of the liberation of the occupied territories. The German Government has greeted with satisfaction the warm sympathy of the government of the U.S.S.R. in this historic event.'[2]

This was the penultimate event when Russia and Germany felt as one. The final event was occasioned by the Briand Plan for a United Europe. There was nothing surprising in this identity of view. The Plan was a last desperate attempt by France to preserve her continental hegemony, undermined though this was

---

[1] *F.Z.*, June 15, 1930.
[2] *Mezhdunarodnaya Politika v 1930 godu* (*International Politics in 1930*), ed. A. V. Sabanin, Moscow, 1932, pp. 165-166.

by Locarno and all the consequences of Locarno. In specific terms, it presupposed the territorial *status quo* in Europe. On this issue of whether the continent was to be dominated by a single power there was, as might be expected, Russo-German harmony of interest. It contradicted the prime Russian aim of keeping her enemies divided; and it would have effectively put a stop to German revisionist claims against Poland. This is again the familiar picture of Russia and Germany finding a common platform, the first for defensive reasons, the second for offensive reasons.

Briand's memorandum on his scheme was at first addressed only to the European members of the League. To counteract this exclusion of Russia (and of Turkey, though this was of lesser importance) the German reply urged the claims of both these countries to a seat on the proposed study commission. The Italian reply did likewise.[1] The move was successful and Litvinov got another opportunity to stride the European stage. He used the opening to advocate a pact of economic non-aggression which would, *inter alia,* forbid differential economic treatment amongst the members of the proposed Union on the grounds of their differing régimes.

While these manoeuvres were proceeding, Litvinov on July 25, 1930, was promoted to *de jure* Commissar of Foreign Affairs. His first press conference in this new capacity affirmed that no change in policy was contemplated. It would continue to defend the revolution, to defend peace and to create the conditions facilitating the building of socialism in one country. In a world of which the socialist one-sixth was surrounded by the capitalist five-sixths, this could be best achieved by eliminating all friction between the two systems. Litvinov also took occasion to explain the basis of the Union's policy towards Germany. 'In view of our natural sympathy for the countries where the burdens, which have been imposed upon them, lie like a heavy weight especially on the workers and also because the states interested in the perpetuation of the consequences and the injustices incorporated in the above-mentioned treaties [*i.e.,* the peace treaties] simultaneously pursue an extremely aggressive and hostile policy towards our Union also, a certain community of interests has grown up between the Soviet Union and the countries suffering from the war.'[2]

---

[1] International Conciliation Pamphlets, No. 265, pp. 685 and 668-669, 1930; see also Curtius's remarks to the Reichstag (Reichstag Debates, Vol. 444, p. 877).

[2] *Mezhdunarodnaya Politika v 1930 godu,* ed. A. V. Sabanin, Moscow, 1932, pp. 238-240.

Litvinov's promotion was the occasion of a minor reshuffle in Narkomindel's upper ranks. Krestinsky left the Berlin Embassy to occupy Litvinov's former position as Senior Deputy Commissar for Western affairs. This was interpreted as a strengthening of pro-German influence by Dirksen.[1] Litvinov's uninterrupted tenure of high office from 1919-1939 and from 1941-1943 as Ambassador to the United States suggests that he was well in with Stalin. Not only was Litvinov distinguished by receipt of the Order of Lenin in 1935, on his sixtieth birthday, but also, in the later 1930's when so many of his colleagues in Narkomindel lost their heads, Litvinov was one of the few who survived. His favourite diplomat was Talleyrand, of whose life Litvinov made a close study.[2] But Litvinov was a modest man—'If I look back', he wrote to Stalin, 'I am chiefly proud of having done my whole party work of forty years under the immediate guidance of our great teachers Lenin and Stalin. If there are any successes in my diplomatic work they must be attributed to the strong and wise leadership of the man who is responsible for the successes in all fields of socialist reconstruction—Stalin.'[3]

Khintschuk succeeded Krestinsky in Berlin. He was primarily an economist and had been one of Krassin's collaborators. He had also been trade representative in London and a member of the Soviet delegation to the World Economic Conference of 1927. He was latterly employed in the foreign trade division of Narkomindel. His association with the German economy dated from 1928 when, as President of the Council of the Russian Chamber of Commerce, he had inaugurated its German section. This was the first foreign section. Khintschuk had then voiced the hope 'that the German section of the Chamber of Commerce would on both sides further a knowledge of the forms of trade between both countries and thus contribute in a concrete way to the consolidation of the relations between them'.[4] The new ambassador's economic background was a recognition of the importance of Russo-German trade as the First Five Year Plan got under way.

Khintschuk handed over his credentials to Hindenburg in December 1930. The following March at the 6th Congress of Soviets Molotov summed up the state of relations with Germany in rather complacent tones: 'The two years that have passed

[1] H. von Dirksen, *Moskau-Tokio-London*, Stuttgart, 1949, p. 95.
[2] A. U. Pope: *Maxim Litvinoff*, New York, 1943, p. 189.
[3] Quoted ibid., p. 191.
[4] Quoted in *Osteuropa*, Jg. 4, Heft 5, pp. 329-330.

since the 5th Congress of Soviets can be divided into two periods.
The first period covers the end of 1929 and the beginning of 1930.
In my report to the Congress of Soviets I cannot pass over in
silence the fact that, to our deepest regret, in the first period I
mentioned German governmental and social circles were seized
by a wave of the anti-Soviet "crusade". For a time this was a
threat to the cause of consolidating and developing Soviet-German
relations. However, from the middle of 1930 there set in the well-
known favourable turning-point in U.S.S.R.-German relations
which I note with satisfaction. The basic line of German foreign
policy towards the U.S.S.R. has recently been one of friendly
collaboration and of further consolidation of our relationship . .
The visit to Moscow of a delegation of the most powerful leaders
in German industry is one more proof of the understanding
displayed by Germany's leaders of the importance and value
of Soviet-German economic co-operation. Permit me to express
my conviction that the visit of this delegation and the negotiations
directly with the leaders of Soviet industry will bring fruitful
results and strengthen even further our economic relations.'[1]

The delegation referred to by Molotov was indeed impressive.
It included some of Germany's most powerful industrialists.
Present were directors of Krupp's, the A.E.G., Demag, Klöckner,
Otto Wolff, Siemens, and Borsig. Peter Klöckner, a self-made
Ruhr magnate came to Moscow in person. Dirksen saw the visit
as the climax of his ambassadorship.[2] The industrialists were also
happy. 'The more the general economic outlook darkened
throughout the whole world, the more the enthusiasm of the
Reich Union of German Industry increased for the Russian plan
[of Industrialisation].'[3]

Three months later, on June 24, the Berlin Treaty was renewed
by a protocol signed in Moscow between Krestinsky and Dirksen.
The terms of the Treaty remained unaltered but two new
provisions were added. Firstly, the duration of the Treaty was
made indefinite. On the other hand either party could denounce
it at one year's notice, though in any case not before June 30, 1933.
Secondly, the protocol added that the Conciliation Convention
of 1929 was to hinge on the renewed Berlin Treaty and only to be
valid whilst the latter remained in force. *Izvestya* devoted an

[1] *Izvestya*, March 11, 1931.
[2] Dirksen, op. cit., p. 115.
[3] Ibid., p. 108.

enthusiastic leading article to the renewal: Germany, it wrote, had thereby shown its understanding 'of the indispensability of friendly relations with the only great power to be an opponent of the Versailles system, an opponent of the exploitation of one country by another. . . . This Treaty strengthens the position of the Soviet Union in her struggle for the execution of the Five Year Plan, in her struggle for peace. It also strengthens the position of Germany in her fight against those grievous consequences of the war, which prevent the German people from developing their technical, economic and cultural possibilities.'[1]

These brave words were the swan-song of Rapallo. During the next few months the Soviet Union ceased to be a supporter of Germany in her struggle against Versailles. This was a veritable revolution in the principle that had informed Soviet foreign policy since 1921. It had a corollary no less revolutionary—the quest for a *rapprochement* with the Western Powers.

---

[1] *Izvestya,* June 26, 1931.

CHAPTER IX

The End of Rapallo (1931-1934)

THE Prolongation of the Berlin Treaty was not ratified until May 1933, by which time it was devoid of significance. From 1931 onwards and until 1939 German policy, apart from an ephemeral phase in 1933, disinterested itself in Russia entirely and turned resolutely Westwards. Russian policy also, cautiously began to disentangle itself from the collapsing Rapallo edifice and to seek re-insurance in the West against German defection. Prosaically, without drama, and with no specific turning-point, the ways of the Rapallo partners began unmistakably to diverge.

Broadly speaking, the Soviets always considered as their principal enemy at any particular time that power which was temporarily dominant in Europe. Thus, until 1924 Soviet policy was primarily anti-French; until 1930 it was primarily anti-British. Now it began to turn against Germany. In each of the two earlier cases it could make use of the German *point d'appui*. But against Germany it obviously had to resort to a different *point d'appui*—to a *rapprochement* with the West. This is precisely what happened.

In all probability—though it must be emphasised that there is nothing but circumstantial evidence to this effect—it was the attempt made by Curtius and Brüning to declare an Austro-German Customs Union that showed the Soviets the red light. In the light of Litvinov's congratulations to Curtius on 'the restoration of the rights of the German people in the Rhineland' and of repeated Soviet denunciation of the injustices of the peace treaties, it would have been consistent to welcome the Brüning-Curtius move as a further assertion of German rights, as a further effort to undo the wrongs of Versailles. But nothing of the kind happened. The projected Customs Union, which would in fact have been equivalent to an Austro-German economic union, did not evoke a protest in Russia as it did in France. Nevertheless, the key-note of press treatment was caution. The plan was seen by *Izvestya* as a sympton of the increasing self-assertion of German capitalism in its struggle against France. It would bring Germany economically into contact with Italy, Jugoslavia and Hungary with inevitable political consequences. At the same time it would also increase German pressure on Poland and Czechoslovakia. France, on the other hand, had no justifiable *locus standi* for her protest. The German move was nothing more than the objective reply to the Briand Pan-Europa Plan.[1] Radek devoted a lengthy analysis to the plan. He came to the general conclusion that it was only to the South that Germany could expand. To both the East and West the path was barred by France. Germany was seeking to expand her influence in the Balkans and Italy, thereby returning to the Mitteleuropa war-aim of German imperialism. He ended with a hint that France, in order to combat German expansionism, might have to call in Russian aid.[2]

In any event, whether or not the Customs Union was the impelling factor, it is from about the middle of 1931 that the Soviets began to seek re-insurance against Germany. This is a tribute to Soviet diplomacy. In the perspective of some twenty years it is clear that the Russian appreciation of the situation was basically correct. The reason for this is Russian weakness. They had no reserves of strength to fall back on. Stalin and Litvinov had to be quicker on the uptake than anyone else for the simple reason that they could not afford to make a mistake.

The Russo-German situation now began to resolve around Poland. There were two reasons for this: firstly, the fact that at long last Russo-Polish and Russo-French non-aggression pacts were becoming practical politics; secondly, the fact that national-ism in Germany was becoming more and more strident in its *insistence* on the return of the Polish Corridor.[3] At this time there could hardly have been a thornier subject for Russia to grasp than the Polish question. Yet she showed no hesitation in doing so.

On the whole, relations between Russia and Poland were an index to Russia's relations with Germany. When hostility prevailed between Russia and Poland, friendship prevailed between Russia and Germany and *vice versa*. Thus the war between Russia and Poland in 1920 was overwhelmingly important in creating Rapallo; Rapallo itself was accompanied by expressions

[1] *Izvestya*, March 24, 1931.
[2] Ibid., May 1, 1931.
[3] See, for example, various despatches rom Sir Horace Rumbold, the British Ambassador in Berlin to Arthur Henderson, the Foreign Secretary (*Documents on British Foreign Policy*, Series II, Vol. I, ed. Woodward and Butler, London, 1946, pp. 490-501).

of Russian hostility towards Poland; and in 1923 when the Ruhr occupation pushed Russia and Germany closer than ever together, Russia had envisaged renewed war against Poland. Conversely, the temporary estrangement between Russia and Germany over Locarno had led to Chicherin's sudden visit to Warsaw with the offer of a non-aggression pact. In short, it was impossible for Russia to be simultaneously on friendly terms with both Germany and Poland.

The Soviets always claimed, of course, that their friendly relations with Germany did not cut across their efforts to establish friendly relations with the other capitalist powers. This had been a feature of Trotsky's comment on Rapallo in 1922; and when the Berlin Treaty was signed in 1926 Litvinov had voiced an identical view: 'Our friendship with Germany does not in any way exclude our efforts to establish friendly relations with other countries.'[1] But it is impossible to test the truth of this assertion for the simple reason that apart from Germany, the Soviets encountered well-nigh constant hostility from the principal capitalist powers. Whether the Soviets were willing or not, they never had the chance to initiate a French or a British 'Rapallo'. Litvinov was quite correct in stating that the Russo-German community of interest was partly based on 'the extremely aggressive and hostile policy' pursued *vis-à-vis* Russia by those states interested in the maintenance of the post-war *status quo*. In 1927, it is true, Litvinov had broached with Briand the subject of an Eastern Locarno but this, at the time, never went very far. The Soviets had never been forced to choose between Germany and Britain and France. They had had no choice but to lean on Germany. Now however, they showed that they would use the opportunity for *rapprochement* with France and Poland—when it did at last come—even if this meant jeopardising Rapallo.

It was in March 1931, at the Sixth Congress of Soviets, that Molotov voiced the Soviet desire for friendlier relations with France. In May, conversations were held in Paris between Dovgalevski the Russian Ambassador, and Berthelot the Secrétaire Général at the Quai D'Orsay. In August a Russo-French Non-Aggression Treaty was initialled and ready for signature.[2] At the

[1] *Izvestya*, April 25, 1926. For Trotsky see above p. 55.
[2] Otto Hoetzsch: *Le Caractère et la Situation Internationale de l'Union des Soviets*, Geneva, 1932, pp. 55-56.

same time France removed her ban on Soviet imports, imposed
the year before on allegations of Russian dumping. In the event
the Russo-French Treaty was not actually signed until November
1932. This was not Russia's doing however, but France's, and
drew a Russian protest.[1] There is no reason to suppose that the
Russians would not have been willing to sign in 1931. At the same
time Herbette, the anti-Soviet French Ambassador in Moscow,
was removed to Madrid. This did not go unnoticed in Germany,
still less the new development in Franco-Russian relations.[2]

Parallel with the Russo-French talks went Russo-Polish talks,
which were also aimed at the conclusion of a non-aggression pact.
These talks, together with similar negotiations between Russia and
her other Western neighbours, were considered in Germany as a
breach of the spirit of Rapallo, though not of course of its letter.[3]
It almost looked as though Russia were choosing a roundabout
way of signing the Versailles Treaty. Thus the prolongation of the
Berlin Treaty in June 1931 was the occasion of much anxious
German enquiry as to the value of Rapallo altogether. Hoetzsch
wrote: ' . . . the Treaty naturally presupposes that Russian
policy does not veer into the line of French policy'.[4] The question
was raised in the most acute form possible by *Germania* of June 18,
1931 in an article 'generally assumed to have had official
inspiration'.[5]

The writer asked: 'Is Russia required to give guarantees that
the talks with France will not lead to a basis for further, more
comprehensive conversations in the East, under Franco-Polish
auspices, which would then inevitably lead to the Eastern Locarno
desired by Poland without Poland fulfilling Germany's conditions

[1] See *Izvestya*, April 5, 1932.
[2] For example, Adolf Grabowsky in *Zeitschrift für Politik*, Heft 4, July, 1931, pp.
229-230: 'That same France, that since Rapallo has wanted to put Germany under
control on account of our supposedly obscure relations with the Soviet Union, would
like to tighten the ring round Germany still more by developing contacts with the
Soviet Union. A Franco-Russian trade treaty and non-aggression pact are in
preparation. Jean Herbette who is strongly anti-Soviet and who was for many years
French Ambassador in Moscow has been transferred to Madrid. . . . France would
like . . . to bring about a Franco-Polish-Soviet Union combination in which Russia
would guarantee the Polish frontiers. . . . '
[3] H. von Dirksen: *Moskau-Tokio-London*, Stuttgart, 1949, p. 97. Dirksen adds
(ibid.) that it was in 1928 that the German Foreign Office was informed of the Russian
intentions re Poland. This date is an obvious error since, although the original
Russian offer to Poland of a non-aggression treaty dates back to 1925, it was not until
1931 that the treaty became practical politics.
[4] *Osteuropa*, Jg. 6, Heft 11, p. 672.
[5] *The Times*, June 20, 1931. *Germania* was the organ of Chancellor Brüning's
Centre Party.

for such an Eastern Locarno, *i.e.* the return of Upper Silesia and the Corridor.' The writer continued with the assertion that Russia had given 'binding assurances' on this point. But without them, he ended ominously, the prolongation of the Berlin Treaty would be 'a song without words'. The whole of the Russo-German relationship 'would lose its meaning'.[1] The *Frankfurter Zeitung* wrote in identical terms: 'Two things must be said—the Berlin Treaty is only of value to Germany if Russian policy *vis-à-vis* Poland and France does not swing into a position where it supports the basic idea of French policy as we encounter it everywhere in Europe, *i.e.* the idea that all international politics only exist in order to perpetuate the decrees of the Versailles Treaty. Secondly, we must add our conviction that in the German view Russian policy had not made any such turnabout nor has it intended to do so.'[2] It is not surprising that *Izvestya's* Berlin correspondent reported to his paper that all news of the Russo-Polish talks was being followed with great anxiety in Germany.[3] It was at last becoming clear that Russian policy was not only fundamentally self-defensive but also quite satisfied with the European *status quo*, whereas German policy was aggressive and revisionist. This contrast had always been in existence but it had always been masked by German weakness and Russian isolation. As these two factors gradually disappeared, the incompatibility of the two Rapallo partners slowly rose to the surface.

For Germany the consequence of all this was the virtual death of Rapallo. Stalin adopted a more cautious attitude—he redefined Rapallo so as to deprive it of its pro-German intent. It now became no more than one example of the non-aggression pacts to which the Soviet Union had recourse in order to normalise its relations with the capitalist world. Rapallo was drained of its pro-German slant and became one non-aggression treaty along with many others. Stalin and Litvinov were not such fools as to desert a German horse that, however strangely it might be behaving at the moment, had at least borne them through almost a

[1] This article is not available in London. Extensive extracts from it are given in *Frankfurter Zeitung* and *The Times*, both of June 20, 1931.

[2] *F.Z.*, June 20, 1931. Two months later the *Frankfurter Zeitung* returned to the point. 'The German standpoint in relation to our Eastern frontiers can only be this: if we do not see any possibility in the forseeable future of revising them, then at least nothing must happen that would make a further settlement difficult or impossible. Our good relationship with Russia would have no value if it did not leave us this door open into the future.' (*F.Z.*, August 28, 1931.)

[3] *Izvestya*, August 27, 1931.

decade of ups and downs, in favour of a Franco-Polish steed of doubtful antecedents and unknown future; or, to change the image, Stalin was not going to buy a Polish pig in a French poke. He had to be absolutely certain that Rapallo was dead before he could drop it entirely. Until then, had Stalin not done so, he might easily have cut off his line of retreat should the new *rapprochement* with France and Poland not come to anything. On the other hand, there would have been no prospect at all of a Western rapprochement had Stalin not dropped the pro-German slant of Rapallo and re-defined the Treaty as a simple Russo-German non-aggression pact.

The characteristic of Soviet policy is its caution. This twilight, intermediate stage of a Russia between Germany and the West lasted almost three years—from the second half of 1931 to the beginning of 1934. It is the exact reverse of the position obtaining in the summer of 1939. In 1939 it was a question for Stalin of considering the possibility of lining up with the West, whilst being prepared, should these efforts fail, to fall back on Germany. In 1931-1934, on the other hand, Stalin hung on to Germany as long as he could until switching over to the Western Powers. The overriding necessity in both cases was to have a *point d'appui* in either of the capitalist camps. Which particular one was of no consequence. It was the principle that counted.

At the end of August 1931 Litvinov came to Berlin to put Curtius *au courant* of the Russo-Polish talks. At the same time he enunciated by implication the new Soviet view of Rapallo, *i.e.*, as an ordinary non-aggression pact. He told a press conference that though Russo-Polish relations were still at the stage they had reached in 1927, he had every hope of putting them on to a friendlier basis. This would bring Poland into line with these other countries that had already signed non-aggression pacts with Russia, such as Germany, Turkey, Lithuania, Persia and Afghanistan.[1] What a fate for the signatories of Rapallo and Berlin to be reduced to the same level as Persia or Afghanistan, let alone Poland!

At the end of the year, Stalin gave an interview to Emil Ludwig, the German best-selling author. At this time it was virtually unprecedented for Stalin to receive visiting literati or newsmen— a fact which did not go unnoticed by Dirksen.[2] This was on December 12, 1931. Ludwig said to Stalin: 'Serious fears have

[1] *Izvestya*, August 30, 1931.
[2] Dirksen, op. cit., p. 119.

recently been expressed by certain German politicians that the traditional policy of friendship between the U.S.S.R. and Germany may be forced into the background. These fears arose as a result of the negotiations between the U.S.S.R. and Poland. Should the present frontiers of Poland be recognised by the U.S.S.R. as a result of these negotiations, it would cause severe disillusionment among the whole of the German people, who have hitherto believed that the U.S.S.R. is opposed to the Versailles system and has no intention of recognising it.'

Stalin replied: 'I know that a certain dissatisfaction and alarm is noticeable among certain German statesmen who fear that the Soviet Union in its negotiations, or in any treaty that may be concluded with Poland, may take some step that would imply that the Soviet Union gives its sanction to, or guarantees the possessions or frontiers of Poland. In my opinion such fears are groundless. We have always declared our willingness to conclude pacts of non-aggression with any government. We have already concluded such pacts with a number of countries. We have openly declared our desire to sign a pact of non-aggression with Poland. As soon as the Poles declared their willingness to start negotiations with us regarding a pact of non-aggression, we naturally consented and began negotiations.

What, from the point of view of the Germans, is the most dangerous thing that might happen? A change of attitude towards the Germans for the worse? But there is no foundation for that. We, like the Poles, must declare in the pact that we shall not resort to force, or aggression in order to change the frontiers of Poland bordering the U.S.S.R., or to violate their independence. Just as we make such a promise to the Poles, so they must make a similar promise to us. Without such a point, namely to the effect that we shall not resort to war in order to violate the independence or the integrity of the frontiers of our respective states, no pact could be concluded. . . . Does that mean recognition of the Versailles system? It does not. Does it mean guaranteeing frontiers? It does not. We never have been guarantors for Poland and never shall be, just as Poland has never been and never will be a guarantor of our frontiers. Our friendly relations with Germany will remain what they have hitherto been. That is my firm conviction.'[1]

---

[1] Stalin: *An interview with the German author Emil Ludwig*, Engl. trans., Moscow, 1932, pp. 13-15.

What is most noteworthy about Stalin's remarks is what they omit to say. They are a model diplomatic statement in seeming to say more than they actually do. As late as June 1931, as shown above, Russia had come out in opposition to the Versailles Treaty, in opposition to 'the exploitation of one country by another'. Only six months later Stalin makes no mention of this. Russia is not recognising the Versailles system, but Russia is also not opposing the Versailles system.

The Russo-Polish non-aggression pact was eventually signed in January 1932 and ratified in July 1932. It was apparently the Russian intention to incorporate in this pact a reference to a guarantee of Poland's frontiers as was the case in respect of Russia's non-aggression treaties with Esthonia, Latvia and Finland. But on German insistence this guarantee was omitted.[1] On the other hand, no formal reservation of this kind could get away from the fact that the treaty *was* signed—even though it 'profoundly worried' the German Foreign Office.[2] In the Reichstag Brüning came in for sharp attacks for the way things were shaping. This was justified for it was Brüning who apparently never even considered ratifying the prolongation of the Berlin Treaty and, in fact, did all he could to hush up the mere fact of prolongation.[3] The Nationalist Freiherr von Freytagh-Loringhoven said to Brüning, the German Chancellor, in the course of a long attack on his policy: 'Since Rapallo and since the Berlin Treaty it was always one of the ideas of German policy that Russia did not belong to our Western neighbours, that Russia formed a sort of counter-balance to them and that, moreover, through Russia Poland was tied down.' But, the speaker went on, in the summer of 1931 came the news of the Franco-Russian talks: 'It was clear that this was a move in the great French game, that Poland was to be drawn

---

[1] H. von Dirksen: *Moskau-Tokio-London*, Stuttgart, 1949, p. 120. The difference between Russia's treaty with Poland and the Treaties with Esthonia and Finland emerges clearly from a comparison between the 1st Article of each. In the case of Finland and Esthonia respectively this runs: 'The High Contracting Parties mutually guarantee the inviolability of the existing frontiers between the Union of Soviet Socialist Republics and the Republic of Finland. . . . ; Each of the High Contracting Parties guarantees to the other party the inviolability of the existing frontiers between them. . . .' The Russo-Polish Pact contains no reference of this kind and its first Article runs: 'The Two Contracting Parties, recording the fact that they have renounced war as an instrument of national policy in their mutual relations, reciprocally undertake to refrain from taking any aggressive action against or invading the territory of the other Party.' (*L.N.T.S.*, Vol. 157, p. 395; Vol. 131, p. 305; Vol. 163, p. 49.)

[2] Dirksen, op. cit., p.119.

[3] Ibid., pp. 115-118.

into this non-aggression pact as an ally of France, and that thereby the French system of double pressure would assert itself—from the west France, from the east Poland. We warned against this at the time.' The immediately following remarks were so offensive that Brüning left the Reichstag.[1] The next day he returned, in part to answer the attack on his policy: 'I cannot agree,' he said, 'with the assumption that the Russo-Polish non-aggression pact will have the effect feared by Herr von Freytagh-Loringhoven. I only need to point out that should Poland attack a Third State, Russia, in accordance with Article II of the Treaty, retains her freedom of action. There is therefore, no reason to bring any change into the German-Russian relationship.' This legalistic defence did not satisfy Freytagh-Loringhoven, and he repeated his attack, terming Brüning's defence an attempt to throw sand in the eyes of the Reichstag: ' . . . it is perfectly clear that the French are setting their pincer system in motion against Germany, and that for this reason Poland must have its Eastern flank free and that it is therefore necessary to bring about a non-aggression pact between Poland and Russia.'[2]

In a brochure published very early in 1933 Seeckt flatly stated that an ambiguous German policy was responsible for Russia's pacts with France and Poland. Russia had been pushed into altering her policy.[3]

When the Russo-Polish pact was signed in July 1932, *Izvestya's* comment went a long way towards justifying the fears of Seeckt and Freytagh-Loringhoven. It actually treated the new Treaty as a Polish 'Rapallo'. The original Rapallo had laid the basis for model relations between Germany and Russia; the new Treaty fulfilled the same function for Poland and Russia.[4]

In the meantime, in April 1932, three separate incidents illustrate the extent of the degeneration of Rapallo. At Geneva there occurred the first clash between the Russian and German delegations to the Disarmament Conference. Proposals advanced by Litvinov for the proportionate reduction of existing armed forces were criticised by Nadolny, the leader of the German delegation, on the grounds that they were based on 'the principle

---

[1] Reichstag Debates, Vol. 446, pp. 2290-2291.
[2] Ibid., pp. 2325 and 2355.
[3] H. von Seeckt: *Deutschland zwischen Ost und West*, Hamburg, 1933, p. 45. This brochure is also notable for its vision of the future: 'Shall Poland advance to the Oder? Such possibilities assume tangible form if we leave Russia out of our calculations' (ibid.).
[4] *Izvestya*, July 30, 1932.

of purely mechanical reduction'.[1] The contrary doctrine enunciated by Nadolny—*i.e.* that of recognising the individual requirements of each state—won universal acceptance with the sole exception of Litvinov who voted against Nadolny's resolution.[2]

Geneva in April 1932 was also the scene of a Litvinov-Brüning clash. On the tenth anniversary of Rapallo, Litvinov suggested to Brüning that a lunch be arranged and speeches exchanged in celebration of the jubilee. Brüning, wishing to soft-pedal the occasion, agreed to the lunch but not to the speeches. In the afternoon Litvinov had his revenge. He summoned the German press representatives in Geneva and held forth in what was considered in Germany an unpleasant manner.[3] He began by the usual mention of the advantages brought by Rapallo to both countries. Then he cleverly developed this theme into an appeal for more 'Rapallo's'. Not only had the Treaty conclusively shown that the Soviet could co-operate with a bourgeois state but it had also acted as one of the pillars of European peace. 'If there were more such pillars, then peace would be more stable. It is therefore to be regretted that the other participants in the Genoa Conference did not conclude a general agreement on the principle of Rapallo.' Litvinov also pointed out that Germany should have no other wish than to be on as friendly terms with the capitalist powers as she was with the Soviet Union.[4]

The same day in Moscow saw yet a further development in the Soviet move away from Germany. On the anniversaries associated with Rapallo it was the usual custom to produce a speech or article that was a re-hash of this theme: Rapallo is an expression of Russia's sympathy for those states suffering from the burdens of the imperialist peace of Versailles, or those states unfairly treated, or those states who find themselves opposed to the prevailing union of capitalist powers. The feature common to all such euphemisms was a distinction, explicit or implicit, between victors and vanquished in the Great War, with Russia favouring the latter. The tune now changed. Only the slightest mention was made of the common interests of Russia and Germany, or of the suffering Germans, or of Russian opposition to Versailles. On the contrary, what received most stress was the

[1] See Minutes of General Commission, Series 'B', Vol. I, pp. 46 and 75.
[2] Ibid., p. 93.
[3] Dirksen, op. cit., pp. 77-78.
[4] *Berliner Tageblatt, Le Temps,* both of April 18, 1932.

L

universal validity of Rapallo, coupled with the assertion that individual arrangements on such a basis could not be expected to last for ever: 'Above all, the historical significance of the Rapallo Treaty lies in its being a model of how it is possible to construct mutual relations between two countries with opposed socio-political systems but with common economic and foreign-political interests *over a given period of time.*' Then followed a quotation from the original resolution of the Central Committee welcoming Rapallo in 1922. The keynote of this resolution was the essentially temporary nature of such arrangements.[1] Later in the article the identity between the Berlin Treaty and the Soviets' other non-aggression pacts was stressed. This was linked to a highly ambiguous reference to the future of the Berlin Treaty itself. 'In its struggle for peace the Soviet Union tries as far as possible to normalise its relations with the individual capitalist countries. To this end it has recourse to bilateral pacts of neutrality and non-aggression. On the tenth anniversary of Rapallo it is worth emphasising that six years ago, on the basis of this Treaty, another Soviet-German agreement was concluded —the so-called Berlin Treaty of Neutrality, *the prolongation of which is at the moment being shaped.*' The only reference to the 'enslavement' of Germany came in the last paragraph—but this was counter-balanced with a plea for the universal application of Rapallo: 'At the present moment, ten years after Rapallo, when the imperialists are once again preparing an intervention against the U.S.S.R. and, by using the world crisis, are once again trying to enslave Germany politically and economically, it is more than ever essential to base the relation between the peoples on the principles of Rapallo.'[2]

At the beginning of June 1932 Papen replaced Brüning as German Chancellor. The new Government was no more relished in Moscow than its predecessor.[3] At Geneva, Boris Stein the secretary of the Russian delegation to the Disarmament Conference told von Weizsäcker, a colleague in the German delegation: 'German-Russian friendship is now at an end.'[4] This extreme distrust of Papen was, it may be assumed, intensified when the latter, at the Lausanne Conference, propounded to Herriot his

---

[1] See above pp.54-5.
[2] *Izvestya*, April 16, 1932. The italics have been added.
[3] Julius Curtius: *Sechs Jahre Minister der deutschen Republik* Heidelberg, 1948, p. 248; Dirksen, op. cit., p. 118.
[4] Weizsäcker, op. cit., p. 99.

plan for a military alliance against the Soviet Union in return for French concessions to Germany. Litvinov later called Papen 'the advocate of a conservative entente between France and Germany, the spearhead of which was to be directed against the Soviet Union'.[1]

The full consequences of this awareness were not immediately drawn. The most glaring example of this is the fact that not until after Hitler's advent to power were the military contacts broken off. Diplomatically, on the other hand, in the second half of 1932 the state of affairs between Russia and Germany went from bad to worse. In private, of course Litvinov continued to assure the German Foreign Office that Russia remained loyal to Rapallo.[2] But actions speak louder than words. At Geneva the clash between Litvinov and Nadolny that had first appeared in April widened in July. This was occasioned by the so-called Benes resolution, an attempt to tabulate progress in the disarmament measures already agreed to. Litvinov and Nadolny were the only two delegates to vote against this resolution. But this superficial agreement concealed fundamental divergence. Litvinov voted against it because the resolution was not sufficiently positive. He tried in vain to strengthen it by inserting a definite provision for a one-third reduction in armaments of all kinds. Nadolny's grounds for rejecting the resolution were just the reverse. He quite categorically stated that this rejection was caused by the lack of any provision for German equality of rights: ' . . . despite its grave objections . . . the German delegation might perhaps have been content with a simple abstention or might even have found it possible to accept the resolution . . . had it recognised the principle without which no result from the Conference would be acceptable to Germany—namely the principle of equality of rights.'[3]

Germany now withdrew from the Conference and was not present when the Bureau met in September. This did not prevent Litvinov from urging that the delegates should nevertheless proceed with the examination of the various disarmament plans already before them.[4] This was not done. As a substitute, informal talks at Geneva, in which Russia did not participate, produced a patched-up formula enabling Germany to return. This was to

[1] See Litvinov's speech of December 29, 1933, quoted pp. 171-2 below.
[2] Dirksen, op. cit., p. 119.
[3] Minutes of General Commission, Series 'B', Vol. I, p. 187, Geneva, 1932, p. 187.
[4] Minutes of the Bureau, Series 'C', Vol. I, IX Disarmament, Geneva, 1935, pp. 8-9.

the effect that one of the principles of the Commission's work would henceforth be to grant to Germany 'equality of rights in a system which would provide security for all nations'. When the full Commission met in December this was noted but no further significant developments took place till February 1933.

In the meantime, the Russian press had used various opportunities to voice the revised Soviet conception of Rapallo. The most noteworthy of these was *Izvestya's* leader on the ratification of the Russo-Polish non-aggression pact, in the course of which it denied that Soviet policy had ever had a pro-German slant. This was a logical development of the interpretation of Rapallo as a common or garden non-aggression pact. The article began by comparing Rapallo and Berlin to the Russian non-aggression treaties with Turkey, Persia, Afghanistan and the more recent ones with Latvia, Lithuania and Esthonia. It went on: 'the signature and ratification of the non-aggression pact with Poland has given rise to rumours in the international bourgeois press of a re-orientation of Soviet foreign policy. These rumours reveal either complete misunderstanding of the basis of the foreign policy of the U.S.S.R. or express the desire to make even non-aggression pacts—these actions in our struggle for peace— a *point de départ* to badger us, a means to strain the relations of some countries with others. Soviet foreign policy was never based on any other "orientation" than on its own strength. . . . We extended our hand and offered a peaceful policy to all states and if some gave us a friendly answer earlier than others, then it is only possible to talk of their re-orientation. The Soviet Union does not require to make any change in its policy. We want to live in peace and to co-operate on a basis of mutual advantage with all states.' This, *Izvestya* stressed, was independent of their structure.[1]

A few days later, when the Russo-French non-aggression pact was signed, the attitude of denying any previous orientation in foreign policy led to this rather artificial argument: 'In the same way as Germany's signature in Locarno of a similar pact did not remove these interests on which were based the friendly relations between the German people and the Soviet Union, the policy of *rapprochement* between France and the Soviet Union must also not harm these relations.'[2]

Intense agitation prevailed in Moscow when it was known that

---

[1] *Izvestya*, November 28, 1932.
[2] Ibid., November 30, 1932.

Hindenburg was planning for Hitler to replace Papen as Chancellor. When Schleicher was appointed instead, the Soviets had
a breathing space.[1] It is this background, perhaps, that accounts
for the complacency of a speech by Molotov on January 23, 1933,
only a week before Hitler's accession to power. The Soviets may
also have been encouraged by the two million drop in the Nazi
vote in November 1932 and by a rise of seven hundred thousand
in the K.P.D. vote, giving the party a hundred deputies for the
first time. Perhaps too, Molotov was hoping for an affirmative
response from a Germany where for all practical purposes Rapallo
had ceased to exist. In any event, the general tone of this speech
remains surprising, even though its references to Germany were
perhaps rather ambiguous. Molotov began by speaking of 'a
substantial strengthening of the international position of the
Soviet Union'. Russia's relations with foreign powers 'have, as a
rule, developed perfectly normally, despite changes in the governments of various countries'. Germany was mentioned as occupying
'a special place in these inter-relationships'. He then seemed to
qualify this remark with a differentiation between Russia's
economic and Russia's diplomatic relations with Germany: 'of
all the countries with which we have diplomatic relations, it is
with Germany that we have had and continue to have the firmest
economic ties. And this is not accidental. It flows from the
interests of both countries.' This was the only reference to Germany. The rest of the speech was devoted to self-congratulation
on the successes achieved by the Soviets' peace policy. This was
evidenced in the whole series of non-aggression pacts. Several
gaps still remained to be filled, however. Rumania had not
signed at all. France had not yet ratified, and the U.S.A. and
Czechoslovakia had not even recognised the U.S.S.R.[2]

A week after this speech Hitler came into power in Germany.
There was no change in Russian policy, merely a different
emphasis. As before the Soviets continued to hope that it would
be possible to re-invigorate Rapallo; as before they continued with
their efforts to re-insure themselves against its possible demise.
They continued to hold out a fraternal hand to Hitler while
trying to join the Franco-Polish security system. These two
policies were incompatible—a fact which was not unknown to
the Soviets as the Stalin-Ludwig interview shows.[3] But Stalin

[1] Dirksen, op. cit., p. 118.
[2] Vlast Sovietov (The Power of the Soviets), No. 4, February 10, 1933, pp. 4-5.
[3] See also Dirksen, op. cit., p. 119.

had no choice. Until he knew which policy would give him what he wanted, he had no alternative but to try at one and the same time to run with the hare and hunt with the hounds. During this awkward transitional period, the fiction of no pro-German orientation was maintained. The pretence was maintained that all Russia wanted to do was to live in amity with all nations. In actual fact the Russian need was to find a *point d'appui* amongst the Western capitalist powers, should the German *point d'appui* give way.

The first awareness of this need made itself felt in the second half of 1931. Not until some three years later was the die unequivocally cast in favour of the West. What prolonged this waiting period was Hitler's attempt at a *détente* with Russia. It did not impress the Soviets much but it must have undoubtedly contributed to Stalin's caution. Hitler's problems were different from Stalin's. Far from wishing to stabilise the European situation the German problem, as the Nuremberg documents reveal, was to decide whom to attack and when. To this end Hitler needed to keep the situation as fluid as possible with the important exception of Polish-German relations. Until these were settled by the German-Polish non-aggression pact of January 1934, Hitler maintained that his fight against Communism at home need not interfere with his desire for friendly relations with Russia. But by January 1934, when the Polish Pact safeguarded the German rear, Hitler could proceed with the revision of Versailles under a gigantic smoke-screen of anti-Bolshevism at home and abroad.

But in 1933 Stalin did not see the pattern of future events so clearly. For a whole year he said not a word on foreign policy. He was waiting to see which way the cat would jump. In the meantime, lesser figures such as Litvinov, Molotov and Radek had their say. The shape of their remarks produced a pattern that corresponded to the line taken prior to Hitler, *i.e.* it was up to Germany to choose. If she genuinely chose the former path of Russo-German collaboration, then Russia desired nothing better. If, on the other hand, Germany chose hostility, Russia would line up with the Versailles Powers.

While the Soviets waited for the German response and in order that they should not take any more chances than necessary, they devoted the interval to attempts at stabilising the European situation, especially in Eastern Europe. Germany was able to participate in these arrangements or not. If she did, *tant mieux*. If not, then she would brand herself as the breaker of the peace. Whether the Soviets expected that it would be possible for Germany to work with them on these terms is an open question. All that can be said is that the attempt was made. Perhaps the most likely explanation is that the Soviets' aim was to put Germany in as awkward a position as possible.

During 1933 the terms required by the Soviet Union became progressively higher. Less than a fortnight after Molotov's speech and a week after the Nazi advent to power Litvinov made a careful speech at the Disarmament Conference at Geneva in which he broke more decisively than ever before with his previous pro-German and anti-French policy. The speech focussed, aptly enough, on the security question. Litvinov stated that he remained as convinced as ever 'that the best if not the only guarantee of security for all nations would be total disarmament, or at least the utmost possible reduction of armaments in the shortest possible period. . . . '

'But apparently there is no escape from this problem [of security] if only because it has been raised by a great and powerful state, whose representatives have declared that until it is solved they cannot undertake any obligation with regard to the reduction of armaments. If therefore we want to advance . . . we shall have to consider with all seriousness the French proposals and make up our minds whether there is any possibility of reaching an international agreement based upon these and other proposals which may be made on security by other delegations, proceeding subsequently to questions of disarmament.'[1]

The next day Litvinov introduced a convention for the definition of aggression. This was hailed by *Izvestya* as a charter of the rights of peoples to security and independence. It left the door open for frontier revision but only by peaceful means—'for any frontier changes by violence only create the causes of new wars'. This whole article breathed an unusual respect for international agreements.[2]

Hitler, meanwhile, was at pains to assure Russia that her fears of a re-orientation of German policy were unjustified. For his first year of power he was feeling his way forward, without

[1] Records of the Conference for the Reduction and Limitation of Armaments, Series 'B'—Minutes of the General Commission, Vol. II, Geneva, 1933, p. 235.
[2] *Izvestya*, February 8, 1933.

committing himself either in the East or in the West. He required for the moment to retain his liberty of action. He accordingly tried to lull Russian suspicions of his intentions. His only anti-Russian outburst as distinct from anti-Bolshevik outburst was on March 2, 1933.[1] This at once drew violent Russian protests.[2]

Henceforth Hitler insisted that his campaign for the crushing of the K.P.D. must be separated from foreign policy. The first must not be taken to imply any influence on the second. On March 23, he said: 'The Government of the Reich are ready to cultivate with the Soviet Union friendly relations profitable to both parties. It is above all the Government of the National Revolution who feel themselves in a position to adopt such a policy with regard to Soviet Russia. The fight against Communism in Germany is our internal affair in which we will never permit interference from outside. Our political relations with other powers to whom we are bound by common interests will not be affected thereby'.[3] This was echoed by such representative Nazi figures as Goering, Papen and Alfred Rosenberg.[4]

None of this disarmed Russian suspicions. *Izvestya* replied to Hitler's speech of March 23, with the comment that the Soviets did not think the speech would 'clear the path for good-neighbourly relations'. The value of French friendship was also emphasised.[5]

In the middle of March, Khinchuk was recalled from Berlin to Moscow for consultations.[6] Their purport is unknown. Presumably they were concerned with the German situation. On April 28, Khinchuk was received by Hitler for the first time. He was informed that the Reich was fully aware of its community of interests with Russia.[7] In conformity with this, Hitler authorised that the redemption of various Soviet bills falling due in March and April 1933 be deferred until a date more convenient to the Soviets.[8] A week later he ratified the prolongation of the Berlin Treaty and the Conciliation Convention—outstanding since 1931. This action was accompanied by an official communiqué stating that it was in the interests of both countries.[9]

[1] *Hitler's Speeches*, Vol. I, ed. N. H. Baynes, London, 1942, pp. 257-258.
[2] See *Izvestya*, March 4 and 9, 1933.
[3] Baynes, op. cit., Vol. II, p. 1019.
[4] For Goering, see *F.Z.*, March 21, 1933; for Papen *The Evening Standard*, May 6, 1933; for Rosenberg *Le Temps*, November 1, 1933.
[5] *Izvestya*, March 28, 1933.
[6] *The Times*, March 18, 1933.
[7] *Völkischer Beobachter*, May 7-8, 1933.
[8] Dirksen, op. cit., p. 122.
[9] *D.A.Z.*, May 6, 1933.

This also cut no ice with the Russians. *Izvestya* commented: 'Whilst welcoming the prolongation of the Berlin Treaty, Soviet public opinion fully realises that treaties have that meaning with which the concrete practical activity of the contracting parties endows them.'[1]

Hugenberg's action at the World Economic Conference in London was too indicative of Nazi 'concrete practical activity' to allow the Soviets to take seriously Hitler's protestations of friendship: for Hugenberg, German Minister of Economics, produced memoranda demanding Germany's right to expand into the Ukraine. *Izvestya*, in its reply to this, said that 'the popular masses of the Soviet Union will see in the circles responsible for these memoranda, their immediate enemy'.[2]

A further Russian reply was made at the Economic Conference itself. It was less direct but had the same anti-German connotation. Litvinov, the chief Soviet delegate, prevailed on the signatories of the Litvinov Protocol of 1929 to sign a multi-lateral Treaty of Non-aggression. This ultimately embraced the U.S.S.R. the Baltic States, Poland, Finland, Rumania, Jugoslavia, Czechoslovakia and Turkey. Germany, Radek emphasised, was also free to join in this arrangement and thereby show her wish to abstain from adventures *à la* Rosenberg.[3]

During the rest of 1933 this sort of tenuous long-range contact continued at intervals. The Nazis, except for occasional outbursts, tried to convince the Russians of their peaceable intentions whilst the Russians refused to take these professions at their face value. Under these circumstances, the mutual expulsion of press correspondents at the end of the year—they were later readmitted—and German measures against Derop, the organisation selling Russian fuel throughout Germany, were obviously minor matters. They were enormously overshadowed by the fact that the author of *Mein Kampf* was in power in Germany.

The Soviets knew as little as anyone else how much of the *Mein Kampf* programme Hitler would try to achieve. Some of their measures to guard against the possibility of its remaining in force have already been mentioned. To these were added on the Soviet initiative the dissolution of the Reichswehr—Red Army contacts.[4] Ideological preparation on the same lines went hand

[1] *Izvestya*, May 6, 1933.
[2] Ibid., June 20, 1933.
[3] Ibid., August 6, 1933.
[4] Dirksen, op. cit., pp. 124-125.

in hand with the various political measures. A lot of words now had to be eaten. The Soviets had to revise their views of the many Western institutions they had hitherto reviled and decried, as soon as it was seen how these institutions might serve *their* purposes and not those of their enemies. Foremost amongst such institutions were Poland, the Peace of Versailles and the League of Nations. If Paris was worth a Mass. . . .

Litvinov at Geneva had already called France 'a great and powerful state.' Radek now proceeded to sing the praises of Poland, the one-time vassal of one-time French imperialism. 'The Soviet Union', he wrote, 'not only has no aggressive intentions of any kind towards Poland but, on the contrary, welcomes the re-emergence of an independent Poland as one of the progressive facts created by the world war in Central Europe, independently of the will of its organisers'.[1] Versailles came in for similar re-habilitation. 'The Peace of Versailles may not be a basis for good relations between the peoples but that peace which would be imposed on humanity by the victorious fascist Vikings would certainly be even worse than the present position. Besides, it would cost humanity a war.'[2] On the heels of Poland and Versailles, there followed the League of Nations. In muted tones Stalin sang the praises of what Lenin had once called 'a den of robbers'. On December 25th, 1933, he was asked this question by Walter Duranty, the American journalist: 'Is your attitude towards the League of Nations a negative one always and under all circumstances?' 'No', answered Stalin patiently, 'I do not think you quite understand our viewpoint. Despite the German and Japanese exit from the League, or perhaps because of it—the League may well become a brake to retard or hamper military action. If that is so, if the League is even the tiniest bump somewhat to slow down the drive towards war and help peace, then we are not against the League. Yes, if such will be the course of historical events, it is not excluded that we shall support the League despite its colossal deficiencies.'[3] After this it is not surprising that even Churchill—on account of his opposition to German revisionism—began to get a good press in Russia.[4]

[1] *Izvestya*, August 29, 1933.
[2] Ibid., August 9, 1933.
[3] Stalin, Molotov, Litvinov: *Our Foreign Policy*, Engl. trans., Moscow and Leningrad, 1934, p. 9.
[4] *Izvestya* for example (March 30, 1933) in its report of a House of Commons debate contrasted Churchill very favourably with Macdonald in view of their respective attitudes to treaty revision.

At the same time as these declarations were being made, Radek was also making it clear that the swing in Russian policy was involuntary and forced on her by Germany. To this end he twice quoted the brochure *Deutschland Zwischen Ost und West* of his old friend von Seeckt. In March, in an article in *Izvestya* entitled 'Where is Germany Going?' he quoted with approval Seeckt's view that only Germany bore the responsibility for Russia's change of front. Two months later Radek again referred to Seeckt's view that Germany would never succeed, in the last resort, in playing off Britain against France. In the long run the two countries would stick together in opposition to Germany.[1]

The German position formed the burden of the speeches delivered at the end of 1933 and the beginning of 1934 by Molotov, Litvinov and Stalin. All spoke in substantially the same terms: although Russia wished to continue on a friendly basis with Germany, she could not ignore these changes in German policy which made this aspiration increasingly unrealisable. This was Molotov's *leitmotiv* on December 28.[2] The next day Litvinov dwelt at greater length on the same theme. Over the past year, he said, Russo-German relations had become 'unrecognisable'. But he did not automatically exclude the possibility of their rehabilitation. In the name of Bolshevik realism he went on to wash his hands of the German Marxists, now getting their first taste of Nazi concentration camps.

'Of course we have our opinion of the German régime, of course we sympathise with the sufferings of our German comrades but we Marxists are the last people who can be reproached for allowing our feelings to prevail over our policy. The whole world knows that we can and do maintain good relations with capitalist

[1] *Izvestya*, March 22 and May 18, 1933. Seeckt's pamphlet seems to have made something of a stir at the time. Apart from Radek's two references, M. Zaretzki quotes it as evidence of continuing German friendship for Russia in a paper read to the Moscow Institute of World Economics and World Politics in May 1933 (See *Krizis, Fashizm i Ugroza Voini* (*Crisis, Fascism and the Threat of War*), Moscow, 1933, p. 43, n.l.). It is also referred to favourably by *Die Deutsche Tageszeitung* quoted in *Le Temps*, March 1, 1933. In *Osteuropa* (Jg. 8, Heft 8, pp. 482-483) Hoetzsch includes a reference to the brochure in a quotation from a work by General von Neidermayer, entitled *Wehrgeographische Betrachtung der Sowjetunion* (*Military-geographical reflections on the Soviet Union*). 'Germany cannot but welcome and further the peaceful reconstruction of the gigantic empire to her east for the reasons so pointedly outlined by General von Seeckt in his latest brochure *Germany Between East and West*. Russia needs our political and technical help for her internal reconstruction in the same way as we need her help and friendship in the struggle against Versailles.'

[2] This speech is contained in Molotov's: *V Borbe za Sotsializm* (*In the Struggle for Socialism*), Moscow, 1935, pp. 484 ff.

states of any régime, including the Fascist. This is not the point. We do not interfere in the internal affairs of Germany, nor in those of other countries, and our relations with her are determined not by her internal but by her external policy.' He ended by saying that 'we desire to have with Germany, as with other states, the best of relations. Nothing but good can result from such relations both for the Soviet Union and for Germany.'[1]

In Stalin's speech to the 17th Party Congress all the themes dominating Soviet foreign policy in the previous two and a half years were recapitulated and developed—the Soviet struggle for peace as evidenced in the Russian non-aggression pacts, the *rapprochement* with France and Poland partly on account of 'the growth of revanchist and imperialist moods in Germany', the lack of any orientation for or against Versailles, and the absence of any reluctance to let the issue of fascism interfere with a possible Russo-German reconciliation. He ended with the customary reiteration of the Soviets' peace policy and of their readiness to defend themselves if necessary—'those who try to attack our country will receive a stunning rebuff to teach them not to poke their pig's snout into our Soviet garden again'.[2]

It is difficult to see on what basis the reconciliation between Soviet Russia and Nazi Germany, as desired by Stalin, Litvinov and Molotov, could have taken place. But in actual fact, the question never arose. On the contrary, not only did the Nazis cold-shoulder all the Russian approaches but their first diplomatic step of any consequence was the most anti-Russian act conceivable: the German-Polish declaration of non-aggression, announced in January 1934. In the same way as Russo-Polish amity was a blow to Germany, German-Polish amity was a blow to Russia. In the latter case it acted as a lever in German hands to break up any Russian-inspired stabilisation in Eastern Europe. It also enabled the Nazis to prevent Russia using Poland as a bridge over which to cross into the Western camp, and, finally, it brought the danger of aggression to the very borders of the Soviet Union, for the Nazis encouraged Polish designs on the Ukraine. As far as Poland was concerned, the move signified a far more definite change in her policy *vis-à-vis* Germany, than her non-aggression treaty had signified *vis-à-vis* Russia.

---

[1] M. Litvinov: *Vneshnaya Politika S.S.S.R.* (*The Foreign Policy of the U.S.S.R.*), Moscow, 1935, pp. 66 ff.
[2] J. Stalin: *Report on the Soviet Union*, Engl. trans., London, 1934, pp.14-18.

The wisdom of this Nazi move was shown on each occasion that Litvinov made desperate efforts to freeze the *status quo* in Eastern Europe. In one way or another, these amounted to four, over a period of less than a year. At the end of 1933 Litvinov proposed to Warsaw that she join Russia in a joint guarantee of the integrity of the Baltic states. To this Poland agreed on condition that the Baltic states were unanimous in accepting the offer. But Finland refused after 'unambiguous and definite declarations' by Germany.[1] The next attempt was made in March 1934. Litvinov proposed to Nadolny, the new German Ambassador in Moscow that Russia and Germany pledge themselves to respect the independence and integrity of the Baltic States. This was rejected by Germany.[2] *Izvestya* commented: 'The whole world will remember that the U.S.S.R. put forward a concrete method to create a healthier atmosphere in Eastern Europe and that Germany rejected this method.'[3] In April and May, Litvinov then took the unusual step of securing the premature renewal of the Russian non-aggression pacts with Poland and the Baltic States. (They were not due to expire until 1935.)

In Germany meanwhile, there was in practice remarkably little active opposition to the end of Rapallo. Some leading Nazis would apparently have preferred a Russian pact to a Polish pact;[4] and the views of such generals as Seeckt and Niedermayer ran on the same lines.[5] Nevertheless, such opposition as there was came to a head in June 1934. In that month Nadolny, who had only been German Ambassador in Moscow a little over six months, since his appointment at the end of 1933, resigned from his post after quarrelling over Eastern policy with Hitler and Neurath.[6] On June 30, 1934—'the night of the long knives'— a situation arose which was described by Hitler as follows: 'I had gained the impression that by certain unscrupulous elements a Nationalist-Bolshevist rising was being prepared which could only bring untold misery upon Germany.'[7] The most notable casualties

[1] *Osteuropa*, Jg. 9, Heft 5, pp. 299-301.
[2] See the Tass communiqué in *Izvestya*, April 27, 1934.
[3] *Izvestya*, Apri 28, 1934.
[4] H. Rauschning: *Germany's Revolution of Destruction*, London, 1939, pp. 272-273.
[5] See above pp. 171.
[6] Erich Kordt: *Wahn und Wirklichkeit*, Stuttgart, 1947, pp. 63-64. Dodd, the U.S. Ambassador in Berlin, states that Nadolny was dismissed following a dispute over a projected Russo-German commercial treaty (*Ambassador Dodd's Diary*, London, 1941, p. 132). In neither case is the significance of Nadolny's departure, whether dismissal or resignation, at all questioned.
[7] Baynes, op. cit., Vol. I, p. 315.

of the resultant shootings were Schleicher and his wife, killed on their own doorstep. This was the consequence of a quarrel with Hitler over Rapallo.[1] Other notable victims were the leaders of the S.A. and left-wing, anti-capitalist section of the Nazis—Röhm and Gregor Strasser. Lieutenant Scheringer, who was dismissed from the Reichswehr in 1930 for spreading Nazi propaganda and then joined the K.P.D. was another victim. He too, was in contact with the S.A. hoping to capitalise their disillusionment in Hitler's socialist claims for communist purposes.[2]

This was the moment Moscow had been waiting for. From its inception in 1930, the internal German political crisis was followed as attentively in Russia as were the changes in German foreign policy. It was consistently argued that any Nazi seizure of power would be essentially ephemeral. It would only lead to a rapid polarisation of political forces whereby the Social-Democratic masses under the combined pressure of Nazis and communists would lose their reformist illusions. They would flock to the K.P.D. and the victory of the counter-revolution would be transformed into its antithesis—the victory of the revolution. Thus, the events of June 30, 1934, when Hitler suppressed the Nazi left-wing, were interpreted in Moscow as the culminating point of the class-struggle in Germany. The Nazi régime had at last thrown off its pseudo-socialist mask and stood revealed in all its nakedness as a military dictatorship by the forces of capital. No further illusions could now prevent the workers from rallying to the Communists and turning defeat into victory.

This attitude towards the Nazis is equivalent to saying that a defeat is a victory, or that it at least contains within itself the seeds of victory. The first occasion, apparently, when this theory was put

---

[1] *Les Relations Polono-Allemandes et Polono-Soviétiques 1933-1939*, Receuil de Documents Officiels, Paris, 1940, pp. 45, 47, 51, 60 and 246.

[2] See the last letter written by Scheringer before his death, quoted in *The Manchester Guardian*, July 20, 1934. The whole episode of 'The night of the long knives' has been summed up by Johannes Wüsten, a student of the German working-class movement who was in Germany at the time, as follows: Röhm, the S.A. chief, was to become Minister of War as the result of an armed rising by his supporters. 'Röhm would have signified an Eastern policy, *i.e.* the attempt would have been made to continue the former policy of *rapprochement* with Russia. The first active conflicts took place in April 1934. Probably a wave of disintegration was to precede the actual rising. This had been the acknowledged method of recent years. What happened next was reported correctly abroad, as far as dates were concerned and only one thing was surprising. The list of those shot was so confused as to appear the work of personal revenge which it was only in part. For on June 30, all who were at that time well known and influential advocates of an Eastern orientation were liquidated.' (*Mass und Wert*, May and June, Heft 5, Zurich, 1939, pp. 616-617.)

forward, was in a pamphlet by Paul Levi discussing the history of
the Bavarian Soviet Republic of 1919. Commenting on the Reichwehr's invasion and the overthrow of Eisner and his colleagues,
he wrote: 'even the victorious counter-revolution and the military
dictatorship are a progress in revolution; they bring the class
conflict clearly and sharply to light. . . . '[1] In Lenin's interpretation of Kapp as a German Kornilov, the same attitude is
implicit. In the same way as Kornilov opened the eyes of the
Russian masses to the real nature of the old régime, would Kapp
similarly cause the scales to fall from the eyes of the German
masses.

This accounts for the extraordinary complacency with which
the rise of Hitler was viewed. It also accounts, to some extent,
for the communist attacks on the Social-Democrats and the consistent refusal to form any sort of United Front. Had they done
so, they would have reinforced reformist illusions. This did not
prevent, however, each step on the Nazi road to power being
accurately charted, even though the wrong conclusion was almost
invariably drawn.

From the angle of analysis, a good start was made. On the
morning of September 14, 1930—the fateful day when the number
of Nazi Reichstag Deputies leaped from 13 to 105, *Izvestya* wrote:
'The elections of September 14 are not only the next elections.
In the consciousness of the bourgeoisie they are also the turning
point in the post-war development of Germany. Their result will
not decide anything but will only accelerate the ripening of the
crisis.'[2]

During the year following, Brüning was only able to rule with
the aid of emergency decrees. He also came under increasingly
sharp Nazi attacks. The opposition to Brüning came to a head
on October 11, 1931, when the 'Harzburg front' of Nazis,
Nationalists and Stahlhelm, a reactionary organisation of ex-
servicemen, was formed to co-ordinate the activities of all Brüning's
right-wing opponents. On that same day Radek wrote: 'The
struggle of the Brüning Government with Hitler and Hugenberg
is not the struggle of bourgeois democracy against fascism but a
struggle between different methods of creating a fascist Germany. . . . '[3]

---

[1] P. Werner (*i.e.* Paul Levi): *Die Bayrische Räte-Republik*, Leipzig, 1920, p. 64.
[2] *Izvestya*, September 14, 1930.
[3] Ibid., October 11, 1931.

From now on the possibility of Nazi participation in the Government was reckoned with. Each time it was maintained that Hitler would lack the mass basis required for strong government. If he tried to secure this mass basis through naked terror, he would drive the working class into the Communist ranks. Thus, ' . . if the National-Socialists do take part in the government then it will soon become clear that they do not in any way dispose of the means to free Germany from the noose [of reparations.] Government by Hitler would be a government of open fascism and of an even intensified dictatorship of finance capital. A Hitlerite government would sharpen to an unprecedented degree the German internal position and as a result the Hitlerites would not be in the position, even if they wanted to, to oppose French imperialism.'[1]

The next elections took place at the end of July 1932. Their effect was to confirm Papen in the power with which President Hindenberg had vested him in May of the same year. The Nazi vote reached 230. For the moment Hitler, despite this tremendous accession of power, remained outside the government. Nevertheless, Radek felt able to write that if he did achieve power his Nazi movement would never be broad enough to serve as the political basis for the rule of German monopoly capital. If Hitler tried to rule through naked terror, he would only weaken his position. ' . . . Such a policy will only thrust the Social-Democratic masses into the Communist camp.'[2]

Finally there came the elections of March 1933. Despite the Nazi terror, there was still scope for political opposition. The Nazi votes numbered seventeen and a quarter million, those of the K.P.D. nearly five million. These five million votes were termed by Radek 'a brilliant victory,' 'a Marne defeat' of the fascists. 'The failure of the fascists to break the compactness of the Communist masses strengthens the tendency amongst the Social-Democratic workers towards a united front with the leading portion of the working class. This means that the fascists will have to go over to a regular siege, to trench warfare against the working class. Time is now the decisive factor and time is not on the side of the fascists but on the side of the Communist party, for every month of fascist policy will inevitably strengthen centrifugal tendencies in the petty-bourgeoisie, to whom the fascists can offer

[1] *Izvestya*, December 29, 1931.
[2] Ibid., August 2, 1932.

nothing, and will continue to increase the friction inside the fascist bloc itself.'[1]

From then on comments on internal German developments were absent from the Soviet press. In the publications of the Comintern, the same optimism continued to prevail, and on several occasions, the K.P.D. was congratulated on the loyalty with which it had fulfilled the directives of the Comintern. This was the situation when there came the shootings of June 30, 1934. At long last the wait was over ! At long last the moment had come when the pseudo-socialist mask of Nazism was thrown aside to reveal the reality of terror ! At long last the K.P.D., now underground, would claim its inheritance of victory. Radek wrote: 'This is the crisis in Fascism. . . . The German fascist government is destroying its mass petty-bourgeois basis.

All this is taking place because outside the party there are ten million German workers who have not capitulated before fascism.

Fascism has not been able to guarantee the stability of the bourgeois régime even by unleashing a wave of terror against the working class. Still less will it be able to achieve this aim by using terror against its own petty-bourgeois basis. The tempo of Germany's historical development has shown itself to be quicker than might have been anticipated.'[2]

The absurd optimism of the Comintern would be incomprehensible were it not for the widespread belief in Germany that the Nazi power would be no longer lasting than its predecessors. Brüning lasted two years, Papen six months, Schleicher a bare two months. Who could say that Hitler would have a longer life ? In actual fact, of course, the events of June 30, 1934 proved to be insignificant. Though it seems likely that there actually was some sort of conspiracy by elements favourable to Russia, it had not the slightest resemblance to the evolution expected in Moscow.

As a result it was the Nazis with whom Litvinov had again to deal. His last attempt to draw them into a plan to stabilise the European situation was made in conjunction with France. The vehicle was the so-called Eastern Security Pact. It provided for Russia, Germany, Poland, Czechoslovakia and the Baltic States to enter into an agreement for consultation and mutual assistance. Russia and France were further to enter respectively the Locarno

---

[1] *Izvestya*, March 7, 1933.
[2] Ibid., July 2, 1934.   Other Soviet press comment to the same effect is quoted in *New York Times* and *Le Temps* both of July 3, 1934.

M

Treaty of 1925 and the new Eastern Pact as additional guarantors. But in September 1934 Germany rejected the plan and a little later Poland did likewise. In that same September, Germany finally left the League and Russia entered it. The ways of the two Rapallo partners had definitely parted. They were not to meet again until 1939.

BIBLIOGRAPHY

I. Autobiographies, Biographies, Diaries, Memoirs, etc.

Bajanov, Boris: *Stalin—der rote Diktator*, Berlin, 1931.

Bauer, Col. Max: *Das Land der roten Zaren*, Hamburg, 1925.

Berndorff, H. R.: *General Zwischen Ost und West*, Hamburg, 1951.

Bernstorff, Count: *The Memoirs of Count Bernstorff*, Engl. trans., London, 1936.

Bessedovsky, Gregoire: *Oui, j'accuse*, Paris, 1930.

Bisschof, Major J.: *Die Letzte Front*, Leipzig, 1935.

Blücher, Wipert von: *Deutschlands Weg nach Rapallo*, Wiesbaden, 1951.

Buckrucker, Major: *Im Schatten Seeckts*, Berlin, 1928.

Curtius, Julius: *Sechs Jahre Minister der deutschen Republik*, Heidelberg, 1947.

D'Abernon, Lord: *An Ambassador of Peace*, London, 1929-1930.

D'Abernon, Lord: *The Eighteenth Decisive Battle of the World*, London, 1931.

Dirksen, H. von: *Moskau-Tokio-London*, Stuttgart, 1949.

Dodd: *Ambassador Dodd's Diary*, London, 1941.

Fischer, Louis: *Men and Politics*, London, 1941.

Fischer, Ruth: *Stalin and German Communism*, Harvard, 1948.

Goltz, R. von der: *Als Politischer General im Osten*, Leipzig, 1936.

Helfferich, K.: *Der Weltkrieg*, Vol. III, Berlin, 1919.

Just, A. W.: *The Red Army*, Engl. trans., London, 1936.

Kessler, Harry: *Walter Rathenau—His Life and Work*, Engl. trans., London, 1929.

Kordt, Erich: *Wahn und Wirklichkeit*, Stuttgart, 1947.

Krassin, Lyubov: *Leonid Krassin*, London, 1929.

Laukhard, Peter: (*i.e.* Edgar Stern-Rubarth): *Brockdorff-Rantzau Contra Versailles*, Berlin, 1935.

Lüttwitz, Gen.: *Im Kampf gegen die November-Revolution*, Berlin, 1934.

Morgan, J. H.: *Assize of Arms*, London, 1945.

Nollet, Gen.: *Une Expérience de Désarmement*, Paris, 1932.

Okay, Kurt: *Enver Pasha—der grosse Freund Deutschlands*, Leipzig, 1935.

Pope, A. U.: *Maxim Litvinoff*, New York, 1943.

Rabenau, F. von: *Seeckt—Aus Seinem Leben 1918-1936*, Leipzig, 1940.

Raphael, Gaston: *Le Roi de la Ruhr—Hugo Stinnes*, Paris, 1924.

Rathenau, Walter: *Politische Briefe*, Dresden, 1929.

Rauschning, H.: *Germany's Revolution of Destruction*, London, 1939.

Reynolds, E. E.: *Nansen*, Penguin ed., London, 1949.

Schmidt-Pauli, Gen. von: *Seeckt*, Berlin, 1937.

Sender, Toni: *The Autobiography of a German Rebel*, London, 1940.

Stein, Ludwig: *Aus dem Leben eines Optimisten*, Berlin, 1930.

Stern-Rubarth, Edgar: *Graf Brockdorff-Rantzau*, Berlin, 1929.

Stresemann, G.: *Vermächtnis*, Vol. II, Berlin, 1932.
Stresemann, G.: *Diaries, Letters and Papers*, Engl. trans., London, 1935-1940.
Thyssen, F.: *I Paid Hitler*, London, 1941.
Troeltsch, E.: *Spektator-Briefe*, Tübingen, 1924.
Trotsky, L. *Stalin*, London, 1947.
Vallentin, A.: *Gustav Stresemann*, Engl. trans., London, 1931.
Weizsäcker, E. von: *Erinnerungen*, Munich, 1950.

II. ARTICLES, PAMPHLETS, SPEECHES, ETC.

Chicherin, G. V.: *An die deutschen Arbeiter*, Moscow, 1919.
Chicherin, G. V.: *Vnyeshnyaya Politika Sovetskoi Rossii za dva goda*, Moscow, 1920.
Chicherin, G. V.: *The Foreign Policy of Soviet Russia—Report of Narkomindel to 7th All-Russian Congress of Soviets*, Engl. trans., London, 1920.
Baynes, ed: *Hitler's Speeches*, London, 1942.
Joffe, A.: *Ot Genui do Gaagi*, Moscow, 1923.
Kuusinen, O., etc.: *The Errors of Trotskyism*, Engl. trans., London, 1925.
Lenin, V. I.: *Sochineniya*, Vols. 23, 25, 26, 27, ed. Adoratski, etc., 3rd ed., Moscow, 1935.
Lenin, V. I.: *Left-Wing Communism—An Infantile Disease*, Engl. trans., London, 1947.
Litvinov, M.: *Mirnaya Politika Sovietov*, Moscow, 1929.
Litvinov, M.: *Vnyeshnyaya Politika SSSR*, Moscow, 1935.
Luxemburg, Rosa: *Die Russische Revolution*, ed. Paul Levi, Berlin, 1922.
Maisky, I.: *Vnyeshnyaya Politika R.S.F.R.S. 1917-1922*, Moscow, 1922.
Molotov, V. M.: *V Borbe za Sotzializm*, Moscow, 1935.
Radek, K.:*Die Russische und die Deutsche Revolution und die Weltlage*, Berlin, 1919.
Radek, K.: *Zur Taktik des Kommunismus*, Berlin, December, 1919.
Radek, K.: *Die Auswärtige Politik des deutschen Kommunismus und der Hamburger National-Bolschewismus*, Berlin, 1919.
Radek, K.: *Die Auswärtige Politik Sowjetrussland*, Hamburg, 1921.
Radek, K.: *Deutschland und Russland*, Berlin, 1920.
Radek, K.: *The Winding Up of the Versailles Treaty—Report to the Fourth Congress of the Communist International*, Engl. trans., Hamburg, 1922.
Radek, K.: *The International Outlook—Radek's Report to E.C.C.I. at the 6th Session June 15, 1923*, Engl. trans., London, 1923.
Radek, K. and others: *Leo Schlageter—Kommunismus und Nationale Bewegung*, 3rd ed., Berlin, 1923.
Rakovsky, Kh.: *Liga Natsii i SSSR*, Moscow, 1926.
Rathenau, Walter: *Gesammelte Reden*, Berlin, 1924.
Reventlow, Graf E.: *Völkisch-Kommunistische Einigung?*, Leipzig, 1924.
Seeckt, Gen. H. von: *Deutschland zwischen Ost und West*, Hamburg, 1933.
Stalin, J.: *Leninism*, Engl. trans., London, 1928.

Stalin, J.: *An Interview with the German author Emil Ludwig*, Engl. trans., Moscow, 1932.

Stalin, J.: *Report on the Soviet Union—Speech to the 17th Congress*, Engl. trans., London, 1934.

Stalin, Molotov, Litvinov: *Our Foreign Policy*, Engl. trans., Moscow, 1934.

Stalin: *Sochineniya*, Vol. 5, Moscow, 1947.

Stresemann, G.: *Essays and Speeches on various subjects*, Engl. trans., London, 1930.

Werner, P. (*i.e.* Paul Levi): *Die Bayrische Räte-Republik*, Leipzig, 1920.

Zaretski, M. and others: *Krizis, Fashizm i Ugroza Voini*, Moscow, 1933.

Zinoviev, G. and others: *Die Lehren der deutschen Ereignisse*, Hamburg, 1924.

III. DOCUMENTS, DESPATCHES, DEBATES, ETC.

1. BRITISH

Cmd. 1614 ⎫
Cmd. 1621 ⎬ 1922
Cmd. 1667 ⎭

Documents on British Foreign Policy, ed. Woodward and Butler:

    1st Series, Vol. 1, 1947
    1st Series, Vol. 2, 1948
    1st Series, Vol. 3, 1949
    2nd Series, Vol. 1, 1946

House of Commons Debates:

    Vol. 148, 1921
    Vol. 154, 1922

2. FRENCH

Herbette, Jean: *Un diplomate français parle du péril bolchévique*, Paris, 1943.

3. GERMAN

Documents and Materials relating to the eve of the Second World War, Vol. 1, trans., Moscow, 1948.

Bericht über den Gründungsparteitag der K.P.D., Berlin, n.d.

Bericht über die Verhandlungen des III (8) Parteitags der K.P.D., Berlin, 1923.

Der Internationale Kampf des Proletariats gegen Kriegsgefahr und Faszismus—Protokoll der Verhandlungen, Berlin, 1923.

4. POLISH

Les Relations Polono-Allemandes et Polono-Soviétiques 1933-1939—Reveuil de documents officiels, Paris, 1940.

5. RUSSIAN

Mezhdunarodnaya Politika Noveshevo Vremeni, ed. Klyuchnikov and Sabanin, Vols. II and III, Moscow, 1926-1928.

Mezhdunarodnaya Politika v 1930 godu, ed. Sabanin, Moscow, 1932.
Protokolli VIII Syezda R.K.P. (b), ed. Em. Yaroslavski, Moscow, 1933.
Protokolli IX Syezda R.K.P. (b), ed. N. Meschtcheryakov, Moscow, 1934.
Protokolli X Syezda R.K.P. (b), Moscow, 1921.
Protokolli XI Syezda R.K.P. (b), ed. N. Popov, Moscow, 1936.
Protokolli XIII Syezda R.K.P. (b), Moscow, 1924.
Protokolli XIV Syezda V.K.P. (b), Moscow, 1926.
Protokolli XV Konferentzi V.K.P. (b), Moscow, 1927.
Protokolli XV Syezda V.K.P. (b), Moscow, 1928.
Protokolli Zasedanii T.S.I.K. Sovetov—
    2 sozyv 2 sessiya, Moscow, 1924.
    2 sozyv 3 sessiya, Moscow, 1935.
Protokolli IX Vseyrossisski Syezd Sovetov, Moscow, 1922.
IV Vseymirni Kongress Kommunisticheskovo Internatsionala—
    izbranniye dokladi, ryechi i rezolutsii, Moscow, 1923.
V Vseymirni Kongress Kommunisticheskovo Internatsionala—
    stenographicheski otchet, Pt. I, Moscow, 1925.
Kommunisticheski Internatsional v dokumentakh, ed. Bela Kun, Moscow,
    1933.

6. UNITED STATES OF AMERICA
Foreign Relations of the United States, Paris Peace Conference, 1919,
    Washington, 1942.
Hale, Robert: *Report of the Mission to Finland, Latvia, Lithuania and Esthonia
    on the situation in the Baltic Provinces*, Washington, 1919.
Official Transcript of the American Military Tribunal No. III-A in the
    matter of the U.S.A. v. Gustav Krupp von Bohlen und Halbach *et. al.*

7. DOCUMENTS OF THE PREPARATORY COMMISSION FOR THE DISARMAMENT
    CONFERENCE
Series V, Minutes of the 4th Session.
Series VI, Minutes of the 5th Session.
Series VIII, Minutes of the 6th Session (First Part).
DOCUMENTS OF THE CONFERENCE FOR THE REDUCTION AND LIMITATION
    OF ARMAMENTS
Minutes of the General Commission, Series B, Vol. I.
Minutes of the General Commission, Series B, Vol. II.
Minutes of the Bureau, Series C, Vol. I, IX.

8. MISCELLANEOUS
International Conciliation Pamphlets, 1930, No. 265, Carnegie, New York.
The Treaties of Peace 1919-1923, Vol. I, Carnegie, New York, 1924.
Verlauf und Ergebnis der internationalen Wirtschafts-konferenz zu Genf,
    ed. Respondek, Berlin, 1927.

IV. Press, etc.

1. British: *Birmingham Post, Evening Standard, Manchester Guardian, Morning Post, Daily Telegraph, The Times.*

2. French: *Le Temps.*

3. German: *Berliner Börsenkurier, Berliner Tageblatt, Deutsche Allgemeine Zeitung (DAZ), Frankfurter Zeitung (FZ), Kölnische Zeitung, Der Mona Osteuropa, Die Reichspost, Die Rote Fahne, Vorwärts, Die Weltbühne, Zeitschrift für Politik.*

4. Russian: *Izvestya, Krasnaya Nov, Mezhdunarodnaya Zhizn, Pravda, Russian Information and Review, Soviet Russia, Vlast Sovetov, Aus der Volkswirtschaft der Ud.S.S.R.*

5. United States: *Journal of Modern History, New York Times.*

V. Miscellaneous

'Augur': *Germany and Europe*, London, 1927.

Beloff, Max: *The Foreign Policy of Soviet Russia 1929-1941*, Oxford, 1947, 1949.

Bergmann, Carl: *The History of Reparations*, Engl. trans., London, 1927.

Carr, E. H.: *German-Soviet Relations between the two World Wars*, Baltimore, 1951.

Churchill, W. S.: *The World Crisis—the Aftermath*, London, 1929.

Erusalimski, A.: *Germaniya, Antanta i S.S.S.R.*, Moscow, 1928.

Fischer, Louis: *The Soviets in World Affairs*, London, 1930.

Flechtheim, O. K.: *Die KPD in der Weimarer Republik*, Offenbach, 1948.

Francois-Poncet, A.: *De Versailles à Potsdam*, Paris, 1948.

Hoetzsch, O.: *Le Caractère et la Situation Internationale de l'Union d s Soviets*, Geneva, 1932.

Jahrbuch für Auswärtige Politik, Berlin, 1931.

Lucien-Graux, Dr: *Histoire des Violations du Traité de Paix*, Vol. I, Paris, 1921.

Mills, J. Saxon: *The Genoa Conference*, London, 1922.

Milukov, P.: *La Politique Extérieure des Soviets*, Paris, 1934.

Morrow, Ian: *The Peace Settlement in the German-Polish Borderlands*, London, 1936.

Reichskriegsministerium: *Die Rückführung des Ostheeres*, Vol. I, Berlin, 1936.

Stampfer, Fr.: *Die Vierzehn Jahre der ersten deutschen Republik*, Karlsbad, 1936.

Tanin, M.: *Desyat Let Vnyeshnyei Politiki S.S.S.R. 1917-1927*, Moscow, 1927.

Zitelmann, F. C.: *Russland im Friedensvertrage von Versailles*, Berlin, 1920.

IV. PRESS, &TC.

1. British: Manchester Post, Evening Standard, Manchester Guardian, Morning Post, Daily Telegraph, The Times.

2. French: Le Temps.

3. German: Berliner Börsenzeitung, Berliner Tageblatt, Deutsche Allgemeine Zeitung (DAZ), Manchester Zeitung (?), Nachrichten, Catmor, Der Monat, Osteuropa, Die Reichspost, Die Rote Fahne, Vorwärts, Die Weltbühne, Zeitschrift für Politik.

4. Russian: Izvestia, Nov, Mezhdunarodnaya Zhizn, Pravda, Bureau Information and Antang Sovu, Rusja, Vlast Sovietov, für der Föderation Sowjets der U.S.S.R.

5. United States: Journal of Modern History, New York Times.

V. MISCELLANEOUS

Angell, Norman: Germany and Europe, London, 1932.

Beloff, Max: The Foreign Policy of Soviet Russia 1929-1941, Oxford, 1947-1949.

Bergmann, Carl: The History of Reparations, Engl. trans., London, 1927.

Carr, E. H.: German-Soviet Relations between the two World Wars, Baltimore, 1951.

Churchill, W. S.: The World Crisis: the Aftermath, London, 1929.

Eudin, Xenia J.: Soviet Russia : U.S.S.R., Moscow, 1928

Fischer, Louis: The Soviets in World Affairs, London, 1930.

Flechtheim, O. K.: Die KPD in der Weimarer Republik, Offenbach, 1948.

François-Poncet, A.: De Versailles à Potsdam, Paris, 1948.

Hoetzsch, O.: La Guerre et la Situation Internationale de l'Union des Soviets, Geneva, 1932.

Niedermayer, R.: Sowjetrussland, Berlin, 1931.

Laufenberg, ...: La Traité de Paix, Vol I, Paris, 1921.

Mills, J. Saxon: The Genoa Conference, London, 1922.

Milioukov, P.: La Politique Extérieure des Soviets, Paris, 1934.

Morrow, Ian: The Peace Settlement in the German-Polish Borderland, London, 1936.

Reichsministerium: Die Rückführung der Ostheere, Vol I, Berlin, 1936.

Stampfer, F.: Die Vierzehn Jahre der ersten deutschen Republik, Karlsbad, 1936.

Beloff, Max: Foreign Policy Soviet S.S.S.R. 1917-1927, Moscow, 1947.

Zuchmann, F. C.: Russland im Friedensvertrage von Versailles, Berlin, 1930.

INDEX